Southern North West

SNW

Training Partnership

251,
8
SUR

Signposts in Theology

Theology and Religious Pluralism
Gavin D'Costa

Theology and the Problem of Evil
Kenneth Surin

Other titles in preparation

Theology and Feminism
Daphne Hampson

Theology and Philosophy
Ingolf Dalferth

Theology and Politics
Duncan Forrester

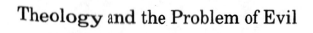

Theology and the Problem of Evil

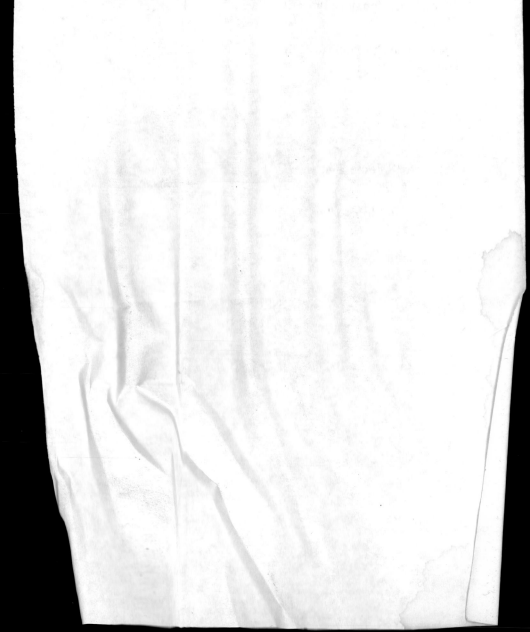

Theology and the Problem of Evil

KENNETH SURIN

Wipf & Stock
PUBLISHERS
Eugene, Oregon

Wipf and Stock Publishers
199 W 8th Ave, Suite 3
Eugene, OR 97401

Theology and the Problem of Evil
By Surin, Kenneth
Copyright©1986 by Surin, Kenneth
ISBN: 1-59244-981-6
Publication date 10/29/2004
Previously published by Basil Blackwell, Ltd, 1986

Always historicize!
Frederic Jameson

There is at least *one* authority that we should never reject
or despise – the authority of those who suffer.
Johann-Baptist Metz

Just as machinery has embodied ideas of good, so the
technology of destruction has also acquired a metaphysical
character. The practical questions have thus become the
ultimate questions as well.
Saul Bellow

To make oneself concretely aware that the Nazi 'solution'
was not 'final', that it spills over into our present lives is
the only but compelling reason for going back or, perhaps,
forward into the non-world of the sealed ghetto and
extermination camp.
George Steiner

Only lightening bolts of knowledge are saturated with
memory and prescience.
T.W. Adorno

For Fiona

Contents

Foreword

The ideas formulated in this book are in large part the distillate of a number of seminar papers, lectures and articles dealing with various aspects of the 'problem of evil' that I have produced over the last decade or so. Many people, whether directly or indirectly, have influenced my thinking on this subject. Nothing in this book is original. Everything that I have to say has already been said by someone else in one way or another. This book ranges rather widely. But it is simply impossible, these days especially, to engage in the area of theological reflection covered by this book without discussing ideas and themes that properly belong to other disciplines: philosophy, literary theory, semiotics, historiography, political theory, social theory, and so forth. I have tried to avoid being 'merely' eclectic. Nevertheless, a little book like this does not give its author room to formulate the precise relationships that exist between the different thinkers to whom he is indebted. Thus, for example, I am well aware that I have borrowed from Paul Ricoeur and Michel Foucault alike, and that in the process I might have appeared to under-emphasize or even ignore the undeniable differences between these two thinkers. I have tried to avoid any blatant inconsistencies in my borrowings, but recognize at the same time that my manner of proceeding will probably fail to satisfy those who staunchly believe that intellectually indebted authors should always have as few creditors as possible.

Many people who attended seminars and lectures given at Birmingham, Cambridge, Duke and Yale provided me with the opportunity to discuss earlier and more rudimentary versions of some of the ideas formulated in this book. My special debt, however, is to the following for their valuable criticisms and comments: Brian Hebblethwaite, Frederick Herzog, John Hick, C.T. Hughes, Werner Jeanrond, Gerard Loughlin and David Nicholls. Colin Terrell, David Miall and Greg Chirichigno provided vital technical assistance during the production of the final draft. The library staff at the College of St Paul and St Mary, Cheltenham, dealt courteously and efficiently with a plague of requests for bibliographical information and for books and periodicals from other libraries. But my greatest debt by far is to my wife Fiona, who gave me invaluable support throughout the time when this book was being written. Without her devotion and very practical assistance, especially when it came to being a surrogate father for our son Alastair (who was born in the final stages of its composition), it would not have been written. I dedicate this book to her.

It would be quite difficult to write a book on the problems of evil and suffering without being forcefully reminded of the terrible and seemingly endless succession of catastrophes that have befallen so many parts of our planet. When I first began to take a more than casual philosophical and theological interest in the problems that fall under the rubric of theodicy, the initial reports of the appalling deeds of Pol Pot were just beginning to filter out of Kampuchea. Since then hardly a week has passed without report of some new calamity or atrocity: the civil wars in the Lebanon, El Salvador and Sri Lanka, the Iranian revolution and its terrible aftermath, the 'forgotten' civil war in East Timor, the 'forgotten' Iran–Iraq war, the famine in the arid zones of Africa, the Bhopal disaster, the two Bangladesh tidal waves, the earthquake in Mexico City, the volcano in Armero, the suppression of Solidarity in Poland, the daily shooting of unarmed demonstrators in South Africa, murderous attacks on innocent bystanders at several European airports, oppression and injustice meted out to masses of peasants and slum-dwellers throughout Latin America, the growing and systematic immiseration of the Third World; the now commonplace harassment, sometimes with death-dealing consequences, of Asian families by racist gangs in the East End of London. The list seems virtually unending. These events have taken place at a time when the two superpowers are spending ever greater sums of money on weapons of mass destruction; when the British budget for overseas aid has been trimmed throughout the present government's period of office (a government which excuses itself by invoking the slogan 'we need to get value for our money'); when cynical Conservative politicians advocate a tough 'immigration policy' in the name of a 'realism' calculated to appeal to the basest instincts of their supporters; when the national interest ('batting for Britain') is invoked to justify the indiscriminate selling of arms to repressive regimes in the Third World; and so on. And throughout this time the unspeakable events associated with the Nazi slaughter of millions of Jews maintain their grip on the reality of the present: the pending trial of Klaus Barbie for war crimes, the revelation that the West German police were until very recently abetting the Mengele family in their attempts to thwart the arrest of Auschwitz's 'angel of death', the shameful visit by President Reagan to the SS war cemetery in Bitburg, are salutary reminders that here is one place where the past cannot be allowed to bury itself.

At the same time, I could not help being aware of a stark contrast, namely, that I was able to compose this book in the comfort of a book-lined study; that at a time when nearly four million people were unemployed in Britain, I had a job which *paid* me to produce articles and books; that as a middle-class, professional, 'non-ethnic' citizen-consumer my lot in life was certainly very different from that of the mass of people who are consigned to the margins of British society today.

To be 'situated' thus, and to write about evil and suffering, is to feel a tension born of the realization that while the truest words about the materialities addressed by this book are those uttered in the autobiographical mode, its author has mercifully been spared the necessity of having to speak about his subject in this most direct and pressing of voices. An author can perhaps be forgiven for producing so many sentences on evil and suffering if he strives to meet one requirement: namely, that none of these sentences should obscure or efface the lived experience of those who happen to be victims. Any author who intends to write on this subject is constrained and challenged, by the barely audible murmurings of something approximating to a 'morality of knowledge' (to borrow a phrase of Van Harvey's), to make his or her book a historically situated text; a text which permits the *reinscription* of the historically-contingent experiences of those whose screams our society will not allow itself to heed. That this particular book has in fact met this condition is of course not something that its author is in a position to decide.

I am grateful to the editors and publishers of the following journals for allowing me to reproduce material from some of my previously published articles: 'The Impassibility of God and the Problem of Evil', *Scottish Journal of Theology*, 35 (1982), pp. 97–115; 'Atonement and Christology', *Neue Zeitschrift für Systematische Theologie und Religionsphilosophie*, 24 (1982), pp. 131–49; 'Theodicy?', *Harvard Theological Review*, 76 (1983), pp. 225–47; and 'Atonement and Moral Apocalypticism: William Styron's *Sophie's Choice*', *New Blackfriars*, 64 (1983), pp. 323–35.

Kenneth Surin

Introduction

Theodicy, in what is usually taken to be its classical or canonical form, is a philosophical and/or theological exercise involving a justification of the righteousness of God. This justification requires the theodicist to reconcile the existence of an omnipotent, omniscient and morally perfect divinity with the existence and the considerable scale of evil. However, as the long and involuted history of theodicy shows, this project has never really been a unitary and homogeneous undertaking. Indeed, this history indicates that it would be less misleading if theodicy were seen as a designation which covers a number of diverse and sometimes even incompatible undertakings. Thus, for example, some theodicists (John Hick and Richard Swinburne come readily to mind) take the question of the *existence* of God to constitute the heart of theodicy; while others (e.g. the exponents of 'process' theodicy) consider theodicy's main problem to be that of determining whether (an *already* existing) divinity can justifiably be said to be responsible for the existence and the sheerly destructive nature and magnitude of evil. It would not therefore be misleading to say that theodicists do not even have a consensus on the question of the kind of primary *agenda* which confronts them. And it goes virtually without saying that these manifold and seemingly irreconcilable differences become more profuse and complex when theologians and philosophers proceed to 'answer' the many questions which they see as being raised by the theodicy-problem.

The so-called 'problem of evil' is deemed by its proponents to have a venerable ancestry, and was apparently first formulated by Epicurus (341–270 BC) in the form of a dilemma which perhaps receives its most succinct formulation in the words of David Hume (1711–76):

Is he willing to prevent evil, but not able? then he is impotent. Is he able, but not willing? then he is malevolent. Is he both able and willing? whence then is evil?[1]

The prevailing consensus among those who operate within theodicy's canonical tradition holds that a long strand in the history of theology – stemming from St Augustine via St Thomas Aquinas and the Reformers to Schleiermacher and modern times – has addressed itself to the task of reconciling God's omnipotence, omniscience and benevolence with the existence and the considerable scale of evil. This received view declares, or covertly assumes, that *all* these philosophers and theologians were addressing themselves to essentially the same *unchanging* set of problems – problems invariably believed to cluster round the dilemma enunciated by Hume. This declaration or unstated assumption is a terribly important one, and it needs to be probed a little more deeply.

Despite the irreducibly complex and diverse 'answers' provided by its many adherents, this scholarly consensus – which constitutes the heart of theodicy's canonical tradition – simply takes for granted that all these varied 'answers' can be fitted into the framework of a single problematic, an overarching schema that can in principle be understood and evaluated in entirely contemporary terms. Countless works on theodicy are written on the wholly unquestioned assumption that there is nothing problematic about treating, say, St Augustine (354–430) and Austin Farrer (1906–68), or St Irenaeus (c. 135 – c. 202) and Friedrich Schleiermacher (1768–1832), as if they were contemporaries. The thinkers who endorse this consensus are disposed to regard the ancient figures in these two juxtapositions as the 'senior partners' of a dialogue that has a timeless reality: the 'problem of evil', they would have us believe, was the 'same' for Irenaeus and Augustine as it subsequently was for Schleiermacher and Farrer (and, by implication, as it is for us today). Subject to one proviso, the great dead theodicists are thought to warrant our attention because they happen to take up positions that have an undoubted relevance for contemporary discussion. The caveat in question is one which imposes on contemporary theodicists the duty to root out the many 'mythological' elements which are alleged to pervade (and thus to vitiate) the writings of their bygone colleagues. The assumption here is that even the most enlightened authors of past times could not help believing things that are manifestly erroneous in the light of what we know today. (And here of course even those great pioneers Irenaeus and Augustine are no exception.) The authors of past ages are thus assumed to provide a rich stock of atemporal resources for the present-day theodicist who is prepared to do some preliminary 'demythologizing'; they become timeless grist for her ahistorical mill. More will be said about this ahistorical approach to theodicy later in this chapter. For the time being it need only be noted that the canonical tradition of theodicy seems to have an understanding of its own past which the historically minded student is likely to find somewhat problematic. Indeed, such a student might say that this tradition has radically misperceived the history of its own formation and development, and that any attempt to 'do' theodicy in the canonical sense of the term must therefore be treated with the utmost caution.

It will be a central thesis of this book that the 'doing' of theodicy in this canonical sense (i.e. a sense which, among other things, treats theodicy as if it were an essentially 'theoretical' and ahistorical activity), not only frustrates historically situated reflection on the manifold forms and occurrences of evil, but also militates against a properly Christian response to the 'problem of evil'. It is my conviction, a conviction that I hope to bear out later in this book, that this misperception and misappropriation of theodicy's own past, benign though it might appear to be, is nonetheless a symptom of a deeper and more pervasive failure, a failure which betokens the lack of a true and sustained historical consciousness. But this is to anticipate matters. Our more immediate need is to attend, albeit somewhat briefly, to a few miscellaneous considerations with a material bearing on the course of our discussion.

'PHILOSOPHICAL THEISM'

Since about the seventeenth century, when the canonical (i.e. the current) form of the theodicy-problem began to acquire its decisive formulation, the 'God' of theodicy has very much been the divinity known as 'the God of the philosophers'. During this time, the 'problem of evil', almost imperceptibly and with the tacit consent of theodicists, has become 'the problem of the God of philosophical theism'.

How is this philosophical theism appropriately to be characterized? In Walter Kasper's words, it is 'the abstract theism of a unipersonal God who stands over against man as the perfect Thou or over man as imperial ruler and judge'.[2] Kasper finds this modern philosophical theism to be ultimately untenable for a number of reasons:

> For one thing, if we imagine God as the other-worldly counterpart of man, then despite all the personal categories we use we will ultimately think of him in objectivist terms as a being who is superior to other beings. When this happens, God is being conceived as a finite entity who comes in conflict with finite reality and the modern understanding of it. Then we must either conceive God at the expense of man and the world, or conceive the world at the expense of God, thus limiting God in deistic fashion and finally eliminating him entirely with the atheists. This conversion of theism into a-theism also takes place for another reason: theism almost necessarily falls under the suspicion voiced by the critics of religion, that the theistic God is a projection of the human ego and a hypostatized idol, or that theism is ultimately a form of idolatry.[3]

It is certainly no exaggeration to say that virtually every contemporary discussion of the theodicy-question is premised, implicitly or explicitly, on an understanding of 'God' overwhelmingly constrained by the principles of *seventeenth and eighteenth century* philosophical theism. Since the outcome of any investigation of the canonical form of the theodicy-problem will be signally affected by the stance that the investigator adopts towards this pervasive philosophical theism, it behoves us to indicate from the outset what our attitude towards it will be.

Here I must confess to sharing the convictions of Walter Kasper, Nicholas Lash and D.Z. Phillips, namely that *this* theism (and, *ex hypothesi*, its negations) are both profoundly unchristian (Kasper and Lash) and conceptually confused (Phillips).[4] The specific target of the criticisms of Lash and Phillips is the theistic system adumbrated by Richard Swinburne, who of course also happens to be a notable contemporary theodicist. According to Swinburne, 'theism postulates a person of a very simple kind – a person who is essentially omnipotent, omniscient, and perfectly free and who is eternal, perhaps essentially so. Such a being will be a necessary being and will necessarily be an omnipresent spirit, creator of all things, and . . . perfectly good. [Theism] only postulates one entity, [and] that entity has control over and knowledge of all other things'.[5] Against this theism, it could be argued, as Lash in fact does, that to divide the beliefs that Christians (and Jews and Muslims) have about God into a 'central core'[6] with a surrounding periphery, is to traduce and distort the belief of Christians (and Jews and Muslims). To quote Lash:

> The belief (for example) that God is his Word, eternally uttered and addressed to us in time; or the belief that that God is his self-gift, his joy, animating, transforming and healing all nature and history; these beliefs are not, as Swinburne claims, 'further' beliefs which may be 'added to' and, by addition, 'complicate', a prior set of convictions concerning an entity with all the interesting characteristics listed by him.[7]

The divinity of modern theism thus turns out to be '*a*' being (an implicit stress is invariably placed on the indefinite article), a rare and fascinating 'entity', possessing a number of clearly specifiable characteristics. Theism is then simply to be understood as a hypothesis about this most sublime 'entity'. When the theist feels the pressure of certain 'problems' – e.g. the 'problem of evil' – she might be disposed to counter these difficulties by adding supplementary hypotheses to theism. Swinburne counts as auxiliary the hypotheses of bad angels, life after death and incarnation.[8] These *prima facie* admissible 'hypotheses', however, are said by Swinburne to be peripheral to the business of 'evidencing' theism. For there is, by and large, enough 'evidence' to 'confirm' the theistic hypothesis unconditionally without the theist having to get too involved in the business of addressing, and wrestling with, the (non-primary) hypotheses of incarnation, Holy Spirit and Trinity. All that this philosophical theist need do is to get on with the task of finding out what kind of 'object' God is. It might be reassuring to the religious person to hear that Swinburne is willing to accept that it is possible for this divine object to have 'good' and 'abundant' reason to 'bring about' a redemptive incarnation and life after death, etc. This consoling thought, though, is destined to be short-lived, for Swinburne proceeds to counsel *against* adding these ancillary hypotheses to theism. He believes that if the theist did resort to these extra hypotheses 'theism then becomes a more complicated hypothesis, and hence has a less prior probability and so needs more in the way of confirming evidence to raise its over-all probability in evidence . . .'.[9]

The theisms of Alvin Plantinga and John Hick (though to a much lesser extent where the latter is concerned) have several close affinities with the system formulated and defended by Swinburne. Common to these theisms are the core assumptions: (1) that to assert the existence of God is somehow to help render the things of the world rational, meaningful and explicable; and (2) that because this God is a unipersonal being, it is somehow not essential for the theist to understand divinity in an irreducibly *trinitarian* way.[10] It would be beyond the scope of this book to present in great depth or detail a properly Christian (i.e. a trinitarian) doctrine of God: all that we can do here is to acknowledge, via an invocation of the work of Kasper, Lash, Phillips, Turner, et al., that the classical Christian view of God is 'intelligible' and that there can be a responsible and patient theological discourse which allows something of the irreducibly trinitarian reality of the mystery that we call God to be communicated. Unlike the theistic philosopher, this position would not purport to communicate lots of interesting snippets of information acquired in the course of 'exploring' a certain 'entity'; 'evidence' that will subsequently be used by the philosophically competent theist to confirm a set of 'core hypotheses' about this 'thing' and its 'activities'.[11] Quite simply, a disciplined theological speech, a *theo*-logic in the true sense of the term, would be one that had at its heart the principle that we do not know what God is. *This* speech would therefore forbear to identify the divine mystery with a 'thing', and in so doing it would inhibit and resist our insatiable yearning for an absolute locus or repository of meaning and significance, that is, the very 'thing' to which philosophical theists give the name 'God'. To seek an understanding of 'God' which conforms to this repudiation of idolatry would willy-nilly be to find oneself being disposed to use a quite different kind of 'God-language' from the one employed and sanctioned by the modern theist. But this is where the student of the theodicy-question has a real problem to face and an important decision to make. Our representative modern theists – Swinburne and Plantinga – are also renowned for their attempts to deal with the 'problem of evil'. It consequently goes without saying that the God they seek to justify is the very 'thing' that the adherent of a properly Christian 'understanding' of God will find herself being disposed to abjure. However, at the same time, one cannot even begin to make sense of what Swinburne et al., have to say about the 'problem of evil' without presupposing the God of philosophical theism. I shall therefore grant to these theodicists all the linguistic and conceptual resources needed to motivate and underpin their 'theism', while at the same time not endorsing the 'descriptions' of the 'God' that is posited by their discourse. Thus, when I say, in the context of my discussions of Swinburne, Plantinga or Hick that God is X, or Y, or Z, this statement should really be glossed as: 'Swinburne (or Plantinga or Hick) *mean* that God is X, or Y, or Z'. This 'bracketing' of the descriptions generated by 'theistic' discourse is 'grammatically' justified because this discourse, in viewing God as an 'object' (albeit a *very* special kind of 'object'), shows itself to be fundamentally incapable of serving as a 'logical grammar' of 'the pedagogy of salvation';[12] the very 'pedagogy' that (as we shall see later in the case of Augustine and Irenaeus) is the springboard of the Christian's response to the world's pain and suffering. This theism, a commodity of the Enlightenment, is a philosophical construction which fails signally to grasp that most elementary of rules in the 'logical syntax' of a properly-formed theological speech, namely, that logically (and not merely 'theologically') there can be no 'order' or 'ratio' between finite and infinite.[13] Any theology which does not incorporate this rule is one that effectively prevents the reality of God from being spoken. To think that God can be understood as some kind of 'thing' or 'entity', one could say, is to have the most profound misunderstanding of who God is. It is to leave theological utterance in irreparable disarray.[14]

THEODICY'S UNDERSTANDING OF ITS OWN PAST

I have already suggested (see p. 2 above) that theodicists who operate in the tradition of Anglo-American analytic philosophy tend invariably to locate the 'problem of evil' in an apparently static analytical scheme. Thus, Alvin Plantinga (1932–) incorporates into his celebrated 'free will defence' St Augustine's proposition that a great deal of the evil that exists can be ascribed to the work of fallen angels. That is to say, all instances and forms of natural or physical evil can in the end be said to constitute a subset of the set of moral evils. In Plantinga's submission, therefore, if it is *possible* that natural evil orginates in the actions of such 'significantly free but non-human persons' (i.e. devils), then 'perhaps it is not within God's power to create a set of such persons whose free actions produced a greater balance of good over evil'.[15]

Likewise, John Hick (1922–) locates his 'soul-making' theodicy in a school of theological thinking deemed to have been inaugurated by St Irenaeus. According to Hick's rendition of this 'Irenaean' strand of thought, human beings were not created as perfect creatures, but as a race of finite and fallible (but nonetheless perfectible) beings who needed to be schooled towards the future perfection that awaited them. In the 'Irenaean' scheme of things, this 'pedagogy' takes the form of a slow and gradual process that will culminate only at the consummation of history, when the human creature will, through the grace of God, come to be in the glorious 'likeness' (and not just the 'image') of her Maker.[16]

Similarly, Richard Swinburne (1934–), while he does not align the tenets of his theodicy with the views of any specific theologian or philosopher of the past, does nonetheless cast his work in a tradition which he associates with Thomas Aquinas, Duns Scotus, Berkeley, Butler and Paley.[17] He also maintains that the methodological convictions which underlie his theistic system are ones that were 'explicitly acknowledged by the vast majority of Christian (and non-Christian) philosophers from the thirteenth to the eighteenth centuries; and . . . shared, although acknowledged less explicitly, by many Christian (and non-Christian) philosophers from the first to the twelfth centuries'.[18] The implication, whether stated or undeclared, behind the claims made by Plantinga, Swinburne and (to a far lesser degree) John Hick, is that their respective methodological convictions, and the notions which they discuss under the rubrics of 'theodicy', 'the free will defence' and 'soul-making', are more or less the 'same' as the methodological principles and notions found in Irenaeus's *Adversus Haereses*, Augustine's *Enchiridion*, Aquinas's *Summa Theologiae*, Butler's *Analogy*, Paley's *Natural Theology*, and so on.

This strategic invocation by our representative modern theodicists of the concepts, themes and procedures employed by Irenaeus, Augustine, Aquinas, Duns Scotus, et al., overlooks, and thus neutralizes, certain vital differences in religious and cultural context; differences which indicate that the deployment of these concepts in any modern theodicy has to be radically different from their use in the thought and practice of bygone epochs. Alasdair MacIntyre is one of the very few philosophers belonging to the Anglo-American philosophical tradition to have noticed, and taken seriously, the fact that the contradictions of a benevolent divine omnipotence and the existence of evil were not seen by the Christian thinkers of the Middle Ages as an obstacle to belief. MacIntyre makes the fruitful suggestion that this pre-modern state of affairs is very different from the situation which came to prevail after the seventeenth century (when 'the problem of evil' metamorphosed into the problem of the coherence and intelligibility of Christian belief per se). Pre-seventeenth century Christian thinkers were certainly not unaware of the conceptual difficulties that these antinomies generated; but, unlike their post-seventeenth century counterparts, they did not regard these problems as constituting *any* sort of ground for jettisoning their faith. For MacIntyre, this discrepancy must raise the question:

> ... why do the same intellectual difficulties at one time appear as difficulties but no more, an incentive to enquiry but not a ground for disbelief, while at another time they appear as a final and sufficient ground for scepticism and for the abandonment of Christianity?[19]

To this pertinent question MacIntyre gives a tantalizingly suggestive answer:

> ... the apparent incoherence of Christian concepts was taken to be tolerable (and treated as apparent and not real) because the concepts were part of a set of concepts which were indispensable to the forms of description used in social and intellectual life.[20]

A historically-minded scrutiny of the relevant writings of the Christian thinkers of antiquity and the Middle Ages will show MacIntyre's explanation to contain a lot more than a grain of truth.

A historicizing investigation of the kind just proposed will show that the appropriate context of Augustine's treatment of the causes and nature of evil, and (absolutely crucially for Augustine) the means of its transformation and overcoming, is that of *conversion*, of the soul's ascent to God. Within this (properly) Augustinian intellectual context, evil is treated in explicitly psychological terms, and little or no scope is allowed for any of the metaphysical or ontological stratagems that are inextricably bound up with the typically modern enterprise of theodicy.

Augustine tries to account for evil's intractable quality by resorting to the notion of a human propensity that is driven ever deeper by habit (*consuetudo*), a propensity whose destructive power is enhanced by the human memory (*memoria*). The gratifications provided by past deeds are implanted in the memory, thereby ensuring their continued existence.[21] The memory's capacity to reinforce illicit pleasures is accompanied by a seemingly inexhaustible perversity which impels the individual to repeat, and thus to remember ever more vividly and insistently, the delight gained from every wicked deed of the past. In this way, the individual becomes habituated to wickedness.[22] Augustine's anthropology thus sees the individual as a being hopelessly constrained by the continuity of memory. This intractability of her inner life creates a 'chain of habit' which saps her very capacity to think and will properly. She surrenders to her compulsions, and delights increasingly in evil:

> The enemy held fast my will, and had made of it a chain, and had bound me tight with it. For out of the perverse will come lust, and the service of lust ended in habit, and habit, not resisted, became necessity. By these links, as it were, forged together – which is why I call it 'a chain' – a hard bondage held me in slavery.[23]

The 'problem of evil' is therefore not to be solved by resorting to philosophical manoeuvres. Even if philosophical acumen could assist in the formulation of a solution, it cannot be overlooked that philosophy has a merely provisional and secondary status. Its true goal, the goal of the true *Christian* philosophy, is the attainment of blessedness, and there is no way to blessedness except that which God has revealed in Jesus Christ. What is more, we can cleave to this way, and so attain to blessedness, only because God has wrought his gracious work of redemption in Christ.[24] The only realistic hope for a solution to the 'problem of evil' lies therefore in the unfathomable will of the ultimately nameless God. The human creature is utterly dependent on this Liberator for the grace that will transform her willing and thinking. In the words of Gillian Evans:

> As he came to be more and more firmly of the opinion that some direct action by God is necessary, Augustine moved towards an extreme position. His developing conception of the huge generosity of the Creator in helping man's damaged will to function properly, gradually blotted out any notion that man might contribute to his own salvation by trying hard; if a man could deserve God's grace that would make grace a lesser thing; only if it is utterly undeserved is it truly a free gift. And if man has no say in the matter it is also a gift he cannot refuse. It is a gift which compels him to be saved.[25]

So it is conversion – which comes about when the human will co-operates with divine grace – that solves the 'problem of evil'. Without conversion, the very *process* of seeking an answer to the question 'whence is evil?' will be undermined by the distorted thinking of a crippled intellect. For the perversion of the human will is complemented by a perversion of the memory and the intellect ('the eye of the mind'); and so evil, inevitably and paradoxically, comes to be yet more deeply entrenched in the unconverted person's attempts to find a solution to this 'problem'. The unconverted person's endeavours to resolve the 'problem of evil', no matter how sincere and intellectually gifted this person might be, are doomed ultimately to be self-defeating. Only faith in Christ makes possible the cleansing of our vision, a cleansing regarded by Augustine as the necessary preliminary to the vision of God. It is this saving vision, whose possibility depends on divine illumination, which enables us, damaged souls that we are, to discover the true answer to this most perplexing of questions.[26]

Augustine's treatment of evil has to be located in its proper historical context, a context in which Christianity had come to an accommodation with the Roman Empire. In the fourth century Constantine's decision to legalize the Christian religion ended the era of persecution, and Christians were no longer compelled to live as members of an outcast eschatological community. After the Edict of Milan (313),Christianity – which had hitherto been marginalized by the prevailing social and political order – came to enjoy official patronage and subvention. Martyrdom ceased, and Christians were able to occupy positions of power and privilege. The church and the 'world' were in a position to accommodate each other. This imperial assimilation of Christianity, which culminated in 389 with Theodosius' decree that Christianity was henceforth to be the official religion of the Empire, meant that

> [the] Christian's worst enemies could no longer be placed outside him: they were inside, his sins and his doubts; and the climax of a man's life would not be martyrdom, but conversion from the perils of his own past.[27]

Augustine's reflections on the 'problem of evil' must be situated in *this* historically contingent cultural and religious milieu if we are not to misunderstand them. His reflections are intended for the spiritually damaged subject, the *servus Dei* or 'servant of God', who is engaged in a restless quest for the healing of her soul, a healing that will come about only when the subject has a right spiritual and cognitive relationship with God.

Furthermore, Augustine's treatment of this 'problem' has as its proper locus a *theology of history* which views history as both a work and a sign of God's providence.[28] Evil deeds, and the divine work of redemption which overthrows them, can be properly interpreted only when seen from the standpoint of the global hermeneutic supplied by this theology of history.

In addition, Augustine's approach to 'the problem of evil' presupposes an epistemology which pivots on the neo-Platonist notion of a divine illumination of the human mind. Without this illumination, the conversion that is the basis of the soul's deliverance from the power of sin cannot even begin to take place[29] For Augustine, therefore, the solution to 'the problem of evil' must await God's triune revelation of himself. It cannot (and on this he is most insistent) be sought anywhere else.

The subject of the post-Leibnizian metaphysical theodicy – that is, the type of theodicy enunciated by Swinburne, Plantinga and Hick – is a very different kind of figure. (A post-Leibnizian theodicy is one that views theodicy as an essentially rational or *theoretical* enterprise. As such it would have no implications for any *practical* strategies intended to overcome evil.) This post-Leibnizian subject is not in any way to be identified with the Augustinian *servus Dei*. Instead, she has to be seen as a 'text' that is 'scripted' by Enlightenment and post-Enlightenment thought. That is to say, from the epistemological standpoint (a standpoint valorized by the 'Cartesian' legacy of the Enlightenment), this subject is the putatively rational and autonomous individual who confines herself to the entirely *worldly* discipline of 'evidencing' and 'justifying' cognitive formations, formations which, moreover, are restrictively derived from reason and sense-experience. This worldly discipline, which finds its authoritative manifestation in common-sense rationalism and empiricism, would cease to be what it essentially is if it were required to posit a subject whose self-definition required her to *live* and *think* as a 'servant of God'.

Moreover, this metaphysical theodicy, which perceives itself as the instrument of a technicalizing philosophy, does not approach 'the problem of evil' in a way that *demands* that this problem be seen as a constituent of an all-encompassing theological (or even a philosophical) reading of history. Indeed, the very idea of such an uncompromising hermeneutical globalism will be deeply alien to its post-Leibnizian practitioners, who tend invariably to approach the 'problem of evil' in terms which do not require any kind of interpretation of historical processes. This theodicist, we have seen, views theodicy (in its ideal form) very much as an ahistorical and individualistic quest for logically stable notions, exact axioms, and rigorous chains of deductive inference. Unlike Augustine, the post-Leibnizian theodicist does not feel constrained to understand history as *anything* possessing an intrinsic *thematic* importance, let alone as a history which is the work of the very God who reveals himself in Jesus Christ, and which is a determining element in the subject's self-definition. Such a 'reading' of history is claimed to be superfluous: (1) because it is a further (and dispensable) hypothesis which serves only to complicate the theistic hypothesis (Swinburne); or (2) because the theological impulse which motivates this 'reading', and the theological 'syntax' and 'semantics' which govern its articulation, are typically and irreducibly *Christian*, i.e., items that are 'culture specific' when seen in the light of our inescapably pluralistic religious and theological world (Hick).

Finally, the epistemological paradigm which dominates post-Leibnizian theodicy is strictly incommensurable with the Augustinian definition of knowledge as a divine illumination of human mind. The understanding of reason promoted by the Enlightenment and post-Enlightenment viewed the human animal as part of nature, and so, inevitably, it came to see her cognitive activities as part of nature too. The paradigm of knowledge sponsored by Enlightenment and post-Enlightenment thought is one that sought, essentially, to explain 'knowledge' in terms of 'mental processes' (Locke), 'processes' which take place in a non-physical substance called 'the mind' (Descartes).[30] This post-seventeenth century 'theory of knowledge' – in effect a context-free empiricism and rationalism with unrelentingly terrestrial horizons – had no need to invoke anything approximating to Augustine's essentially Platonic conception of a *divine* illumination of the human mind.[31]

If the foregoing is remotely plausible, then it has to be acknowledged that the forms and presuppositions which underlie Augustine's treatment of evil are so crucially different from those of the modern (i.e. post-Leibnizian) theodicist that the place of evil in this theodicy has to be entirely different from that of *malum* in Augustine's thought and practice. What we have here is not only a vivid example of the metaphysical theodicist's inability to confront modes of thinking and doing prevalent in the very culture whose intellectual legacy provides the linguistic and conceptual resources that make modern theodicy possible, but also a salutary reminder of how themes and ideas, when abstracted from their historically particular intellectual contexts, will merge into a discourse of free-floating abstractions, the kind of discourse which the post-Leibnizian metaphysical theodicy is in constant danger of becoming.

The same lamentable inattentiveness which leads the metaphysical theodicist to treat Augustine as if he were a contemporary figure is displayed by those writers who, when finding that they are dissatisfied with the 'Augustinian theodicy', cite the work of Irenaeus as the *locus classicus* for an alternative answer to 'the problem of evil'. The resultant answer incorporates a 'pedagogy of salvation' premised on a slow progression on the part of the human creature towards perfect communion with her Creator. Roughly the same (negative) historiographical points made above in connection with the so-called 'Augustinian' pattern of theodicy can be made with regard to its supposed 'Irenaean' counterpart.

The proper, historically constituted context of Irenaeus's ideas was one in which the early church's dominant concern was the need to transmit the primitive Apostolic faith in all its purity and wholeness to the pagan who had resolved to become a Christian. The theology of Irenaeus is thus to be placed in a *Sitz im Leben* which accorded a certain primacy to catechesis.[32] This context was one in which Gnosticism was seen as the major threat to the integrity of the primitive Apostolic tradition, and the refutation of Gnostic heresies therefore became an integral part of the catechetical work undertaken by the post-Apostolic church.[33]

The distinctive feature shared by the many versions of Christian Gnosticism was their heterodox emphasis on a sharp distinction between creation and redemption, an emphasis which led Gnostic thinkers to distinguish between the inferior Demiurge responsible for the creation, and the Supreme God responsible for its redemption. The God of the Old Testament was identified with the lower Demiurge, who was characterized as an enemy of the Supreme God of the New Testament. The inevitable outcome of this dualism was a denial of the continuity of the two covenants, which in turn involved a denial that the Jewish dispensation had any place in the economy of salvation. The theologian who (like Irenaeus) wanted to combat this Gnostic heresy would therefore find himself confronted with the task of having to define *both* the differences *and* the continuity of the two Testaments. It was precisely in order to break the back of the Gnostic antinomy of the two Testaments that Irenaeus invoked the doctrine of the progressive education of the human race towards salvation.

In repudiating the teaching of Gnosticism, Irenaeus affirmed that there are not two separate and antagonistic creations, but a single creation in which human beings advance towards God:[34]

[God] created all things, since He is the only God, the only Lord, the only Creator, the only Father, alone containing all things, and Himself commanding all things into existence.'[35] The Gnostic Demiurge is neither God nor Father, but possesses these titles merely by courtesy (*Against Heresies*, IV, 1, 1). There are two covenants, of course, but they have the same Author and they share the same end (IV, 32, 1, and IV, 36, 2; IV, 9, 1). Both covenants were prefigured in Abraham (IV, 25, 1), and we 'possess the same faith as Abraham' (IV, 5. 4). Because 'the Lord was not unknown to Abraham' (IV, 5, 5), 'Abraham desired to see that day [when] he might himself embrace Christ' (IV, 7, 1). Marcion's attempt to exclude Abraham from the salvation wrought by Christ was therefore vain and misguided (IV, 8, 1). In contradiction of the heretics, 'God chose the patriarchs for the sake of [our] salvation' (IV, 14, 2). The prophets even predicted the advent of Jesus Christ (IV, 34, 3), and the Son of God is 'shown forth' by Moses, who was not ignorant of the day of the Son's passion (IV, 10, 1). Moreover, 'the precepts of an absolutely perfect life . . . are the same in each Testament' (IV, 12, 3), for Christ did not cancel the Law (IV, 16, 5). In refuting Gnosticism, Irenaeus saw himself as having no choice but to safeguard the unity of the two Testaments, and (given the Gnostic bifurcation of the Godhead) the ultimate unity of divinity itself.[36]

Irenaeus's task, of course, was to affirm the unity of the Testaments in a way that did not obscure or overlook the undeniable differences between them. The significance of these differences for salvation simply cannot be gainsaid. Thus, Irenaeus claims that God used the Law to draw 'slaves' to himself, but afterwards 'conferred upon them [the freedom]' of the new dispensation (*Against Heresies*, IV, 13, 4); so that although 'all natural precepts are common to us and to them (the Jews) . . . in us they have received growth and completion' (IV, 13, 4), 'for the Law does not confer perfect righteousness' (IV, 16 1). The old covenant, while it is an inalienable part of the economy of salvation, is nevertheless a merely preparatory stage that the human race had to pass through in the course of its journey towards the unique and unsurpassable moment in which it encountered the God-man:

> . . . the new covenant [was] known and preached by the prophets, He who was to carry it out according to the good pleasure of the Father was also preached, having been revealed to men as God

pleased; that they might always make progress through believing in Him, and by means of the [successive] covenants, should gradually attain to perfection (*Against Heresies*, IV, 9, 3).

The principle of a slow and progressive perfecting of the human race by God in Christ is the lynchpin of Irenaeus's *apologia* against Gnostic dualism. The Gnostic denial of the inseparability and the ultimate harmony of the Old and the New Testaments, and its concomitant denial of the unity of God, is countered by a sustained theological argument in which Irenaeus purports to show that because God is one, the God who is at work in Noah, Abraham, Moses and the prophets is precisely the God who was proclaimed by Jesus of Nazareth and who in turn was proclaimed in Jesus by Christians, and vice versa. The advance from the Old to the New Testament is not, as the Gnostics argued, a transition from one God to another; it is, rather, a continuous movement in which the out-reach of divine grace is extended from its original locus in one nation (Israel) to the historical moment when it comes to encompass the whole world. The difference between the two Testaments is thus emphatically not a difference between two entirely different things:

'[the words] *greater* and *less* are not applied to those things which have nothing in common between themselves, and are of an opposite nature, and mutually repugnant; but are used in the case of those of the same substance, and which possess properties in common, but merely differ in number and size; such as water from water, and light from light, and grace from grace' (*Against Heresies*, IV, 9, 2).

This understanding of the relation between the two dispensations is not confined by Irenaeus to the level of exegesis; the exegesis which he undertakes subserves and augments the elaborate theology of history at the heart of his theological vision. The key to this theology of history is the event of incarnation, that is, the mystery in which the God-man 'recapitulates' all things, including humanity, in himself.[37] In his own person Christ, the representative of all humanity in a concrete, historical form, sums up, transforms, consummates and restores all aspects of humanity. The covenant inaugurated by Christ, who is the absolute and ultimate disclosure of God, is the most decisive of the four covenants given to the human race:

> ... one, prior to the deluge, under Adam; the second, that after the deluge, under Noah; the third, the giving of the law, under Moses; the fourth, that which renovates man, and sums up all things in itself by means of the Gospel, raising and bearing men upon its wings into the heavenly kingdom (*Against Heresies*, III, 11, 8).

Christ, the new Adam, by this 'recapitulation' (*recapitulatio*), recovers everything that humanity has lost as a consequence of the disobedience of the first Adam. The incarnate One, who is God's very image, restores in humanity its original capacity for Godshapedness; and in so doing manifests himself as the redeemer of the whole of humanity.[38]

This theology of history, articulated in an entirely catechetical context (one which, moreover, had as its subject the individual who is in the process of being won over from *false* belief, as opposed to the *non*-believer or sceptic posited by the post-Enlightenment theodicy), has nothing whatever to do with the principle which under-pins those post-Leibnizian theodicies named after Irenaeus, that is, the principle which asserts that the world contains evil because evil is 'logically' required for the moral and spiritual development of souls as they move towards a perfect relationship with their Creator. There is a 'problem of evil' for Irenaeus, but it has absolutely nothing to do with this kind of 'soul-making' or with anything resembling a theodicy. For as Irenaeus sees it, the real problem concerning evil arises in quite another area of theological territory, one occupied by human beings who,

> puffed up by the pretence of knowledge, fall away from the love of God, and imagine that they themselves are perfect, for this reason ... they set forth an imperfect Creator ... It is therefore better ... that one should have no knowledge whatever of any reason why a single thing in creation has been made, but should believe in God, and continue in His love, than that, puffed up through knowledge of this kind, he should fall away from that love which is the life of man; and that he should search after no other knowledge except [the knowledge of] Jesus Christ the Son

of God, who was crucified for us, than that by subtle questions and hair-splitting expressions he should fall into impiety (*Against Heresies*, II, 26, 1).

Or as von Balthasar pithily puts it: where Irenaeus is concerned 'holiness is more important than gnosis'.[39] The real problem of evil, for Irenaeus, arises in connection with the struggle to love God truly in Christ, with being able to hold in check our deep reluctance to abide in the awful darkness of the mystery that is God, a reluctance which makes us turn with relief and in haste to the anodyne intellectual balm proffered by the Gnostic heretics.

I have tried to suggest that the attempt to align this second-century appreciation of the 'problem of evil' with the post-seventeenth century theodicy involves a conflation of two radically different, even incommensurable, intellectual contexts. It is mistaken to assume that Irenaeus and the modern theodicist, deeply immured as she is in 'philosophical theism', are in fact addressing themselves to the same questions; that they are somehow conducting their arguments on the basis of the same presuppositions and concepts (when, evidently, they are not). A comprehensive and detailed comparative study of the formal and semantic conditions of the different texts produced by ancient Christian thinkers and modern theodicists will of course require a great deal more than the cursory sketch I have just provided. It will require nothing less than the hypothetical reconstruction of the materials – content, narrative paradigms, discourse patterns, stylistic and 'grammatical' practices – which must be available in advance in order for a particular text to be produced in its unique historical context.[40] But I think I have done enough to indicate that the modern theodicists who blithely include the 'timeless' writings of Augustine and Irenaeus in the genealogies of their own material, have succeeded only in obscuring the unique historical specificity of these ancient texts. In failing to come to terms with this textual specificity, they have correspondingly failed to bring to light the historically contingent circumstances which surround the production of their own texts. As we shall see in chapter 1, this failure has profound implications for the enterprise of theodicy.

'COGNITIONAL INDIVIDUALISM'

The metaphysical theodicy of the seventeenth century and after takes as its starting-point the individual subject's *awareness* that the presence of evil and suffering in the world constitutes *prima facie* evidence against the existence, and/or the benevolence and/or the omnipotence, of God. The theodicist's aim, of course, is to vindicate God in the face of this *prima facie* evidence. The 'problem' which confronts the theodicist can be expressed most simply in terms of the following inconsistent set:

1 Evil exists on a considerable scale.
2 There is a God.
3 God is all-powerful.
4 God is morally perfect.

This set is held to be inconsistent inasmuch as the truth of (1), which not very many people would be prepared to gainsay, would seem to entail either: (a) that (2) is false (in which case the question of the truth or falsity of (3) and (4) would not even arise); or (b) if (2) is true, then (3) or (and) (4) are false. The Christian theodicist can attempt to banish the inconsistency of this set by: either (i) adding to it one or more propositions which, when taken together with (1)–(4), render these propositions mutually consistent; or (ii) *accepting* the anti-theodicist's denial of the truth of (3), while maintaining at the same time that this denial does not in any way entail the falsity of 'theism'.[41]

The tasks entailed in establishing (i) and (ii) are perhaps best undertaken in the tranquillity of the theodicist's study (a perusal of the writings of theodicists will tend invariably to confirm the suspicion that the study *is* very much the theodicist's domain). For the 'project' of theodicy is essentially a work of solitary reflection, something that can be engaged in by any individual who has the requisite capacity to judge, i.e., to make appropriate assertions and denials. Possessing the capacity to make such assertions and denials, the theodicist, *qua* epistemological subject, proceeds by ascribing truth (or falsity) to *judgements* – in this context judgements of the kind embodied in propositions (1)–(4) above. Judging is an activity of the will, so the diffence between the 'good' and the 'bad' theodicist consists pre-eminently in the former's ability and readiness to withold her judgement when the relevant grounds for assenting to the judgements in question are not forthcoming. Theodicy is thus a way of gathering knowledge, of *justifying* claims to knowledge. The theodicist's fundamental interest is in *cognition*, the kind of clear-headed epistemological activity that can be undertaken by the solitary contemplative subject.[42] Or to put it very briefly: theodicy is formulated when an *individual* turns his or her *mind* to the task of making temporally invariable judgements that serve to justify God and his ways vis-à-vis a world that contains evil. This is not the place to undertake a critique of the Cartesian legacy which bedevils modern theodicy (and much of contemporary theology). I shall restrict myself to making two very general and rather tendentious observations regarding the implications of this legacy for the enterprise of theodicy.

First, it should perhaps be noted that when it comes to the essentially *practical* task of overcoming evil or mitigating its effects, one is talking not so much about an individual epistemological subject, but about the subject of an action or a set of actions. And this subject is very rarely an individual agent (as the late Lucien Goldmann has reminded us):

> When I say the cat catches a mouse, there is no problem: the cat is the subject of this behaviour. However at the level where there is language and symbolic systems the situation is completely changed. A new element appears which . . . is made possible by communication . . . Were one to take the subject in the very strict sense as the agent of the action, if this table is too heavy to be lifted by one person and if two people, say John and James, lift it, it is neither John nor James who lifts the table: it is John-and-James. This is very important, because when it becomes a question of transforming society or modifying a whole combination of interior or exterior givens, there are no longer any individual subjects.[43]

If Goldmann's point is taken (and I am disposed to take it), then we must acknowledge that there is a quite radical discrepancy between the 'explanatory space' occupied by the modern theodicist, for whom theodicy is essentially a matter of making judgements, and the 'explanatory space' inhabited by those who seek actively to combat evil in all its historically particular manifestations. For, quite simply, the subject who occupies the former 'space' is very much the contemplative *individual* subject; whereas the occupant of the latter 'space' is the *trans-individual* subject. The implications of this distinction for theodicy are momentous (to say the least).

The trans-individuality of the subject is constituted by historical processes in such a way that the identity of this subject only emerges within a set of practices. In terms of Goldmann's example: it is only in the *act* of lifting the table that the (trans-individual) subjectivity of James and John comes to be established. Apart from this act there can be no basis for constituting this subjectivity. Hence, the assertion that the identity of the subject is engendered, defined and constrained by such practices carries with it a concomitant refusal to grant any kind of epistemic privilege to the solitary and historically-detached cognitive subject. This refusal, and its warrant, are given succinct expression by T.W. Adorno (1903–69):

> If truth has in fact a temporal core, then the full historical content becomes an integral moment in truth . . . The relation to experience is a relation to all of history; merely individual experience, in which the consciousness begins with what is nearest to it, is itself mediated by the all-encompassing experience of historical humanity; the claim that socio-historical contents are nevertheless supposed to be only indirectly important compared with the immediate life of the individual is a simple self-delusion of an individualistic society and ideology.[44]

This philosophic consciousness, one which is typified by the modern theodicist, 'entertains' judgements from a specious Archimedean or extra-textual standpoint outside the sphere of historical or textualizing activity. However, as Goldmann and Adorno (following the tradition of Vico, Hegel and Marx) remind us, all subjects are, ultimately, the outcome of human productive activity, and as such need to be seen as a kind of ideological text, a text 'scripted' by the subject's affiliations (whether acknowledged or not) with 'institutions, offices, agencies, classes, academies, corporations, groups, guilds, ideologically defined parties, and professions'.[45] The implications of this profound discrepancy between the respective 'explanatory spaces' occupied by the subject posited by the modern theodicy and the trans-individual subject will be discussed in the next chapter; for the time being, it need only be noted that this incommensurability exists, and that its

implications are potentially damaging to the whole enterprise of theodicy.

Second (and this observation is related to the preceding one),
the pursuit of holiness, the engagement in the often costly and
strenuous process of conversion, is not an activity that involves
an isolated human subject. In a properly Christian context,
conversion is inseparable from fellowship, a fellowship which is
at root fellowship with the Father and the Son in the Spirit,
fellowship with the Trinity itself. This fellowship is inseparable
from commitment to a community, a commitment expressed in
sharing its way of life, its customs and practices.[46] To be
converted is to be initiated into a way of life which, in the
context of the Christian faith, is inseparable from the practice of
discipleship. It is not fortuitous, therefore, that Irenaeus' whole
understandings of the economy of salvation should pivot on the
Greek notion of *paideia* ('education into release'), a notion which
defines true humanity in a way that involves an irreducibly
social dimension. *Paideia*, as expounded in the Irenaean scheme
of things, is to be understood in terms of the progressive
re-creation of all human beings, a work which God accomplishes
in and through Christ as he transforms the totality of nature
and history. In this work of re-creation, human beings come to
be shaped in the image of Christ, and in this way are restored to
a right relationship with God and with each other.[47] Likewise,
Augustine portrays the soul's ascent to God in explicitly
trinitarian, and hence social, terms: since God is the Trinity, the
image of God in the human soul is trinitarian, and the human
creature attains to her true humanity only by coming to love,
through the grace of God, this (trinitarian) image in herself.[48]

If Irenaeus and Augustine are right, and holiness and
conversion are the only authentically Christian responses to
'the problem of evil', then the only remotely adequate way of
resolving this 'problem' will be one which begins by moving the
theodicy-question into another, and quite different, theological
context, one which comes under the rubric of (a socially rooted)
redemption. But here we are likely to have a problem. For if my
arguments are correct, the 'cognitional individualism', the
deeply ingrained methodological solipsism that besets the
post-Leibnizian theodicy, must be reckoned to constitute a
grave and even insurmountable obstacle to any move of this
kind. To justify this rather pessimistic proposition, however, we

must first provide a more detailed specification of the proper form of an authentically Christian response to 'the problem of evil'.[49]

NARRATIVES

The exponent of the post-Leibnizian metaphysical theodicy, we have seen, is an essentially contemplative epistemic subject, one whose interests are apparently confined to *arguments* (which can then be tested for their 'coherence' and 'validity'), and *judgements* (which can then be examined for their 'evidentiality'). The highly abstract and thoroughly discursive nature of this activity becomes evident when we consider, concretely, how it is that a particular event, one which brings pain and suffering to an innocent human being, comes to be construed as a 'sign' which seemingly tells against God's righteousness (or in the case of some modern theodicies, against God's existence). The book of Job is a classic study of unwarranted suffering, and we can turn to it for a narrative of one individual's attempts to read the 'signs' that are embodied in his afflictions.[50]

Job, an upright and pious servant of God, enjoys good fortune. Suddenly, this is taken away from him. He finds himself in a new and bewildering situation, where he can hardly account for what goes on around him. The author of the book of Job portrays this as a spiritual crisis, but we can also look upon it as an epistemological crisis: the disasters that befall Job cause him to question the schemata which have previously informed all his interpretations of social and religious life, and especially his understanding of his relationship with God. Job, who attributed his happiness and prosperity to God, now finds that his understanding of this relationship is now longer adequate; his spiritual turmoil is so great that he has no real alternative but to seek a new vision of divinity.[51]

To begin with, he is content to curse the day he was born (Job 3:1), and to wish that God would end his agony by annihilating him (6:8–9). His wife advises him to curse God for afflicting him (2:9), but Job steadfastly refuses 'to sin with his lips' (2:10). However, when his friends Eliphaz, Bildad and Zophar arrive to comfort him, Job finds himself confronted by more than one schema for interpreting his new situation. His impeccably orthodox friends are anxious to justify the ways of God. In a series of homilies they present him with a variety of schemata, each amounting to a kind of theodicy, invoking sins that Job might have forgotten; sins that he might not have been aware of; sins committed by his ancestors; sins committed by his family; sins committed by his people. Job is in a position where he not only has to decide which of these schemata to apply, he has also to address the question: whom now do I believe? My wife? My friends (and if so, which of the several schemata enunciated by them?) Or do I trust my own instincts? Until he has adopted some schema Job will not be able to determine what he should regard as evidence; until he decides what to treat as evidence he cannot be sure which schema is the right one to adopt. As MacIntyre notes, the person undergoing an epistemological crisis is trapped in an 'epistemological circularity' in which 'the general form of her problem is: "What is going on here?"' [52] That this is Job's problem is indicated by his passionate cry to God:

> . . . let me speak, and do thou reply to me.
> How many are my iniquities and my sins?
> Make me know my transgression and my sin.
> Why dost thou hide thy face, and count me as thy enemy?
> (13:22–4)

and further:

> Oh, that I knew where I might find him,
> that I might come even to his seat!
> I would lay my case before him
> and would fill my mouth with arguments.
> I would learn what he would answer me,
> and would understand what he would say to me (23:3–5).

Job's plea that God should reveal to him what is going on around him can be expressed in terms of another question: 'How ought the narrative of these terrible events to be constructed?' Job's problems arise because the dramatic narrative of his life and of the divine economy within which he situates and lives his life has been ruptured by a radical interpretative doubt. In MacIntyre's words (albeit words addressed to the situation of

Hamlet), the task confronting Job is that of needing 'to reconstitute, to rewrite that narrative, reversing his understanding of past events in the light of present responses to his probing'.[53] MacIntyre goes on to say that 'this probing is informed by two ideals, truth and intelligibility, and the pursuit of both is not always easily coherent. The discovery of an hitherto unsuspected truth is just what may disrupt an hitherto intelligible account'. MacIntyre further notes that 'an epistemological crises is always a crisis in human relationships'. This is undoubtedly true in Job's case, though (as I have already indicated) it has to be acknowledged at the same time that his crisis is above all a crisis in his relationship with God.

An epistemological crisis is to be resolved by the construction of a new narrative which makes it possible for the protagonist to understand '*both* how he or she could intelligibly have held his or her original beliefs *and* how he or she could have been so drastically misled by them. The narrative in terms of which he or she first understood and ordered experiences is itself made into the subject of an enlarged narrative'. MacIntyre does not tell us in any detail how this enlarged narrative comes to be composed when an individual seeks to resolve an epistemological crisis, but we can take up his insights by employing the notion of a 'collision' between narratives to thematize the situation in which this more comprehensive narrative comes to be enunciated.[54]

Where Job is concerned, we have a crisis generated by the collision between his *personal* narrative, that narrative which has as its subject a devout and morally upright individual, and an *external* or 'objective historical' narrative, a narrative which recounts, 'historically', the succession of misfortunes that have befallen this seemingly innocent subject. The 'enlarged narrative' advertised by MacIntyre is in effect a rewritten personal narrative in which the recalcitrant external or objective historical narrative has come to be 'sedimented'. In this process of 'sedimentation', the events with feature in the external narrative are reconstructed or 'emplotted' within the new and larger narrative pattern, so that a new manner of speaking about events and individuals becomes possible. A new order of meaning is inaugurated.[55] Job begins to 'write' this more comprehensive narrative when he starts to formulate his rejoinders to his comforters. It is a narrative which shows Job to have moved beyond the faith of his fathers to a new kind of faith, a faith in which Job turns in real hope to the God who speaks 'out of the whirlwind', that is, the holy mystery who is heard through the categories of the concealed, the unexplained, and the arbitrary. His experience has compelled him to tread the path of unknowing. God refuses to give Job the explanations he craves, and Job has to work towards a faith beyond all purely personal concerns. In repenting of his stupidity in speaking of things that he cannot understand (40:3–5; 42:1–6), Job learns that he has to love and worship this hidden and unknowable God for God's own sake. Or to make the same point in terms of a theological 'grammar': Job is brought to the realization that there can be no 'order' or 'ratio' between finite and infinite.[56]

We can generalize the above account by saying that, in an indentifiably Christian context, the 'problem of evil' arises (at least in part) when *particular* narratives of events of pain, dereliction, anguish, oppression, torture, humiliation, degradation, injustice, hunger, godforsakenness, and so on, come into collision with the Christian community's narratives, which are inextricably bound up with the redeeming reality of the triune God. These events, we have suggested, generate epistemological crises in which agents come to realise that the schemata of interpretation on which they have so far relied have broken down irretrievably, a realization which gives an impetus to the construction of more adequate narratives and forms of narrative. The Leibnizian theodicy, I wish to suggest, cannot come to terms with such epistemological crises and their narrative resolutions. For this theodicy has as its sole focus of investigation a range of *arguments* and *judgements*, arguments and judgements which their proponents hold to be true (or false) irrespective of time, place and persons. Thus, for example, Richard Swinburne and Alvin Plantinga would almost certainly hold their theodicies to be valid and cogent for Nelson Mandela and President Botha alike, for the investment banker in Zürich and the nomad in Chad alike, for this present time and, say, the first century AD alike. By contrast, the student of epistemological crises and of the narrative discourses which they engender will be aware that the form and the content of these discourses are essentially such that we can hope to determine their true nature only by scrutinizing the cultural *practices*, the *forms of life* or the *socio-historical* configurations in which these crises and their accompanying discourses are embedded. This student, unlike the metaphysical theodicist, will acknowledge from the outset that all reflection is historically situated.

It will perhaps have crossed the mind of some readers that I have not so far drawn any distinction between those questions that are held to arise for the theodicist because evil *per se* exists and those questions that can properly be held to be posed by the phenomenon of suffering. The problems of evil and those of suffering are of course asymmetrical: thus (and this is a *very* large generalization), not all instances of suffering are in themselves evil, and not all manifestations of evil need be accompanied by suffering (whether visible or otherwise). Nothing that I have said so far has required us to make this evidently important distinction; we shall, however, need to broach it later (in chapter 2).

NOTES

1 David Hume, *Dialogues Concerning Natural Religion*, ed. H. D. Aiken (New York: Harper, 1948), Part X, p. 66. The term 'theodicy' is derived from the Greek *theos* (God) and *dikē* (justice); hence 'demonstrating that God is just'.
2 Walter Kasper, *The God of Jesus Christ*, trans. M. J. O'Connell, (London: SCM, 1984), p. 294. See also p. 295, where Kasper speaks of 'the heresy of theism'.
3 Kasper, *The God of Jesus Christ*, p. 295.
4 For Lash's argument, to which I am greatly indebted, see 'Considering the Trinity', *Modern Theology*, 2 (1986), pp. 183–94. For Phillips's argument, see 'The Friends of Cleanthes', *Modern Theology*, 1 (1985), pp. 91–104. Phillips believes that Swinburne (and his critic J. L. Mackie) 'mislocate the logic of the word "God" because they treat God as an object among objects' (p. 100). Interestingly, Denys Turner has argued that a similar mislocation underlies Don Cupitt's critique of 'objective theism'. See Turner's 'De-centring Theology', *Modern Theology*, 2 (1986), pp. 125–43. It should be acknowledged that our reflections on Swinburne's theism will be deeply indebted to the criticisms advanced by Lash. T. W. Jennings's *Beyond Theism* (Oxford: Oxford University Press, 1985) addresses similar issues, but was not published in time to be considered in this book.
5 Richard Swinburne, *The Existence of God* (Oxford: Clarendon, 1979), pp. 103–6. See also pp. 8–9. See also *The Coherence of Theism*

(Oxford: Clarendon, 1977), p. 1. As will be seen later (in chapter 3), essentially the same kind of theism is sponsored by Alvin Plantinga, John Hick and (with very substantial qualifications) the exponents of the 'process' theodicy.

6 Swinburne, *The Coherence of Theism*, p. 1.

7 Lash quotes from Swinburne, *The Coherence of Theism*, p. 222. Lash wants to argue that Swinburne's understanding of the nature of God would seem effectively to preclude a specifically trinitarian, and hence a properly Christian, understanding of the mystery of God.

8 Swinburne, *The Existence of God*, pp. 221–2. It is perhaps noteworthy that there is no mention of the Holy Spirit anywhere in Swinburne's highly acclaimed trilogy.

9 Swinburne, *The Existence of God*, p. 222.

10 These two assumptions are integral to the positions of Swinburne and Plantinga. Where Hick's theism is concerned, a necessary caveat must be entered with regard to assumption (2). For, as Hick sees it, the infinite divine reality, since it is conceptually 'neutral', can appropriately be 'schematized' or 'concretized' in terms of both personal and non-personal categories. In this scheme of things, a trinitarian understanding of divinity is merely one among the many legitimate, and ineluctably divergent, forms of religious 'experiencing-as'. The obvious corollary is that such a trinitarian conception of divinity is always 'optional', inasmuch as it is an item that is (culturally) specific to a particular, and in Hick's view, limited, tradition of religious awareness and theological conception. For these matters, see Hick's essays, 'Seeing-as and Religious Experience', 'A Philosophy of Religious Pluralism', and 'Religious Pluralism and Absolute Claims', in his collection of essays *Problems of Religious Pluralism* (London: Macmillan, 1985), pp. 16–27, 28–45, and 46–65 respectively. See especially pp. 26–7, 41–4, and 47ff. Hick discusses the Trinity specifically in 'Towards a Philosophy of Religious Pluralism', *Neue Zeitschrift für Systematische Theologie und Religionsphilosophie*, 22 (1980), pp. 131–49. See especially p. 144. But see Hick's contribution to a symposium with Swinburne and D. Z. Phillips, where he explicitly refers to God as an individual centre of 'consciousness'. For this designation of divinity, see Hick's 'The Problem of Evil: Remarks', in S. C. Brown, ed., *Reason and Religion* (London and Ithaca: Cornell University Press, 1977), p. 122. Phillips chides Hick for this anthropomorphism in his 'Postscript', p. 134.

11 For use of the metaphor of 'exploration' in the context of modern theism, see Lash, *'Considering the Trinity'*, pp. 186 ff.

12 On this 'pedagogy', see Lash, *'Considering the Trinity'*, pp. 192–3. In the context of the Christian faith this 'pedagogy' refers to the

arduous and sometimes painful process whereby Christians strive to follow the way of Christ.

13 This 'grammatical' rule, associated with the radical critique of anthropomorphism, has a long and reputable philosophical heritage, going back to Plato's remark in the *Timaeus* (28e) that it is impossible for the discoverer of the Father and Maker of the universe then to speak of him to all and sundry, and to the critique of popular religion associated with Xenophanes. Plato's remark is quoted by a number of Church Fathers, including Clement of Alexandria, Origen and Gregory Nazianzen. Xenophanes is cited by Clement. For references and a splendid discussion of this material, see Frances M. Young, 'The God of the Greeks and the Nature of Religious Language', in W. R. Schoedel and R. L. Wilken, eds, *Early Christian Literature and the Classical Intellectual Tradition: in honorem Robert M. Grant* (Paris: Beauchesne, 1979), pp. 45–74. This rule receives its fullest thematization in the writings of St Thomas Aquinas. See especially *Summa Theologiae*, 1.3. Intro, and 1.3.4.2. Hans von Balthasar has rightly made the point that modern theologians have lost the sense of God's fundamental incomprehensibility. See his 'The Unknown God', in M. Kehl and W. Löser, eds, *The Von Balthasar Reader* (New York: Crossroad, 1982), pp. 181–7. On p. 182 von Balthasar cites Augustine's proposition *Si comprehendis non est Deus* ('If you think you have conceived something, what you conceived was certainly not God').

14 On this point, see my 'Philosophical Reflection and the Trinity', *Modern Theology* 2 (1986), pp. 235–56. See especially pp. 239ff. Space prevents me from discussing the historical factors which were responsible for spawning and legitimizing this philosophical theism. A masterly discussion of the topic is to be found in Jeffrey Stout, *The Flight from Authority* (Notre Dame: University of Notre Dame Press, 1981).

15 See Plantinga's *The Nature of Necessity* (Oxford: Clarendon, 1974), p. 192. For Augustine's proposition concerning the activity of bad angels, see his *Enchiridion*, i–iv, in the translation of the Library of Christian Classics, vol. VII, ed. and trans. Albert C. Outler (London: SCM, 1955), pp. 341–6.

16 For Hick's theodicy, see *Evil and the God of Love* (London: Fontana/Collins, 1968), Parts III and IV. In his more recent essay 'An Irenaean Theodicy', in Stephen T. Davis, ed., *Encountering Evil: live options in theodicy* (Edinburgh: T. & T. Clark, 1981), pp. 39–52, Hick is careful to point out that Irenaeus himself did not formulate a theodicy, and that it would therefore be misleading to attribute such a 'soul-making' theodicy to him. Hick suggests that Irenaeus should instead be seen as the 'patron saint' of this kind of

theodicy. See p. 41. But the implication is clear: if Irenaeus had wanted to develop such a theodicy, it would have been perfectly *possible* for him to have done so. Hick's distinction between the Irenaean and the Augustinian types of theodicy is endorsed in Brian Hebblethwaite, *Evil, Suffering and Religion* (London: Sheldon, 1979), p. 58. For the views of Irenaeus, see his *Against Heresies*, in the translation of the Ante-Nicene Library (Grand Rapids: Eerdmans, 1979), vol. I, pp. 315–567.

17 Swinburne, *The Coherence of Theism*, p. 7.

18 Swinburne, *The Existence of God*, pp. 1–2.

19 Alasdair MacIntyre, 'Is Understanding Religion Compatible with Believing?', in Bryan R. Wilson, ed., *Rationality* (Oxford: Blackwell, 1974), p. 73. See also his American Bampton Lectures, jointly delivered with Paul Ricoeur, 'The Debate About God: Victorian Relevance and Contemporary Irrelevance', in MacIntyre and Ricoeur, *The Religious Significance of Atheism* (New York: Columbia University, 1969), p. 14, where MacIntyre says: '. . . the God in whom the nineteenth and early twentieth centuries came to disbelieve had been invented only in the seventeenth century'.

20 MacIntyre and Ricoeur, *The Religious Significance of Altheism* p. 74. Elsewhere MacIntyre says: 'It is only when theories are located in history, when we view the demands for justification in highly particular contexts of a historical kind, that we are freed from either dogmatism or capitulation to scepticism.' See his 'Epistemological Crises, Dramatic Narrative and the Philosophy of Science', *The Monist*, 60 (1977), p. 471.

21 *Our Lord's Sermon on the Mount*, I, xii, 34, in the translation of the Nicene and post-Nicene Library (Grand Rapids: Eerdmans, 1979), vol. VI, p. 15. For Augustine's analysis of memory, see *Confessions*, X, viii–xxv, in the translation of the Library of Christian Classics, vol. VII, ed. and trans. Albert C. Outler, (London: SCM, 1955), pp. 208–24. All page references given within parentheses are to this translation.

22 On the 'weight of carnal habit', see *Confessions*, VII, xvii, 28 (p. 150). On sin as 'the tyranny of habit, by which the mind is drawn and held, even against its will', see XIII, v, 12 (p. 165).

23 Augustine, *Confessions*, VIII, v, 10 (p. 164).

24 See Augustine, *The Trinity*, XIII, 9, 12, in the translation of the Nicene and Post-Nicene Library, (Grand Rapids: Eerdmans, 1978), vol. VIII, pp. 173–4. See also *The City of God*, X, 29, in the same translation, vol. II, (Grand Rapids: Eerdmans, 1977), pp. 199–200. For a general discussion of this point, see R. A. Markus, 'Marius Victorinus and Augustine', in A. H. Armstrong, ed., *The Cambridge History of Later Greek & Early Medieval Philosophy* (Cambridge: Cambridge University Press, 1967), Part V, pp. 344–5.

25 G. R. Evans, *Augustine on Evil* (Cambridge: Cambridge University Press, 1982), p. 128.

26 To quote Gillian Evans: 'Everything Augustine has to say about evil must be read in the light of one central principle: that the effect of evil upon the world is to make it impossible for the sinner to think clearly, and especially to understand higher, spiritual truths and ideas' (*Augustine on Evil*, p. 29). On faith as the indispensable starting-point of knowledge, see *The Trinity*, XIII, 9, 12 (pp. 173–4). See also IX, 1, 1, (p. 125); and VIII, 4, 6 (p. 118), where Augustine says: 'except He [i.e. God] is loved by faith, it will not be possible for the heart to be cleansed, in order that it may be apt and meet to see Him'. For a penetrating discussion of the relation between faith and vision in Augustine, see Margaret Miles, 'Vision: The Eye of the Body and the Eye of the Mind in Saint Augustine's *De trinitate* and *Confessions*', *The Journal of Religion*, 63 (1983), pp. 125–42, especially pp. 130ff. It is not surprising, therefore, to find that Augustine reserves his discussion of specifically theological topics for the last three chapters of the *Confessions*, implying thereby that he himself had to acquire a profoundly new language for God, and to allow its 'syntax' to penetrate into the deepest reaches of his soul (i.e. he had to undergo conversion), before he was in any sort of position to apprehend the real truth about God. There is a fine discussion of this subject in David Burrell, *Exercises in Religious Understanding* (Notre Dame: University of Notre Dame Press, 1974), pp. 11–41. See especially pp. 21–7. The influence of Plotinus in Augustine's account of life as a progressive liberation from the sensible and material realm has been noted in Robert J. O'Connell, 'Action and Contemplation', in R. A. Markus, ed., *Augustine: A Collection of Critical Essays* (New York: Doubleday/Anchor, 1972), pp. 38–58.

27 Peter Brown, *Augustine of Hippo: A Biography* (London: Faber, 1967), p. 159. A succinct account of this historical background to Augustine's views is to be found in R. A. Markus, 'Marius Victorinus and Augustine', pp. 341ff. Augustine's repudiation of the Theodosian age is expressed most decisively in *The City of God*, XV–XXII. For discussion, see Peter Brown, 'Saint Augustine: Political Society', in R. A. Markus, ed., *Augustine*, pp. 311–29.

28 This is Walter Kasper's characterization of Augustine's theology of history. See *The God of Jesus Christ*, p. 106. The fullest development of Augustine's theological 'reading' of history is of course to be found in *The City of God*.

29 For Augustine's theory of the divine illumination of the human mind, see *The Trinity*, XI, 3, 6 (pp. 147–8); and XII, 15, 24 (pp. 164–5). See also *Retractiones*, I, 4, in *Augustine: Earlier Writings*, in the translation of the Library of Christian Classics, ed. J. H. S.

Burleigh, (Philadelphia: Westminster, 1953), p. 18; *Soliloquies*, I, i, 3 and I, viii, 15, in *Augustine: Earlier Writings*, pp. 24–5 and 32; and *On the Gospel of St John*, XV, 19–20, in the translation of the Nicene and Post-Nicene Library, vol. VII, pp. 103–4. For discussion, see Markus, 'Marius Victorinus and Augustine', pp. 362–74; and Ronald H. Nash, *The Light of the Mind: St Augustine's Theory of Knowledge* (Lexington: University Press of Kentucky, 1969). See also Evans, *Augustine on Evil*, pp. 128ff. On Augustine's 'Christian Platonism', see A. H. Armstrong, 'St Augustine and Christian Platonism', in R. A. Markus, ed., *Augustine*, pp. 3–37.

30 Critiques of this Lockean-Cartesian (and, by extension of this philosophical tradition, ultimately Kantian) 'theory of knowledge' are now playing an increasing part in current philosophical debate, and have become established as a separate and clearly identifiable genre in Anglo-American philosophy. The leading practitioners are commonly thought to be Wilfrid Sellars, Richard Rorty, Alasdair MacIntyre, Ian Hacking and Charles Taylor. See their following works: Sellars, 'Empiricism in the Philosophy of Mind', in his *Science, Perception and Reality* (London: Routledge & Kegan Paul, 1963), pp. 127–97; Rorty, *Philosophy and the Mirror of Nature* (Oxford: Blackwell, 1980); Alasdair MacIntyre, 'Epistemological Crises', pp. 453–72; Ian Hacking, *The Emergence of Probability* (Cambridge: Cambridge University Press, 1975); and Charles Taylor, 'Philosophy and its History', in R. Rorty, J. B. Schneewind and Q. Skinner, eds, *Philosophy in History* (Cambridge: Cambridge University Press, 1984), pp. 17–30. See also the contributions by Hacking, MacIntyre and Rorty in *Philosophy in History*. I am indebted to all these works for various aspects of my discussion.

31 It is true of course that Descartes, in his *Meditations*, posited a deity who underpinned human cognitive mechanisms; and that Locke maintained that 'the belief of a Deity is not to be reckoned amongst purely speculative opinions, for it [represents] the foundation of . . . the whole life and actions of men . . .' (in *Epistola de Tolerantia* (*A Letter on Toleration*), ed. J. W. Gough and R. Klibansky, (Oxford: Clarendon, 1968), pp. 15–16). But this Cartesian and Lockean deity is a mere epistemological (and in Locke's case, an ethical and social) long-stop: this divinity does not transform our thinking and willing in the sense presupposed by Augustine. Besides, as Annette Baier has rightly noted, modern philosophers tend anyway to discard this Cartesian-Lockean invocation of the deity, even while according a canonical status to Descartes and Locke. See her 'Secular Faith', in Stanley Hauerwas and Alasdair MacIntyre, eds, *Revisions: Changing Perspectives in Moral Philosophy* (Notre Dame: University of Notre Dame Press, 1983), p. 203.

32 As indicated by Père Daniélou in his magisterial *Gospel Message and Hellenistic Culture*, trans. John Austin Baker, (London: Darton, Longman & Todd, 1973), p. 166.

33 For summary accounts of Gnosticism see Daniélou, *Gospel Message and Hellenistic Culture*, pp. 82–9; J. N. D. Kelly, *Early Christian Doctrines* (London: Black, 5th ed., 1977), pp. 22–8; Johannes Quasten, *Patrology: vol. 1 (The Beginnings of Patristic Literature)* (Utrecht–Antwerp: Spectrum, 1975), chap. VII; and Harry Austryn Wolfson, *The Philosophy of the Church Fathers* (Cambridge, Mass.: Harvard University Press, 3rd rev. ed., 1970), pp. 495–574. These summaries rely largely on the testimonies of Irenaeus and Hippolytus (died c. 235). For Irenaeus, see *Against Heresies*, I, 1, 1–8. For Hippolytus, see *The Refutation of All Heresies*, VI, 2–37, in the translation of the Ante-Nicene Library, (Grand Rapids: Eerdmans, 1978), vol. V, pp. 74–94. Gnosticism taught that the spirit is redeemed through knowledge or *gnosis* (hence 'gnostic').

34 Irenaeus, *Against Heresies*, II, 9–10.

35 Irenaeus, *Against Heresies*, II, 1, 1. See also II, 9, 1; and III, 1, 2. Irenaeus maintains that this conception of the Creator is acknowledged by Moses (IV, 2, 1) and Jesus (IV, 1, 1). It should be stressed that Irenaeus objected to Gnosticism not so much because it was inherently dualistic, but because he feared that Gnosticism ends up by subordinating God to nature because Gnosticism demanded that the divine will be inserted into the cosmic system. This point is made in Richard Norris, 'The Transcendence and Freedom of God: Irenaeus, the Greek Tradition and Gnosticism', in W. R. Schoedel and R. L. Wilken, eds, *Early Christian Literature*, pp. 87–100.

36 'The affirmation of the oneness of God, imperilled by Gnostic speculation of every sort, was the indispensable premiss for refuting the Gnostic separation of the Testaments, and to demonstrate this oneness was the principle task of Irenaeus and his contemporaries'. J. N. D. Kelly, *Early Christian Doctrines*, p. 69. See also Hans Urs von Balthasar's magnificent essay on Irenaeus in his *The Glory of the Lord: A Theological Aesthetics: vol. II*, trans. A. Louth, F. McDonagh and B. McNeil, (Edinburgh: T. & T. Clark, 1984), p. 42.

37 Irenaeus, *Against Heresies*, III, 16, 6. Daniélou provides a superb exposition of Irenaeus's theory of recapitulation in his *Gospel Message and Hellenistic Culture*, pp. 166–83.

38 On Irenaeus's understanding of Christ as the restorer of our capacity for Godshapedness, see Aidan Nicholls, *The Art of God Incarnate: Theology and Image in Christian Tradition* (London: Darton, Longman & Todd, 1980), p. 63.

39 Kehl and Löser, eds, *The von Balthasar Reader*, p. 44.

40 A procedure for undertaking such a historical reconstruction is outlined in Frederic Jameson, *The Political Unconscious: Narrative as a Socially Symbolic Act* (London: Methuen, 1981), *passim*. I am much indebted to this book, which, while it does not deal with the theodicy-question in any way, nevertheless caused me to understand for the first time its true nature as a mode of discourse. My only reservation about Jameson's book concerns what Edward W. Said has aptly termed its 'religious confidence in the teleological efficacy of the Marxist vision'. See Said's 'Opponents, Audiences, Constituencies, and Community', *Critical Inquiry*, 9 (1982), pp. 1–26, see especially p. 14. Said's essay, which is likewise not concerned with theodicy, is absolutely essential reading for anyone else who writes and thinks about the 'problem of evil'.

41 Theodicists who espouse the latter alternative are therefore prepared to say that evil exists because *it is not in God's power* to bring about its complete eradication. The denial of (4) is far more difficult for the Christian theodicist to accommodate, because it is hard to see how divinity can be recognized in the way that Christians purport to recognize it if it made *sense* to say that God is 'morally imperfect'. The more usual way of dealing with the denial of (4) is to argue that human moral categories do not apply to divinity.

42 Readers familiar with the more recent writings of Richard Rorty and Richard J. Bernstein will recognize the 'Cartesian' ancestry of the modern theodicist's procedure. See Rorty, *Philosophy and the Mirror of Nature;* and Richard J. Bernstein, *Beyond Objectivism and Relativism: Science, Hermeneutics and Praxis* (Oxford: Blackwell, 1983), pp. 115–18. Essential to all the different varieties of Cartesianism is the assumption, whether explicit or tacit, that the mind of the *individual* is the 'place' where understanding occurs.

43 Lucien Goldmann, 'Structure: Human Reality and Methodological Subject', in R. Macksey and E. Donato, eds, *The Languages of Criticism and the Sciences of Man* (Baltimore: Johns Hopkins, 1970), p. 101.

44 T. W. Adorno, 'The Essay as Form', trans. B. Hullot-Kentor and F. Will, *New German Critique*, number 32 (1984), p. 158. Adorno's essay contains a sharp critique of the four rules of epistemological method formulated by Descartes in his *Discourse on Method*. See especially pp. 161–5.

45 On this see Edward W. Said's discussion of Michel Foucault's analyses of how modern subjects come to be 'scripted' by collective organizations, in Said's 'The Problem of Textuality: Two Exemplary Positions', *Critical Inquiry*, 4 (1978), pp. 673–714.

46 Here I am indebted to Andrew Louth, *Discerning the Mystery: an essay on the nature of theology* (Oxford: Clarendon, 1983), p. 75.

47   Andrew Louth correctly suggests that an appropriately Christian
     elucidation of the *paideia* concept will be one expressed in terms of
     the doctrine of creation. See *Discerning the Mystery*, pp. 75ff. I
     argue that the Christian understanding of atonement needs to be
     located in the Irenaean framework of a progressive re-creation of
     humanity in my 'Atonement and Christology', *Neue Zeitschrift für
     Systematische Theologie und Religionsphilosophie*, 24 (1982), pp.
     131–49. There is a masterly conspectus of this concept in Edward
     Schillebeeckx, *Jesus: an Experiment in Christology*, trans. Hubert
     Hoskins, (London: Collins, 1979), pp. 562–70. The definitive
     treatment of the *paideia* concept is Werner Jaeger's massive
     Paideia: the Ideals of Greek Culture (3 vols), (Oxford: Oxford
     University Press, 1944).
48   On the trinitarian image of God in the soul, see *The Trinity*, VII, 6,
     12 (p. 113). Here I follow the account provided in Andrew Louth,
     *The Origins of the Christian Mystical Tradition: From Plato to
     Denys* (Oxford: Clarendon, 1981), pp. 132–58. On p. 136 Louth,
     citing the work of G. B. Ladner, notes that 'an important
     strand . . . in Augustine's thought stresses the social nature of final
     beatitude'. See G. B. Ladner, *The Idea of Reform: its Impact on
     Christian Thought and Action in the Age of the Fathers* (Cambridge,
     Mass.: Harvard University Press, 1959), pp. 282ff. A similar
     estimation of Augustine is to be found in Brown, 'Saint Augustine:
     Political Society', in Markus (ed.), *Augustine*, pp. 311–29. For
     criticism of Augustine's idea that the human soul or person is
     formed in the image of the Trinity, see A. C. Lloyd, 'On Augustine's
     Concept of a Person', in Markus, ed., *Augustine*, pp. 191–205.
49   The philosophical character of this Cartesian-based 'cognitional
     individualism' will be explored more fully on pp. 47–8 below.
50   I am well aware of Brevard S. Childs's reminder that 'few books
     in the Old Testament present such a wide range of critical
     problems as does the book of Job'. See his *Introduction to the Old
     Testament as Scripture* (Philadelphia: Fortress, 1979), p. 528.
     Childs suggests that the sufferings of Job can be seen from two
     perspectives: one which understands Job's plight in terms of the
     wager struck between God and Satan in the book's prologue, and
     the other which views Job's sufferings from his own standpoint,
     that is, one where Job lacked all knowledge of this wager and thus
     of God's will (pp. 533–4). With the needs of our own discussion
     specifically in mind, I shall opt for the second of these perspectives
     in glossing Job's story.
        I am also aware that not everything I have to say subsequently
     will be mentioned explicitly in the book of Job. But no less an
     authority than Paul Ricoeur has said that the book of Job gives its
     reader an 'impulse' which she then has to bring to 'completion' in

herself. He is right. See his *The Symbolism of Evil*, trans, E. Buchanan, (Boston: Beacon, 1969), p. 322.

51 In my characterization of Job's epistemological crisis I am deeply indebted to Alasdair MacIntyre's 'Epistemological Crises, Dramatic Narrative and the Philosophy of Science', especially pp. 454ff. MacIntyre explicates the notion of such a crises via a fascinating case-study of Hamlet. In depicting Job's predicament as an epistemological crisis of the kind delineated by MacIntyre, I do not mean to imply that Hamlet and Job have anything in common apart from their radical need to make sense of what is going on around them.

52 MacIntyre, 'Epistemological Crises,' p. 454.

53 MacIntyre, 'Epistemological Crises,' p. 455.

54 For an account of how this 'collision' between narratives is to be understood in a Christian context, see George W. Stroup, *The Promise of Narrative Theology* (Atlanta: John Knox, 1981).

55 On narrative as the creation of a new order of meaning, see Hayden White, 'The Value of Narrativity in the Representation of Reality', *Critical Inquiry*, 7 (1980), pp. 5–27.

56 I deal more fully with the subject of a faith that is beyond all consolation in my 'Atonement and Moral Apocalypticism', *New Blackfriars*, 64 (1983), pp. 300–15.

CHAPTER 1

The Possibility of Theodicy: I

Confronted with the seemingly innumerable 'solutions' to the 'problem of evil' advanced over the last couple of centuries, the sceptically-inclined historian of theodicy would probably be disposed to claim that Kant's complaint about the metaphysics of his time is just as applicable to theodicy:

> [it] has rather to be regarded as a battle-ground peculiarly suited for those who desire to exercise themselves in mock combats, and in which no participant has ever yet succeeded in gaining so much as an inch of territory, not at least in such manner as to secure him its permanent possession.[1]

While theodicists – in conformity with the post-Enlightenment epistemological paradigm – often display remarkable ingenuity in their attempts to establish the logical invulnerability of their conclusions, these conclusions nevertheless give the appearance of resting on precariously makeshift foundations: the arguments advanced by the theodicist in support of her conclusions seem at times to be no more than ad hoc devices designed to prop up a theoretical superstructure already on the verge of collapse. What intellectual, and therefore ultimately historical, conditions account for and sustain this rather unfavourable initial impression of theodicy's achievements?

An idea or set of ideas is given plausibility and rendered intelligible by the social and material reality in which it is grounded and which it mediates. If these social and material configurations are absent, then the argument which hinges on them is unlikely to survive, even if it is articulated and defended by philosophical and theological virtuosi. The theologian or philosopher who studies the 'problem of evil' at some depth, and who professes to resolve it, will therefore have to make attempts to secure her arguments by making an excursion into the history of ideas. The same path will obviously have to be taken by the critic of theodicy. Both these protagonists will thereby engage in what Michel Foucault (1926–84) has referred to as an 'archaeology of knowledge'.[2] Only in this way will they be able adequately to reflect on the real or historical causes of the failures of those who engage in theodicy.

A study of the history of theodicy conducted in the manner of an 'archaeology of knowledge' will reveal three socio-historical reasons why attempts to formulate a viable theodicy are apt to be unsuccessful (or, at least, to culminate in a merely forensic victory on the part of the theodicist).

THE FIRST PROBLEM: THE INTELLECTUAL LEGACY OF
THE ENLIGHTENMENT

The contemporary theodicist has little alternative but to take seriously the real, because historically generated, possibility that this is an epoch in which it is no longer possible for us to address ourselves legitimately to 'the problem of evil'. That is, it may be that ours is an epoch in which historical conditions are such that it is no longer possible to view evil as 'problem' that can be 'answered' by an essentially intellectual or theoretical undertaking like theodicy. Thus it could be argued that theodicy gets off the ground only if it is granted the supposition that it is possible, in principle, to understand what goes on in the universe in terms of a larger, divine order. Without this supposition (that is, of God as the supreme Architect and Sustainer of the universe) it would be pragmatically futile to seek a justification of God vis-à-vis the fact of evil. (Such an endeavour on the part of the theodicist would be the pragmatic equivalent of trying to get someone to assent to the *truth* of a proposition before he or she had even grasped its *meaning*. Such an undertaking would be hopelessly unavailing from the very outset.) And, our historical objection proceeds, the epoch in which we live is precisely one in which there no longer exist the discursive and non-discursive formations which shape discourses requiring as their absolute presupposition *a God who is an almighty Creator*. According to the proponent of this broadly historical objection, the theodicist is deficient in historical knowledge: she sets out to address a problem which presupposes a *dispositif* or 'apparatus (of intelligibility)' no longer available to individuals living in a desacrilized age.[3] Let me amplify this argument in support of the thesis that historical conditions have generated a set of cultural practices which have effectively made theodicy a futile and unintelligible undertaking.

The Enlightenment was a watershed for theodicy. The revolution in physics and cosmology inaugurated by Galileo and Newton, leading as it did to the break-up of the Aristotelian-Thomist system (the so-called 'mediaeval synthesis'), posed a number of intellectual problems which simply could not have arisen for the theologians and philosophers of the mediaeval world. One of the more formidable of these problems was concerned with the existence of evil.

Galileo (1564–1642), who was already a follower of Copernicus (1473–1543), evolved a scientific procedure that reflected his virtually unconstrained confidence in human reason's capacity to unravel the secrets of nature. His confidence in this procedure prompted him to dispute the authority of Scripture in determining matters of fact:

> ... In discussions of physical problems we ought to begin not from the authority of scriptural passages, but from sense-experiences and necessary demonstrations ... It is necessary for the Bible, in order to be accommodated to the understanding of every man, to speak many things which appear to differ from the absolute truth so far as the bare meaning of words is concerned. But Nature, on the other hand, is inexorable and immutable, she never transgresses the laws imposed upon her, or cares a whit whether her abstruse reasons and methods of operation are understandable to men. For this reason it appears that nothing physical which sense-experience sets before our eyes, or which necessary demonstration proves to us, ought to be called in question (much less condemned) upon the testimony of biblical passages which have some different meaning beneath their words. For the Bible is not chained in every expression to conditions as strict as those which govern all physical effects ...[4]

Hand in hand with Galileo's spurning of Scripture as a basis for determining truth about the physical world went his repudiation of the Aristotelian teleology favoured by scholastic thinkers. In his polemical work *Dialogue Concerning the Two Chief Systems of the World* (which Galileo dedicated to the Pope), the God of final causation, that is, the God who implanted his purposes in the foundations of the universe, was set aside in favour of the God of efficient causation, that is, the deity who created the atoms of a fundamentally independent and self-sustaining natural order. Galileo's cosmology seemingly retains a place for God, who is still required to bring atoms into existence, but divine causal efficacy becomes progressively restricted as subsequent causality within nature is grounded in the activity of already created atoms. The outlines of an essentially deanimated (and hence dedivinized), rational and mechanistic conception of the universe had been etched by Galileo, and others, notably Isaac Newton (born in 1642, the year of Galileo's death), were to complete the project he had embarked upon.

Newton, invoking only the concepts of motion, matter, space and time, showed physical nature to operate according to a single universal law – the law of attraction – which needed God only to create the universe and to intervene from time to time to maintain its stability. E. A. Burtt gives the following vivid characterization of the Newtonian universe:

> In the Newtonian world . . . [the] cosmic order of masses in motion according to law, is itself the final good. Man exists to know and applaud it; God exists to tend and preserve it. All the manifold divergent zeals and hopes of man are implicitly denied scope and fulfilment; if they cannot be subjected to the aims of theoretical mechanics, their possessors are left no proper God, for them there is no entrance into the Kingdom of heaven . . . God, now the chief mechanic of the universe, has become the cosmic conservative. His aim is to maintain the status quo. The day of novelty is all in the past; there is no further advance in time . . . no new creative activity – to this routine of temporal housekeeping is the Deity at present confined.
>   . . . Newton's authority was squarely behind the view of the cosmos which saw in man a puny, irrelevant spectator . . . of the vast, mathematical system . . . The world . . . was a world hard, cold, colourless, silent, and dead; a world of quantity, a world of mathematically computable motions in mechanical regularity.[5]

Newton's invocation of the notion of an intervenient deity does of course forestall an assessment of him as an out-and-out mechanist. But while it would be misleading to represent

Newton as an outright mechanist, his *method* provided the reliable basis for a universal science that would later be employed by his followers to show the world to be so completely regulated by mathematical laws that divine intervention was dispensable. Historically, the proclamation of the superfluity of divine intervention had to await Laplace (1749–1827), who would use Newton's method to demonstrate that the universe was, after all, a self-contained mechanical system.

The problem for the person who accepted Newtonian mechanics was this: if the nature of the world, as represented by this cosmological synthesis, was so precisely ordered, so (seemingly) flawlessly proportioned, then why were there evil and disharmony in the world? The 'problem of evil' still existed, but given this new synthesis, with its deistic, and ultimately even atheistic, implications, it was now difficult to reconcile the existence of evil with the workings of divine providence. This, of course, was one particular aspect of a more general problem posed for philosophy and theology by the thinkers of the Enlightenment, namely, how are morality and faith to be accommodated in a world governed by the laws of a rigidly mechanistic, and ultimately godless, system? The primary intellectual figures of the Enlightenment – Newton, Descartes, Leibniz and, later, Hume, Kant and Hegel – were not of course nihilists or thinkers who perceived themselves to belong to a 'post-theistic' or post-Christian era (in the way that, say, Nietzsche did); nevertheless, they were confronted, or perceived themselves as being confronted, by a problem (that of accommodating morality and religious faith in a mechanistic, dedivinized universe) which simply could not have posed itself to their intellectual forebears, the thinkers of the now superseded 'mediaeval synthesis'.

The thinkers of the Enlightenment perceived the need for a new form of theodicy, one which would enable us to circumvent the problem of reconciling the existence of evil with the existence of an increasingly 'absent' God. As Ernest Becker, in his characteristically trenchant way, puts it:

> Something entirely different had to be done to explain evil in the world, a theodicy without divine intervention. The new theodicy had to be a natural one, a 'secular' one ... Evil had to be explained as existing in the world apart from God's intention or justification.[6]

How was this to be achieved? Becker continues:

> The only way to achieve this new explanation was gradually to
> shift the burden from reliance on God's will to the belief in man's
> understanding and powers. This was a shift that was to occupy
> the whole Enlightenment, and it was not easily accomplished. In
> fact . . . the separate . . . traditions had their own kind of ing-
> enuity, and fashioned quite different notions of 'secular' theodicy,
> or 'anthropodicy'.[7]

The thinkers of the Enlightenment and their successors, having
eschewed the principle of cosmic order (and thus the notion of a
divine Cosmic Orderer), had in this way shifted the burden of
the 'problem of evil' from God to humanity itself. The intellectual thrust of the Enlightenment was, as Becker notes, to
secularize this 'problem', to transform theodicy (properly
so-called) into 'anthropodicy'. This process, which Kant
described as 'man's emergence from his self-imposed tutelage',
was continued as the spirit of the Enlightenment permeated the
other natural sciences before proceeding to affect the social and
human sciences. The upshot was that the individual human
consciousness – the 'I think' of Descartes' *cogito* – came to be
viewed as the absolute origin of thought and action. In this
anthropocentric turn, the *human individual* herself became the
pivot of her thinking about, and doing in, the world. This
anthropocentric attitude received its decisive formulation in
the philosophical programme outlined by Hume, who said:

> 'Tis evident, that all the sciences have a relation, greater or less,
> to human nature; and that however wide any of them may seem
> to run from it, they still return back by one passage or another.
> Even *Mathematics, Natural Philosophy*, and *Natural Religion*,
> are in some measure dependent on the science of MAN; since they
> lie under the cognizance of men, and are judged by their powers
> and faculties.[8]

The concern with human nature voiced by Hume in this passage
is in large part a reflection of the post-Enlightenment individual's new-found identity as self-defining subject. This self-
defining subject regards the world, including the good and evil
contained therein, as an object of control, of *producibility*.
According to Max Weber (1864–1920), the essential manipulability of the world is a concomitant of the 'disenchantment' of

the cosmos, a disenchantment that is the outcome of the progressive rationalization of the world. Weber believed the manipulability of the world to be the principle on which bureaucracy operates; and since the rationalization of the world is inexorable and irreversible, it is only a matter of time before the bureaucratic principle will come to pervade all spheres of human life. The outcome of the inevitable and increasingly dominant operation of the bureaucratic principle was that

> By the time of Hiroshima . . . not only was theodicy long since dead, but the burning problem of good and evil was removed from most people's lives. At best, overcoming evil was a 'job to be done' – someone else's job; and it was not a way of life to heed. And how could it be otherwise? – the world was so matter-of-fact . . .[9]

The Enlightenment, as our cursory discussion indicates, poses a daunting intellectual agenda for the theodicist. After the Enlightenment, and as a consequence of the penetration of social and cultural phenomena by the irrevocable and irreversible process of rationalization sponsored by Enlightenment thought, a hegemonic ideological force is created which throws into question the very possibility of doing theodicy. And yet so many discussions of theodicy proceed as though its proponents were not confronted by the intellectual legacy of the Enlightenment. Theodicists approach the 'problem of evil' as though this 'problem' were not in itself a problem, as though theodicy were not in itself faced by an epistemological crisis generated by the collapse of its 'apparatus (of intelligibility)'. It would seem that the theodicist can hope to do her subject justice only if she takes seriously the historically generated possibility that doing theodicy may in fact presuppose an 'apparatus' which is no longer sustained by existing cultural practices. It is conceivable that the historical conditions associated with the onset and growth of Enlightenment thought have created an 'epistemic rupture' – between an 'apparatus' which *did* incorporate the principle of cosmic order and one (ours) which does not – potentially fatal for (strictly so-called) theodicy.[10]

If this is true, then the theodicist is an anachronism, a creature who could have existed happily in the University of Paris in the thirteenth century, but who has no place in a world which finds it difficult to make sense of the notion of a divine

Cosmic Artificer. In a world where the voice of God can no longer be heard, the theodicist's words can strike no resonance: she shares the fate of her God and she too can no longer be heard. The theodicist, then, overlooks the question of the 'epistemic rupture' created by Enlightenment and post-Enlightenment thought at her own peril. If she does not endeavour to come to terms with the historical forces which generated this 'rupture', she could face intellectual extinction.

The fact that the Enlightenment helped to deprive theodicy of its *prima facie* plausibility and intelligibility (which is what I have been arguing) should not obscure the equally salient fact that Enlightenment thought also served to make theodicy a pressing and significant problem. The thinkers of the Enlightenment, beginning with Spinoza, discredited the notion that nature possessed an immanent teleology. Spinoza (1632–77) denied that the workings of nature were governed by a divine Final Cause, and argued that final causes (or purposes) are fictional, and thus mystifying, expressions of *human* desires:

> Wherefore, a cause which is called final is nothing else but human desire, in so far as it is considered as the origin or cause of anything. For example, when we say that to be inhabited is the final cause of this or that house, we mean nothing more than that a man, conceiving the conveniences of household life, had a desire to build a house. Wherefore, the being inhabited, in so far as it is regarded as a final cause, is nothing else but this particular desire, which is really the efficient cause; it is regarded as the primary cause, because men are generally ignorant of the causes of their desires.[11]

Spinoza's explicit identification of final causation with efficient causation was upheld by Hume, who argued that all causation is derived from the 'constant conjunction' of two objects, from which it follows that there is no justification for accepting the traditional Aristotelian distinction between final, efficient material and formal causes. Kant (1724–1804) did not jettison the idea of final causation, but held that, unlike efficient causation, the idea of a purpose in nature cannot be schematized. To schematize a Category it is necessary to display the temporal conditions which underlie its applicability; temporally specifiable existence in the case of Reality, permanence in the case of Substance, and so on. In Kant's scheme, the Humean principle that a causal connection requires the (empirical) perception of regular succession is accepted with hardly any qualification. It is not possible, Kant avers, to specify the appropriate perceptual condition for the application of the notion 'purpose in nature'. Since this notion cannot be schematized, it can therefore only be grounded beyond the bounds of experience in some supersensible (and thus illegitimate) realm.[12]

Spinoza, Hume and Kant, by challenging the view that nature possessed an immanent teleology, made it less easy for theologians and philosophers to explain occurrences of evil and suffering in terms of a divinely ordained creative process inherent in nature. Evil and suffering thus become more difficult to account for and explain away. The Enlightenment, it would seem, managed at the same time both to make theodicy a *problem* and to deprive its proponents of the intellectual horizon traditionally presupposed by their ancestors in their attempts to solve this problem.

THE SECOND PROBLEM: THEODICY'S ABSTRACT CONCEPTION OF EVIL

Another reason why attempts to formulate a viable theodicy are apt to end in disappointment can be found in the abstract conception of evil invariably employed by the theodicist. The use of an abstract, ahistorical understanding of evil is the unavoidable concomitant of viewing theodicy as an undertaking with exclusively theoretical implications. It seems to be in the very nature of theodicy to have implications that are purely theoretical. To quote Alvin Plantinga:

> Neither a Free Will Defense nor a Free Will Theodicy is designed to be of much help to one suffering from . . . a storm in the soul . . . Neither is it to be thought of first of all as a means of pastoral counselling. Probably neither will enable someone to find peace with himself and with God in the face of the evil that the world contains. But then, of course, neither is intended for that purpose.[13]

The same view is expressed by John Hick:

A Christian theodicy . . . offers an understanding of our human situation; but this is not the same as offering practical help and comfort to those in the midst of acute pain or deep suffering.[14]

There are at least two broadly historical reasons why theodicy has come to be viewed as a merely theoretical undertaking. First, as we have seen, reflection on the 'problem of evil' is governed, tacitly or overtly, by a post-Enlightenment paradigm of knowledge which originates in the thought of Descartes. René Descartes (1596–1650) sought to separate knowledge from error by adverting to the intuitive self-certainty of the human subject. He maintained that this subject can doubt all her thoughts except the thought that she is doubting. To doubt this thought is already to nullify one's own doubt, for in the very act of doubting the truth of my doubt I make it *true* that I doubt. To discover this indisputable truth the human subject has only to turn inward to examine the act of cognition. Descartes thus confined knowledge to the allegedly unmediated transaction between the individual subject and her mental representations; as one of his commentators puts it, for Descartes 'the materials of knowledge are given to the mind by the mind'.[15] Descartes was thus responsible for bringing about a fundamental break with previous epistemological paradigms. Whereas former models had adhered to a conception of knowledge which regarded it as consisting characteristically in the relation between the thinker and the *object* of cognition, Descartes' method attached metaphysical and epistemological primacy to the cognizing *subject*. Descartes' essentially self-reflexive, mentalistic theory of knowledge was shared by Kant, who maintained that the totality of ordered experience is structured by laws imposed on reality by the human subject's cognitive mechanisms. The emphasis on the subjectivity of the individual which characterizes the Cartesian-Kantian view of knowledge has the unavoidable consequence of promoting an understanding of knowledge effectively premised on a denigration of history. Since this approach is moored to the abstract self-reflexivity of the thinking subject, the objective social configurations that are determinative of human subjectivity become hopelessly occluded. The quest is always for the correct, the absolutely correct, model for registering and representing the 'impressions' or 'ideas' that constitute the contents of the mind. The model, because of its putative infallibility, is held to be timelessly valid.[16]

The flight from history represented by this 'turn to the subject' seems to be implicit in the viewpoints of Plantinga and Hick. While they acknowledge that there is a history of theodicy, they nevertheless do not appear to have come to terms with the fact that theodicy has an irreducibly historical core precisely because it is the product of the collision between: (1) *theological* narratives (i.e. certain historically and socially conditioned textual renditions of the (triune) reality of God); (2) *the personal narrative of the theodicist* (whose biography is itself a product and a reflection of historical conditions), and (3) an *episteme* or *historical reality* itself (which, in this post-Enlightenment context, takes the form of a narrative, or set of narratives, that, directly or indirectly, renders problematic the notion that there is a God who is omnipotent, omniscient and benevolent).[17] The required historical consciousness is thus twofold: the theodicist has to be conscious not only of her subject's historicity, but also of the historicity of her *own* appropriation and criticism of this subject (viz. theodicy). Another way of stating this criticism of Hick and Plantinga would be to say that their implied conception of the 'history' of theodicy is simply that of a *chronicle*, that is, a relatively unprocessed historical record of the different doctrines formulated by theodicists over the course of time: they appear to have no conception of the dynamic which underlies and underpins this chronicle. (Acknowledgement of this dynamic would be an instrumental factor in converting this chronicle into a fully-fledged historical narrative.)

Theodicy might be first and foremost a form of rational discourse about the phenomenon of evil, but the theodicist cannot afford to overlook the fact that rationality itself has social roots, and that occurrences of evil and suffering, and human responses to these occurrences, are likewise located in quite specific historical and material configurations. Historically, the philosophical traditions associated with Vico, Hegel, Marx and Nietzsche have placed the emphasis on the social history of human consciousness that appears to be missing in the tradition associated with Descartes, Hume and Kant; and it is perhaps significant that Plantinga and Hick (as well as Swinburne) belong to the latter tradition of philosophy, which eschews the principle that the materials of knowledge are socially created and formed by historical forces. The theodicist, it would seem, can hope to operate with a less abstract and less ahistorical understanding of evil only if she is prepared to accept this principle.

A second reason why theodicy is deemed to be a primarily theoretical undertaking may lie in the fact that its practitioners are virtually constrained to pursue a quite narrow range of intellectual interests. To substantiate this charge would require us to make a fairly lengthy detour into the sociology of knowledge, the sociology of meaning (semiotics), and what can be called a 'politics of interpretation'[18], so I shall confine myself to making a very brief and somewhat impressionistic observation. The narrowness referred to above is reflected in the range of topics discussed by contemporary theodicists, who in the main confine themselves to the articulation of a free will defence, the adequate (i.e., logically coherent) specification of God's attributes, the advocacy of the notion that the existence of evil is required to bring about certain 'second-order' goods, and so on. While consideration of these topics is by no means unimportant, the exclusive focusing of attention on them has been largely responsible for producing a certain barrenness and triteness, so that progress in argument in theodicy invariably consists in the drawing of ever more subtle distinctions, the formulation of appropriate chains of reasoning, and the meticulous refining of existing arguments. This last procedure invariably involves the search for 'auxiliary premises' that will enable the theodicist to bypass the formal, as opposed to the substantive, strictures of opponents who are seemingly just as committed to viewing theodicy as a purely logical exercise.

There is a sense in which scholarly reflection on the 'problem of evil' is a highly ritualistic activity, which requires the theodicist to focus her attention on a number of canonical or 'sacred' texts (Leibniz's *Theodicy*, Tennant's *Philosophical Theology*, Journet's *Le Mal*, and so forth), and to engage in certain professional rituals (writing doctoral theses, submitting articles to learned journals, and producing books!). The professionalization of scholarship is doubtless a phenomenon to be found in other areas of academic life, but its pervasiveness in a sphere concerned essentially with the stark realities of evil and suffering can only serve to promote, even if only indirectly, a culturally-mediated perspective which blurs the complicities that exist between scholarship and these brutal, and brutalizing, realities. To quote Edward Said:

> ... culture works very effectively to make invisible and even 'impossible' the actual *affiliations* that exist between the world of ideas and scholarship, on the one hand, and the world of brute politics, corporate and state power, and military force, on the other. The cult of expertise and professionalism, for example, has so restricted our scope of vision that a positive (as opposed to an implicit or passive) doctrine of noninterference among fields has set in ... [S]pecialists are not always sensitive to the dangers of self-quotation, endless repetition, and received ideas that their fields encourage, for reasons that have more to do with politics and ideology than with any 'outside' reality.[19]

To regard theodicy as a purely theoretical and scholarly exercise is to provide – albeit unwittingly – a tacit sanction of the myriad evils that exist on this planet. Crucial to this argument is the tenet that *all* philosophical and theological reflection, no matter how abstract such reflection may be, inevitably mediates a certain social and political praxis. All significant intellectual visions have a socially-mediated purchase on reality. They thus have the capacity to determine the way(s) in which a certain segment of reality is either to be transformed or else maintained in its existing form. The philosopher and the theologian do not reflect and discourse *in vacuo*: it is their responsibility, therefore, to ask themselves, continually, what particular praxis their work mediates. For it is only by such self-scrutiny that they can avoid being implicated in a rarefied discourse which legitimizes and mystifies the social processes that block the transformation of life and reality.

Fundamental to the above argument is the principle that the text participates in society, that consciousness is not divorced from historical and social forces. The text provides a structured representation of social and historical reality, and its subjectivity is in turn modified or rearranged by the specific arrangement of social and historical materiality.[20] Theodicy, we are arguing, has little alternative but to consider itself a kind of signifying practice. So what social and political practice could possibly be mediated by an approach to the 'problem of evil' which favours an abstract and ahistorical conception of evil? The evil which results directly from the deeds of men and women, and which arises when we compound occurrences of physical evil by our own inhumanity, owes its existence to the deeds of human beings: evil is manifested *in concreto* in the actions of men and women, either individually or in groups; it exists at particular times and in particular places; and it needs its victims and their torturers and executioners. The most terrible visions are conjured up by certain names: the Warsaw ghetto, Auschwitz, the Gulag, the refugee camps of Beirut, Biafra, Pol Pot's 'Year Zero', and so forth. The evil perpetrated in these places and at these times was not abstract: 'annihilation is no longer a metaphor. Good and evil are real'.[21] The evil deeds associated with these places and times were of such a malignant and palpable magnitude that some writers, Sartre for example, have been moved to assert that evil is irredeemable:

> We have been taught to take [evil] seriously. It is neither our fault nor our merit if we lived in a time when torture was a daily fact . . . Dachau and Auschwitz . . . have demonstrated to us that Evil is not an appearance, that knowing its cause does not dispel it, that it is not opposed to Good as a confused idea is to a clear one, that it is not the effect of passions which might be cured, of a fear which might be overcome, of a passing aberration which might be excused, of an ignorance which might be enlightened . . .
> We heard whole streets screaming and understood that Evil . . . is like Good, absolute.
> Perhaps a day will come when a happy age, looking back at the past, will see in this suffering and shame one of the paths to peace. But we were not on the side of history already made. We were, as I have said, *situated* in such a way that every minute seemed to us like something irreducible. Therefore, in spite of ourselves, we came to this conclusion, which will seem shocking to lofty souls: Evil cannot be redeemed.[22]

A theodicist who, intentionally or inadvertently, formulates doctrines which occlude the radical and ruthless particularity of human evil is, by implication, mediating a social and political practice which averts its gaze from the cruelties that exist in the world. The theodicist, we are suggesting, cannot propound views that promote serenity in a heartless world. If she does, her words will be dissipated in the ether of abstract moralizing, and she will become like the persons described by Joseph Conrad in his great short story 'An Outpost of Progress', who 'talk with indignation and enthusiasm; talk about oppression, cruelty, crime, devotion, self-sacrifice, virtue, and . . . know nothing real beyond the words. Nobody knows what suffering or sacrifice mean – except perhaps the victims'.[23]

Theodicy, then, has to engage with the sheer particularity, the radical contingency, of human evil. The theodicist cannot, of course, guarantee that her doctrines will have any real or immediate import for *the victims* of such evil, but she must at least not attempt to disengage herself from their plight by adhering to a viewpoint of specious generality, which effectively reduces theodicy to mere ideology, and which in the process merely reinforces the powerlessness of those who are powerless. If, as Conrad says, only the victims can truly understand what suffering and sacrifice mean, then theodicy must necessarily be articulated from the standpoint of the victims themselves. Otherwise, theodicy will succumb inevitably to what Paul Ricoeur calls 'the bad faith of theodicy': 'it does not triumph over real evil but only over its aesthetic phantom'.[24] A theodicy is not worth heeding if it does not allow the screams of our society to be heard.

But if theodicy did acknowledge the pain and the grief of victims, and what is more, if it then set out to be a discourse which facilitates a practice that *interrupts* the reality which causes victims and torturers to exist and to flourish, would it still be 'theodicy' in the traditional sense? This is a question of some importance that we shall have to attend to later.

PROBLEM THREE: THEODICY AS THE APPLICATION OF
REASON TO THAT WHICH TRANSCENDS RATIONALITY

A third reason why theodicy seems so precarious an enterprise, so incommensurable with the scale of evil and suffering that exists in the world, stems from the fact that theodicy, by its very nature, involves the application of the principles of *reason* to a cluster of problems which are essentially such that they cannot be resolved by the mere application of rational principles. Evil and suffering in their innermost depths are fundamentally mysterious; they confound the human mind. And yet the goal of theodicy is, somehow, to render them comprehensible, explicable. The cornerstone of theodicy is the attempt to provide a *teleology* of evil and suffering, to slot occurrences of evil and suffering into a scheme of things consonant with the essentially rational workings of divine providence. As D. Z. Phillips notes:

> Theodicies are part of the rationalism which I believe clouds our understanding of religious belief. I doubt whether any believer would deny that Jesus faced evil of a certain kind in the Garden of Gethsemane. And in asking that if possible the bitter cup should pass from him, he came to see his own survival as a mere possibility subject to the will of God. He came to see that the will of God meant, for him the Cross. If anyone said that the Son of God met the evil in a reasonable way I would not know what to make of him. And if a philosopher attempts, as John Wisdom did once, to show that the forgiveness from the Cross is reasonable, he gets into terrible trouble. I'd at least venture to say that talk of reasonableness and rationality is not the most natural response of most Christians to the central act of their faith.[25]

The philosophical theodicist, in a real sense, is someone who has taken on the role of spinning words that can be put into the mouths of Job's comforters. She seeks to render the intractable tractable. Confronted by a wordless abyss, she trusts in the efficacy of words. This point can be made more grandiloquently by saying that theodicy promotes an essentially non-tragic vision of the realities of evil and suffering. Paul Ricoeur is therefore entirely correct in stressing that it is one of the functions of the tragic God (and of tragic symbols) to execute an 'iconoclasm' of theodicy, that is, to subvert the tendency of the theodicist to domesticate evil and suffering by viewing them (and God) in merely ethical or juridical terms. In making this point, Ricoeur claims that the sufferings of Job shatter the theodicist's 'ethicizing' vision of the world and divine reality:

> . . . where God is perceived as the origin of justice and the source of legislation, the problem of just sanctions is raised with a seriousness without precedent; suffering emerges as an enigma when the demands of justice can no longer explain it; this enigma is the product of the ethical theology itself. This is why the virulence of the book of Job is without equivalent in any culture;

Job's complaint supposes the full maturity of an ethical vision of
God; the clearer God becomes as legislator, the more obscure he
becomes as creator; . . . it becomes possible to turn the accusation
back against God, against the ethical God of accusation.
Thereupon begins the foolish business of trying to justify God:
theodicy is born.[26]

And the justifiers of God in this context are the comforters of
Job, those prototypical theodicists, who seek to exculpate God
by rationalizing the afflictions of their friend. This they do by
invoking a whole range of transgressions which in their eyes
give a point to what God has done to Job: ancestral sins,
unacknowledged sins, forgotten sins, the sins of the community,
and so on. But Job's pain and anguish, the severity of his
epistemological crisis, thwart any easy incorporation of his
personal narrative into such a comfortable teleological schema.
The causes of his suffering have a surd reality, and as such
frustrate the attempt to make them comprehensible, explicable.
The potential critic of theodicy who is persuaded by Ricoeur's
interpretation of the story of Job wil probably conclude that the
enterprise of theodicy is irreparably broken-backed, and this
precisely because it overlooks the irreducibly tragic quality of
the manifestations of evil and suffering. Theodicy, it could be
said, founders on the 'mystery of iniquity'.

Is there any substance to this (Ricoeurean) objection? And not
just this particular criticism of theodicy, but also the objections
raised in the previous sections of this chapter? Before
endeavouring to evaluate these objections a little more fully, it
is necessary to consider in greater depth and detail exactly what
the theodicist proposes, in principle, to accomplish. This is
necessary, for the opponent of theodicy could be accused of being
able to raise objections such as the three outlined in this chapter
only because she has no real grasp of the true nature of the
theodicist's task. Thus, it might be argued that these three
objections possess a veneer of conviction only because they
assume that the theodicist is proposing to undertake a task
which by its very nature is impossible to accomplish
successfully.[27] It is therefore necessary for us to attempt a
delineation of the aims of the theodicist, as a vital preliminary
to the formulation of a critique of theodicy along the lines
proposed in this chapter. This characterization of the aims of the
theodicist will be undertaken in chapter 2.

NOTES

1 *Critique of Pure Reason*, trans. N. Kemp Smith, (London and New York: Macmillan, 1964), p. 21. Kant had a similarly unfavourable view of theodicy. See his *On the Failure of all Attempted Philosophical Theodicies* (1791), translated as an appendix in Michel Despland, *Kant on History and Religion* (London and Montreal: McGill–Queen's University, 1973), pp. 283–97. One is reminded too of Donald MacKinnon's stricture:

> where the treatment of 'the problem of evil' is concerned, we reach an area in which in very various ways, theologians have allowed apologetic eagerness to lead them to suppose they had reached solutions, when in fact they had hardly begun effectively to articulate their problems.

See his *The Problem of Metaphysics* (Cambridge: Cambridge University Press, 1974), p. 124.

2 Foucault characterizes this 'archaeology' as '[the] analysis of statements, . . . a historical analysis, but one that avoids all interpretation: it does not question things said as to what they are hiding, what they were "really" saying, in spite of themselves, the unspoken element that they contain . . .; but, on the contrary, it questions them as to their mode of existence, . . . what it means for them to have appeared when and where they did – they and no others'. See *The Archaeology of Knowledge*, trans. A. M. Sheridan, (New York: Harper Colophon, 1972), p. 109.

3 Foucault uses the technical term *dispositif* to designate 'discourses, institutions, architectural arrangements, regulations, laws, administrative measures, scientific statements, philosophic propositions, morality, philanthropy, etc.' See his 'The Confession of the Flesh', in Colin Gordon, ed., *Power/Knowledge: Selected Interviews and Other Writings by Michel Foucault, 1972–1977* (New York: Pantheon, 1980), p. 194.

4 Stillman Drake, ed. and trans., *Discoveries of Galileo* (New York: Doubleday, 1957), pp. 182–3.

5 E. A. Burtt, *The Metaphysical Foundations of Modern Science* (London: Routledge & Kegan Paul, 2nd rev. ed., 1932), pp. 236–94.

6 E. Becker, *The Structure of Evil: An Essay on the Unification of the Science of Man* (New York: The Free Press, 1976), p. 18.

7 Becker, *The Structure of Evil*, p. 18. The follower of Foucault will be inclined to dismantle the 'project' of an 'anthropodicy' in the light of Foucault's remark that its historical subject – the 'new' post-Enlightenment man who defines himself in Nietzschean fashion as

'the killer of God' – will in turn die: the death of God (Foucault believes) presages the death of this post-Enlightenment subject. See *The Order of Things: An Archaeology of the Human Sciences* (New York: Vintage, 1973), pp. 384ff.

8 Hume, *A Treatise of Human Nature*, ed. L. A. Selby-Bigge (Oxford: Clarendon, 1888), p. xix. Even more than Hume, Kant was responsible for assigning humankind a pivotal position in the cosmos; his 'Copernican revolution' showed that the objects of the cosmos are thinkable only in so far as they are structured in accordance with the laws of human consciousness.

9 Becker, *The Structure of Evil*, p. 17.

10 I adapt the notion of an 'epistemic rupture' from Foucault, who defines an *episteme* as '. . . the total set of relations that unite, at a given period, the discursive practices that give rise to epistemological figures, sciences, and possibly formalized systems . . . The episteme is not a form of knowledge . . . or type of rationality which . . . manifests the sovereign unity of a subject, a spirit, or a period; it is the totality of relations that can be discovered, for a given period, between the sciences when one analyses them at the level of discursive regularities' (*The Archaeology of Knowledge*, p. 191).

11 Spinoza, *Ethics*, trans. R. H. M. Elwes, in *the Rationalists* (New York: Doubleday, 1960), Part I, Appendix. See also Part IV, Preface. Descartes rejected final causation on somewhat different grounds, contending that teleological explanation was superfluous because nature was explicable in purely mechanistic terms. See the Fourth of his *Meditations*, in F. E. Sutcliffe, trans., *Descartes* (Harmondsworth: Penguin, 1968), pp. 132–41.

12 *Critique of Pure Reason*, pp. 185ff. A Category for Kant, is an *a priori* regulative principle of the human understanding which ensures the objectivity of experience.

13 Plantinga, *God, Freedom and Evil* (London: Allen & Unwin, 1974), p. 29.

14 Hick, 'An Irenaean Theodicy' in Davis, ed., *Encountering Evil*, p. 68.

15 Peter A. Schouls, *The Imposition of Method: A Study of Descartes and Locke* (Oxford: Clarendon, 1980), p. 23.

16 On this see Charles Taylor, 'Philosophy and its History', in Rorty, Schneewind and Skinner, eds, *Philosophy in History*, pp. 17ff. For a socio-historical critique of Descartes' method, see T. W. Adorno, 'The Essay as Form', pp. 161–5. A profoundly important *theological* critique of the Cartesian-Kantian espistemological tradition is to be found in Eberhard Jüngel, *God as the Mystery of the World*, trans. D. L. Guder, (Edinburgh: T. & T. Clark, 1983).

17 Strictly speaking, historical reality is *not* a text; it is intrinsically

non-narrative and non-representational. Nevertheless, it has to be acknowledged at the same time that there can be no access to historical reality except in textual form. I shall follow Frederic Jameson's practice and refer to this historical text as a *subtext*. See his *The Political Unconscious*, chap. 1. Jameson's is a resolutely hermeneutical procedure, which does not sit very comfortably with Foucault's hostility towards hermeneutics. Here my own inclination is to agree with Jameson that Foucault's position, despite the animosity that it displays towards hermeneutics, is a kind of hermeneutic in its own right. Jameson proposes to subsume Foucault's (particular) hermeneutic of 'the decentred subject' under his own global Marxist hermeneutic. On this, see *The Political Unconscious*, pp. 21ff and 124ff.

18 On the 'politics of interpretation', see Edward W. Said, 'Opponents, Audiences, Constituencies, and Community', p. 1.

19 Said, 'Opponents', pp. 1–9. The emphasis is Said's. Said shows how universally, and disastrously, this scholarly attitude pervades the field of Orientalism, in his brilliant *Orientalism: Western Conceptions of the Orient* (Harmondsworth: Penguin, 1985). Pertinent here is Adorno's remark: 'People thinking in the forms of free, detached, disinterested appraisal were unable to accommodate within those forms the experience of violence which in reality annuls such thinking. The almost insoluble task is to let neither the power of others, nor our own powerlessness, stupefy us.' In *Minima Moralia: Reflections from Damaged Life*, trans. E. F. N. Jephcott, (London: Verso, 1974), p. 57.

20 On the relation between text and reality as a two-way process, see Peter Madsen, 'Semiotics and Dialectics', *Poetics*, 6 (1972), pp. 29–42, see especially pp. 35ff. Frederic Jameson characterizes the literary or aesthetic act as a 'textualizing' which involves the active '[drawing of] the Real into its own texture'. See his *The Political Unconscious*, p. 81.

21 Saul Bellow, *Herzog* (Harmondsworth: Penguin, 1965), p. 172.

22 Jean-Paul Sartre, *What is Literature?*, trans. B. Frechtman, (London: Methuen, 1950), pp. 160–2. Sartre, in this passage, is reflecting on his experiences as a member of the war-time Resistance in France.

23 Conrad, *Tales of Unrest* (Harmondsworth: Penguin, 1977), p. 100.

24 Ricoeur, 'The Hermeneutics of Symbols and Philosophical Reflection: I', in Don Ihde, ed., *The Conflict of Interpretations*, (Evanston: Northwestern University, 1974), p. 312. See also p. 314, where Ricoeur argues that theodicy is an expedient of false knowledge because it does not give us an understanding of hope. Pertinent here is Kierkegaard's dictum: 'There are two ways – one is to suffer; the other is to become a professor of the fact that another suffers'.

25 D. Z. Phillips, 'The Problem of Evil: Postscript', in Brown, ed., *Reason and Religion*, p. 139. See also Phillips's earlier response to Swinburne in *Reason and Religion*, 'The Problem of Evil: II', p. 119. John Hick, in his contribution to the same symposium, states explicitly that theodicy is important because '. . . it may show faith in God to be . . . still a possibility for a *rational* person' (p. 123; my emphasis).

26 Ricoeur, *The Symbolism of Evil*, pp. 314–15.

27 The theodicist's task is of course that of enabling us to come to terms not only with the mere existence, but also with the *awfulness*, of evil and suffering; and not only this, but in so doing for the theodicist also to address herself *directly* to the plight of those who are afflicted.

CHAPTER 2

The Possibility of Theodicy: II

The putative objections discussed in the last chapter presuppose a certain as yet unarticulated understanding of the theodicist's task. It is now imperative for us to specify our understanding of the nature of this enterprise. The 'problem of evil', at this rather early stage, seems to be an amalgam or cluster of various *theoretical* and *practical* aspects.

In its theoretical aspect theodicy is ostensibly concerned with three primary questions:

1   Can *evil* in itself be rendered intelligible?
2   Is the existence of *God* logically compatible with the *existence* of evil?

A variant of 2 is:

2a   Is the existence of *God* logically compatible with the *varieties* and the *profusion* of evil?

It is possible to combine 2 and(or) 2a, the *logical* form of the 'problem of evil', with a version of 1, to produce the *evidential* form of the 'problem of evil'. This latter form of the problem can be expressed in terms of:

3   Does the existence of evil constitute *evidence* that counts against (or reduces the possibility of the truth of) theism?

A cursory look at even a small sample of theodicies will show that theodicists differ quite substantially on what constitutes the core of the 'problem of evil', and what is only peripheral to it. Thus David Griffin, a noted process theodicist, has argued that the question of the intelligibility of evil *per se* (i.e. question (1)) is important for theodicy, whereas John Hick, whose work in this area is undeniably central, has been prepared to acknowledge that evil is fundamentally mysterious. Hick, understandably, would not attach quite the same significance to (1) as

Griffin does.[1] It is also important to note that one's perception of the function of theism will affect the significance that one is prepared to attach to these questions. It should also be noted that the theologian or philosopher who believes that theism has an explanatory function will in all probability maintain that it is (3), and not (2) or (2a), which expresses the heart of theodicy. Hick and Richard Swinburne come readily to mind as theodicists who would have this estimation of the significance of (3), whereas Alvin Plantinga, who favours a formal-logical approach, takes the core of the theodicy-question to be constituted by (2).[2]

In addition to questions (1)–(3), there is a practical aspect to theodicy which can be expressed in terms of the following questions:

4   What does *God* do to overcome the evil and suffering that exist in his creation?
5   What do *we* (*qua* creatures of God) do to overcome evil and suffering?

Before discussing the relation between the theoretical and the practical aspects of the 'problem of evil', it is worth noting that the standard distinction between human (or moral) evil and physical (or natural) evil might necessitate a sub-division of question (1) into:

1a   Can *human* evil in itself be rendered intelligible?
1b   Can *physical* evil in itself be rendered intelligible?

It is fairly easy to see that an answer may in principle be available to (1a) but not to (1b), and vice versa. For it is almost certainly the case that, at the very least, something approximating to a general theory of human behaviour will have to be forthcoming before it will be possible for an affirmative answer to be given to (1a). But possessing such a general theory will not provide the basis for an answer to questions about the origins of earthquakes and hurricanes, etc., the kinds of question that come under the rubric of (1b). Only a general *physical* theory of the universe will be able to furnish the answers to such questions about the universe. At the same time, it is evident that there are many cases in which it is impossible to draw a rigid distinction between human and physical evil. For example, the misery and pain caused by a natural disaster are often compounded by the failures of compassion, and at times the sheer murderous incompetence, of other human beings. Nevertheless, the *prima facie* distinction between human evil and physical evil still remains: all else being equal, the baby who dies of a congenital heart defect is the victim of a manifestly different kind of evil from the healthy baby who is battered to death by its parents. This intuitive distinction is reflected in the rather different strategies employed by theodicists when dealing with the two basic kinds of evil. The free will defence (which attributes the existence of human evil to the deeds of free and fallible beings who misuse their freedom) can hardly be used to resolve the problem, or problems, of physical evil. For it would be odd, even misconceived, to attribute *all* defects in the natural order solely to the choices of free but finite agents.[3] It is beyond the scope of this book to dwell at length on the implications for theodicy of the similarities and differences that exist, at a conceptual level, between human and physical evil. But the perspective on evil, suffering and salvation taken in this book requires a number of observations to be made about the problems posed by the two basic kinds of evil.

HUMAN AND PHYSICAL EVIL: SOME MAINLY THEOLOGICAL CONSIDERATIONS

First, given that the primary focus of this book is specifically (but not exclusively) theological, we must concern ourselves principally with the problem of human evil, i.e. *sin*. To accord primacy to the theological sphere in the context of this discussion is simply to acknowledge that our procedures and criteria have to be governed (admittedly in a so far unspecified sense) by the central tenets of the Christian faith; in this case by the affirmation, fundamental to the Christological traditions of the Church, that Christ died on the cross as a sacrifice for sin.[4] To accept that the cross of Christ is theologically normative for any discussion of the 'problem of evil' is to imply that the issue of sin or human evil has a *theological* significance not shared by the question of physical evil. This is not to say that the question of physical evil cannot arise for theology; it is only to say that, for theology, the problematic of the conquest of physical evil is shaped decisively by the affirmation of faith that God overcame sin on the cross of Christ. Only in the light of this truth does it then make sense for theology to discuss the problematic of physical evil.

Secondly, the centrality and primacy of the problem of human, as opposed to physical, evil can also be established in terms of the Christian understanding of divine providence. As Kant rightly indicates in his essay *On the Failure of all Attempted Philosophical Theodicies* (1791), sin or human evil is *absolutely* contrary to divine providence, whereas physical pain and suffering are only *conditionally* contrary to divine purposefulness.[5] Kant argues that God cannot desire sin as either means or end, though he can desire pain as a means (but not as an end). God, for example, can conceivably desire that someone should be subjected to the physical pain of surgery so that she might be cured of an illness, but it is inconceivable, given that sin is the power which disrupts or distorts the relation that creatures have to God, that God, who is love, should in any sense want his creatures to be alienated from him. Helpful though Kant's distinction undoubtedly is, his suggestion that God can desire pain and suffering as a means, attractive though it might seem in the context of an abstract scholarly discussion, should not be pressed too far where actual instances of suffering are concerned: it is a gratuitous insult to those who are afflicted to suggest that their pain and anguish are the means whereby they can become better persons or get closer to their Creator. Thus P. T. Geach's contention that '. . . the best of men . . . gladly accept [suffering] as what shapes their souls into immortal diamond' (*sic*) should be resisted.[6] Human motives are so often profoundly and bafflingly complex; so what one person 'gladly accepts' and what another endures with the utmost reluctance may in truth be a very poor guide to the state or quality of their souls. Certitudes regarding the means chosen by God to shape human souls are perhaps best left to God himself. This makes it necessary for me to qualify our declared intention of giving emphasis to the problem of human, as opposed to physical, evil.

Thirdly, from the standpoint of the individual *victims* of evil and suffering, it may be quite irrelevant whether it is human evil on the one hand, or physical evil on the other, that is more or less difficult to reconcile, *theoretically*, with the existence of a benevolent, omniscient and omnipotent deity. The person suffering from incurable cancer of the liver, if she should find herself confronting the theoretical problem of theodicy, will in all probability to disposed to seeing the question of physical evil as paramount. The theodicist who happens to have been an inmate of Auschwitz or Treblinka, by contrast, would probably be disposed to regard the issue of human evil as primary. If theodicy is a form of explanation, the potentially contrasting dispositions of our hypothetical cancer sufferer and concentration-camp inmate will indicate that explanations are *relative* to the interest of the persons who advance or adopt them. Each person has an (at least implicit) 'image' of the world and a stance with regard to the world (a stance which may or may not be articulated). The person who engages in theodicy, or any other kind of explanation for that matter, will consequently focus on precisely those issues or questions which are posed by, and rooted in, their world-image and the particular stance they have adopted towards the world. Material and ideal interests shape the images that individuals have of the world and the stances they take toward it, and these images and stances in turn circumscribe a 'logical space' within which explanations are sought for and provided. The notion of the 'interest-relativity' of explanation will be elucidated in chapter 5; for the time being it need only be pointed out that it is *not* being suggested here that explanations are merely 'reflections' of certain material or ideal interests, and that what they assert or entail can therefore be reduced to the interests of those who advance or accept them.[7] The thesis of the 'interest-relativity' of explanation is certainly not intended to be reductionist: it merely suggests that their specific situations and concerns, their particular experiences of evil and suffering, are all decisive for the ways in which individuals approach the problems of evil and suffering. Material and ideal interests thus affect even the most abstract and theoretical dimensions of theodicy.

The principle that explanations are relative to the interests of those who seek or advance them demonstrates quite clearly that it is fundamentally misconceived, even futile, to deal with questions concerning the intelligibility of human and physical evil as such in isolation from the circumstances of those who pose these questions. Accepting this principle, however, creates another possibility. It may be that the interests of those who have to confront the more painful manifestations of evil are such that the question of the intelligibility of evil *per se* is (to these persons) a matter of no real consequence; far more important (to these persons) will be the question of how the evils which afflict them are to be overcome or staved off. Thus a person suffering from liver cancer is more likely to be interested in his or her chances of being cured, rather than in finding an answer to the question of the intelligibility of evil *per se*. Citing this example does of course amount to stating a truism, but one has only to read the dozens of books and articles on theodicy that appear each year to realize that there are many writers who are apparently quite unaware of the implications, *for theodicy*, of such commonplace truths about the realities of evil and suffering. But while the question of the intelligibility of evil *per se* may not therefore be all that important to those who are afflicted by evil in its manifold forms, the issue of sin or human evil still remains on the agenda of the theologian who accepts that God's deed on the cross of Christ to overcome the power of sin is determinative for all theological reflection. And this brings us to the second question that falls under the rubric of the theoretical aspect of theodicy, namely, the question whether theism is intelligible in the face of the fact of evil.

THE INTELLIGIBILITY OF EVIL *PER SE* AND THE
INTELLIGIBILITY OF THEISM

In the previous section it was argued that the issues of human evil or sin has a centrality for Christian theology that is not shared to quite the same extent by the problem or problems of physical evil. This argument, however, needs immediate qualification: from the standpoint of the victims of evil themselves, the question of the intelligibility of evil *per se* might not arise at all, or if it did, it is likely to have a merely peripheral or derivative significance. The *practical* problem of eradicating or bypassing the travails in question would be paramount for such persons. Indeed, it is perfectly conceivable that the interests of the victims of evil may be such that the question of the intelligibility of evil *per se* is for these persons irrelevant or even unanswerable in principle. This may be so, but what about the second, and even the third, of the three questions that constitute the theoretical dimension of theodicy, the questions concerning the intelligibility, and the evidentiality, of *theism* vis-à-vis the existence and the profusion of evil? Would the general position arrived at in the last section with regard to the question of the intelligibility of *evil* in itself be just as appropriate for the question of the intelligibility of *theism* in the face of the fact of evil?

It should be acknowledged at the outset that while it may not be really possible, or perhaps even desirable from the standpoint of an 'ethics of judgement' (to appropriate a term of Van Harvey's), to demonstrate that *human evil* in itself is intelligible, theodicist may nevertheless argue that it is theologically necessary to show that *theism* is intelligible in the face of the existence of evil. In fact, this would be one of the more obvious means available to the theodicist who wants to escape Paul Ricoeur's stricture that she is guilty of 'bad faith' because she reduces evil and suffering to an 'aesthetic phantom' in the very process of making them intelligible. Indeed, it is hard to think of an easier way for the theodicist to circumvent Ricoeur's objection than to say that she *can* exhibit the intelligibility of theism in the face of the evil and suffering present in the world *without* needing in any way to establish that human evil is itself intelligible (and in the process of so doing making herself vulnerable to Ricoeur's objection). The follower of Ricoeur may be prepared to counter-argue on his behalf that the intelligibility of theism in a world containing human evil is conditional upon the intelligibility of human evil *per se*, so that, despite the best efforts of the theodicist, the contagion of this 'aestheticization' will be transmitted willy-nilly to theism itself! But this claim, if it were made, would certainly not be self-evidently true. The demonstration of the intelligibility of human evil will take the form of an adequate answer to the question 'Why is there human or moral evil in the world?', but is not at all clear that a plausible answer to this question must necessarily be given *before* the question of the intelligibility of *theism* can properly be answered. (And the same holds for the issue of the evidentiality of theism.) For it might be possible for the theodicist to answer the question 'Why does an omnipotent, omniscient and benevolent God allow human evil to exist?', without being able, or even needing, to answer the question 'Why is there human evil in the world?'. After all, it could be argued that God 'allows' human evil to exist because he has endowed his creatures with freedom (a freedom that is misused by finite and fallible creatures who thereby lapse into wickedness); but it would not follow from this that we know, necessarily, *why* it is that creatures use their God-bestowed freedom to sin.

The claim 'God allows human evil to exist' can be made without the theodicist needing to make the accompanying claim 'We know why human evil exist'; in the same way that I can say to the policeman informing me of my son's car crash 'I allowed my son to drive the family car' without being in the position to make the claim 'I *know* why my son crashed our car'. I may be completely ignorant of the circumstances in which my son crashed the car, though there is no reason why I should not be able to provide an informative account of the circumstances in which I allowed him to use the car. Likewise, it may be possible for the theodicist to demonstrate the intelligibility of *theism* vis-á-vis the fact of human evil without having the means to explain why it is that human evil exists.[8] In which case, the theodicist can affirm the intelligibility of theism in the face of the fact of human evil without laying herself open to Ricoeur's charge that she thereby prevails over an 'aesthetic phantom'.

But the supporter of Ricoeur has not yet been defeated. For she can still retort that the existence of evil is rationalized, and hence domesticated, the moment one tries to locate instances of evil in a theological framework which sanctions the principle that evil is 'permitted' to exist by God. It is salutary to recall that just such a theological framework is implicit in the platitudes of Job's comforters, who insisted that God had 'permitted' evil to befall Job because of the sins that he, or his ancestors, had committed. Their neat theological system, in which the nature and origins of evil and suffering are shorn of any ambiguity, is repudiated by Job. Job finds the mystery of evil to reside precisely in the inescapably tragic and sombre fact that the world is a 'land of gloom and chaos, where light is as darkness';[9] his moralizing friends, however, because they can only see light as light and darkness as darkness, are blind to the nature of Job's epistemological crisis in particular, and to the ethical irrationality of the world in general.[10]

The ethical irrationality of the world subverts all comprehensive theological schemes that purport to explain occurrences of evil in terms of what God is said to 'permit'. It would seem, therefore, that the only way in which the theodicist can hope to avoid objections of the kind posed by Ricoeur is to concede: (1) that evil *per se* cannot be made intelligible; and (2) that it is not possible to display the intelligibility of *theism* in the face of the presence of human evil. And since (1) and (2) comprise the theoretical aspect of theodicy in its entirety, the theodicist, if she makes the concession recommended above, is effectively preparing to evacuate theodicy from the realm of theory in order to relocate it in the realm of practice. At least, this is the thrust of the argument we are developing. In other words: the crux of the theodicy-problem does not consist in any putative resolution of the apparent difficulties that comprise its theoretical aspect, but in seeking a way (or ways) to answer the 'practical' questions:

4 What does *God* do to overcome the evil and suffering that exist in his creation?
5 What do *we* (*qua* creatures of God) do to overcome evil and suffering?[11]

This proposal is hardly original: twentieth-century theologians such as Jürgen Moltmann, Dorothee Soelle and Eberhard Jüngel have developed theologies of the cross which declare or imply that a God of salvation would be justified in creating a world which contained so much pain and suffering only if he were prepared to share the burden of pain and suffering with his creatures. We shall discuss the views of these theologians in chapter 4. Approaching the 'problem of evil' from the standpoint of the theology of the cross will require the acceptance of the principle that the true deity of God is revealed on the cross of the crucified Jesus of Nazareth. It might then follow that the true divinity of the triune God thus revealed is in actual contradiction with the theodicist's essentially *metaphysical* conception of the essence of God, the kind of conception that enables the theodicist to talk about the divine attributes of omnipotence, omniscience and benevolence in isolation from the event of the cross, and from the triune life of (the Christian) God. We have already mentioned the problematic 'philosophical theism' which underlies the post-Leibnizian metaphysical theodicy, and our next task, a complementary one, will be to undertake this critique from the standpoint of the theology of the cross. But this is to anticipate the course of our argument. First it will be necessary to consider a number of approaches to theodicy which evince an essentially theoretical understanding of the 'problem of evil'.

NOTES

1   For Griffin's claim that the issue of the intelligibility of evil *per se* is important, see his 'Creation Out of Chaos and the Problem of Evil', in Davis, ed., *Encountering Evil*, p. 119. For Hick's claims that the nature of evil and suffering is ultimately mysterious, see his *Evil and the God of Love*, pp. 369ff.

2   The distinction between the logical and the evidential forms of the problem of evil is made in William L. Rowe, 'The Problem of Evil and Some Varieties of Atheism', *American Philosophical Quarterly*, 16 (1979), pp. 335–41.

3   This assertion has to be qualified because Alvin Plantinga ascribes the existence of physical evil to the actions of free and rational, but non-human, agents: namely, Satan and his legions. See his *God, Freedom and Evil*, p. 58; *God and Other Minds: A Study of the Rational Justification of Belief in God* (Ithaca and London: Cornell University Press, 1967), p. 149; and *The Nature of Necessity*, pp. 191ff.

4   The affirmation that Christ died for the sin of humankind is integral to the summaries of the articles of faith given in Acts 11: 34–43 (see especially v. 43) and in I Corinthians 15: 3ff. The sacrificial theologies of the Old Testament attach a similar importance to human sinfulness: according to them, sacrifice was the ritual means given by God for the overcoming of sin. For an illuminating discussion of the relation between sin, sacrifice and atonement, see Frances M. Young, *Sacrifice and the Death of Christ* (London: SPCK, 1975).

5   Details of this essay have been given in note 1 of chapter 1, on p. 55 above.

6   P. T. Geach, *Providence and Evil* (Cambridge: Cambridge University Press, 1977), p. 114.

7   As far as I know, Max Weber is the first thinker to have first discovered the 'interest-relativity' of the explanations favoured by theodicists. See his essay 'The Social Psychology of the World Religions', in H. H. Gerth and C. Wright Mills, eds, *From Max Weber* (New York: Oxford University Press, 1958), pp. 267–301. See especially p. 280.

8 Thus Herbert McCabe has argued correctly that there is nothing inconsistent in the idea of a morally perfect God who permits the suffering caused by sin to exist. To quote him:

> ... it is one thing to say that sin is *not a manifestation* of God's goodness and quite another to say that sin is a manifestation that God is *not good.* We do not know why the good God has made a world which does not at all times manifest his goodness, but the notion is not contradictory. Somehow the infinite goodness of God is compatible with his allowing sin. ('God: Evil', *New Blackfriars*, 62 (1981), p. 17.)

Even if its is acknowledged, as I just have, that there is no contradiction in the idea of a benevolent deity who allows human evil to exist (which is McCabe's point as well), it could still be argued that a problem remains *if* if is accepted that God is an *infinitely loving* being: after all, can an infinitely loving being permit the suffering caused by sin to exist while he does nothing about it? It is one of the main theses of this book that human suffering can be reconciled with the existence of a God of love only if this God is a God of *salvation.*

9 The Book of Job 10:22.

10 In my understanding of the Job narrative I have been greatly assisted by Robert Gordis's magisterial *The Book of God and Man: A Study of Job* (Chicago and London: The University of Chicago, 1978). See especially ch. XI.

11 Of these two questions, 4 is more important from the standpoint of theodicy than 5. Even so, there is no warrant for treating 4 and 5 as though they have no real connection with each other. Given the framework of Christian faith, 5 is implied by 4.

CHAPTER 3

Theodicies with a 'Theoretical' Emphasis

In the last chapter it was argued that if the theodicist abandons (or at any rate subordinates) the theoretical aspect of theodicy in favour of its practical dimension, she can go some way towards rebutting the Ricoeurean charge that her doctrines inevitably turn evil and suffering into an 'aesthetic phantom'. Before such a change in strategy can be justified, however, it will be necessary to scrutinize the characteristic features of a number of approaches to theodicy which, implicitly or explicitly, regard the business of providing a philosophical or theological response to the 'problem of evil' as a quintessentially theoretical matter. Each of the approaches to be considered is typically Cartesian (in the sense specified in the introduction and in chapter 1); and each traffics, in one way or another, in the brand of 'philosophical theism' delineated in our introduction.

The four approaches to be considered in this chapter are: the free will defence (as formulated by Alvin Plantinga); the so-called 'natural law' theodicy (Richard Swinburne); process theodicy (A. N. Whitehead and Charles Hartshorne); and the 'soul-making' theodicy of John Hick.[1]

THE FREE WILL DEFENCE

The free will defence has a long ancestry, sometimes alleged to extend as far back as St Augustine. Although this defence has not lacked its exponents in recent years, it is pretty widely agreed that Alvin Plantinga has been by far the most redoubtable of the free will defence's modern advocates.[2] Critics of the defence have acknowledged Plantinga's pre-eminence by dealing almost exclusively with his formulations. We shall do likewise in this section.

Plantinga maintains that the free will defence aims to show that

1 God is omnipotent, omniscient and perfectly good is not inconsistent with
2 Evil exists.[3]

The way to do this, says Plantinga, is to find a third proposition which, together with (1), will entail (2). The third proposition is

3 Evil exists because of the actions of free, rational and fallible creatures.

It is important to stress that Plantinga employs the notion of free will solely in order to construct a *defence*, that is, to show that the assertion that God exists is not logically inconsistent despite the presence and the profusion of evil in the world. He therefore makes no attempt to prove: (a) that (3) is true; or (b) that (3) is *prima facie* plausible; or (c) that we have good grounds for asserting (3). All that is required in order to demonstrate that (1) is not logically inconsistent with (2), is for (3) to be shown to be *logically possible*. For this reason he prefers not to call his argument a 'theodicy': to be a theodicy (in the traditional sense of the term), it will be necessary for the free will defender not only to show that (3) is logically possible, but also that one or more of (a)–(c) above is in fact the case.[4] At the same time, it should be noted that Plantinga does not advance any argument in support of the proposition that human beings have free will. He is content to formulate the notion in a way that shows free will to be a logical possibility. In his words:

> If a person *S* is free with respect to a given action, then he is free to perform that action and free to refrain; no causal laws and antecedent conditions determine either that he will perform the action, or that he will not. It is within his power, at the time in question, to perform the action, and within his power to refrain.[5]

Having stated his objective (i.e. to show that (3) is logically possible), and having provided the above characterization of a free agent S, Plantinga is able to develop his defence in terms of a 'possible worlds' logical semantics. (For our purposes it is not necessary to explore the details of such a semantics. A 'possible world' for Plantinga is '*a way things could have been;* it is a *state of affairs* of some kind'.[6]) The free will defence is then constructed as follows. Suppose there is a possible world, or possible state of affairs, call it W, in which the free agent S will perform action A. God, because he is omniscient, knows that S will do A. God has also created (Plantinga's word is 'actualized') this world W, the world in which S will do A. Plantinga then suggests that it may be *impossible* for God to have actualized another world in which S will *not* do A, even though God may disapprove of S's doing A in the actual world W. Since S is a free being, another possible world (call it W*), like W in every respect, must include S's doing A (though obviously it would not include A if God decided to intervene in W* and prevent S doing A, thus depriving him of his freedom). But since A is a free agent, God cannot (even though he might *want* to) create the world W* and bring it about, in W*, that S does not do A. In short: A's being free places logical limitations on God's power to actualize worlds. In this instance, God cannot actualize W* and at the same time bring it about that S does not do A in W*. God's omniscience is not affected by his inability to actualize W* and to exclude action A in the process, because God knows exactly what will happen in W* (or any other world that he could actualize). Nor is his omnipotence threatened: God still has the *power* to actualize any world he can conceive of. The upshot of this is that God cannot intervene to prevent S from doing A in W*, and this no matter how strongly he disapproves of A, and regardless of how wicked or harmful A is. The free will defence, it would seem, has now been established on solid logical foundations.

(The reader who is daunted by Plantinga's formidable technical skills as a logician, and by his predilection for using logical symbolism to schematize his arguments, will be able to get the gist of this defence if she retains its central insight, that it is *logically impossible* for an agent to create another being such that it is necessarily the case that this being freely performs *only* those actions which are good or beneficial.)

However, arguing, as Plantinga does, that the notion of free will entails logical constraints on what God may do is still not sufficient to vindicate the free will defence. For, as Antony Flew and the late J. L. Mackie have argued, God, since he is omnipotent, will still have the power to actualize a world in which free beings *always* freely choose to do what is right and pleasing to him. In such a world *S* would therefore *freely* abstain from doing anything wicked.[7] To get round this objection, Plantinga invokes the idea of *transworld depravity*. According to Plantinga, it is possible that every human being suffers from a kind of depravity in which he or she will freely go wrong on at least one occasion in every world in which he or she is actualized. This being the case, *S* will perform at least one morally reproachable action in every world in which she exists. And since there is nothing logically inconsistent in the notion of 'transworld depravity', it follows that God, even if he is omnipotent, could not have created any of the possible worlds containing *S*, as well as any other free (and hence transworld depraved) human agents, without these worlds containing at least a modicum of human evil. Using only the assumptions that free agency and transworld depravity are logically possible, and that God has a purpose in actualizing a world with free human beings in it, Plantinga, it would seem, has succeeded in showing that an omnipotent, omniscient and morally perfect God will not necessarily prevent all evil. This God might endow some of his creatures with free will, and making this gift is *not* compatible with preventing *all* evil if human freedom happens to be exercised in a way that results in moral evil. The presence of evil in the world is thus logically compatible with God's existence. The free will defence, in Plantinga's submission, is able to survive the seemingly conclusive objection advanced by Flew and Mackie.

But, the sceptic might object, are there not other significant elements in the 'problem of evil' not so far addressed by Plantinga? What about the sheer variety and the quite considerable amount of human evil? What about the existence of physical evils not caused by human agency, such as diseases, tidal waves, congenital defects, earthquakes and droughts? Plantinga is well aware of this potential objection to his defence, and he argues that it can be modified to take such criticisms into account. Physical evils not caused by human beings can, he believes, be attributed to the agency of another category of free,

finite and fallible beings, namely devils.[8] The haphazard
distribution and scale of evil in the world would not disconfirm
theism, Plantinga says, 'provided there is no possible world God
could have created that contains a better balance of broadly
moral good with respect to broadly moral evil'.[9] Apparently
Plantinga believes that the distribution and magnitude of evil
does not disconfirm the existence of God because it is logically
possible that ours is a world in which, on balance, free agents
perform *more* morally right actions than reprehensible ones; a
world in which, in the final outcome, the good is not outweighed
by the bad.

This very brief sketch of Plantinga's version of the free will
defence hardly does justice to the logical rigour and clarity
displayed by Plantinga in his formulations. Plantinga's work in
this area has been definitive. At the same time, he has certainly
not lacked his critics. It is not possible to discuss all the
objections raised against the free will defence in the space of a
few pages.[10] But, from a distinctively theological standpoint,
there are at least four major objections that can be levelled
against Plantinga's presentation of this defence.

First, the very simplicity of Plantinga's proposal for resolving
the 'problem of evil' is likely to be problematic. His beguiling
'minimalism' seemingly implies that, at a theoretical level at
any rate, nothing more is needed to overcome or circumvent the
'problem of evil' than the hypothesis that the world contains at
least one individual who will perform at least one free act that is
morally wrong. This defence, *if* one is prepared to overlook
Plantinga's contention that a free will defence is quite different
from a theodicy, is in effect a pared-down theodicy acceptable to
the theodicist with greatly reduced or even no real *theological*
expectations. But, and this is one of the main issues considered
in the previous chapter, how plausible is it to claim, or to
assume, that the 'problem of evil' can be disposed of, in this
vastly minimalist fashion, at a purely theoretical or logical
level? And, far more importantly, there is the question whether
Plantinga's somewhat indeterminate Cosmic Actualizer is even
telescopically identifiable as the Holy One who is the Father of
Jesus Christ. Walter Kasper is right when he says that

> The church's profession of faith is not concerned with God in an
> unspecified sense of this word; its faith is in the God of Jesus

Christ, the God who is the Father of our Lord Jesus Christ . . .
The question of God is therefore inseparable from the question of
Christ.[11]

Pursuing and implementing the principle that for the Christian
faith the 'story' of God is irreducibly Christ-shaped, or Christ-
omorphic, will require us to understand God's power in terms of
the powerlessness of Christ on the cross, the manner of his
knowing in terms of knowing of the Nazarene, the character of
his love in terms of the deeds of the crucified Rabbi, and so on. To
speak of God in this way, however, is to speak of him in a way
that has little or no affinity with the modalities of speech
sanctioned by utterance, such as Plantinga's, that is unre-
servedly 'theistic' (i.e. specifically *non*-Christomorphic).

Secondly, there is the question of the acceptability of the free
will defender's tacit assumption that human evil can be
'balanced' or 'outweighed' by human good. Dostoyevsky's
character Ivan Karamazov protested to his brother Alyosha
that it was (morally) unacceptable that *any* alleged good should
be seen as recompense for a single tear of the innocent child who
had been tortured. The theologian who finds herself agreeing
with Ivan would therefore have substantial reservations about
granting the free will defender the assumption, crucial to her
defence, that God is morally justified in creating a world that
contains evil, provided this evil is 'balanced' or 'outweighed' by
good in the final outcome. Ivan's 'protest' or 'moral' atheism has
some very profound implications for the free will defence, and
we shall discuss it later in this chapter.

Thirdly, Plantinga's characterization of human free will
poses a problem for his account of divine omnipotence (which,
for the sake of argument, I shall accept as presented). According
to Plantinga, God is unable to exercise his power to prevent the
performance of morally reprehensible actions once he has
actualized a world populated by creatures endowed with free
will. Nevertheless, says Plantinga, God is morally justified in
creating such a world provided it is logically possible that the
evil actions of free creatures are 'balanced' or 'outweighed' by
their good deeds. But, equally, it is just as possible that the evils
perpetrated by human agents will *not* in fact be balanced or
outweighed by the good done by these agents. It is logically
possible, in other words, for human agents to exercise their

freedom in ways that will ultimately frustrate God's designs for his creation. One of Plantinga's critics, Nelson Pike, has argued that God's omnipotence can be safeguarded only if the free will defender is prepared to say that God has the ability to shape the evil that exists in the world to his ultimate purposes.[12] The God who bestows freedom on his creatures has, in the end, to be the God who takes up this human freedom into his work of salvation. Only then will he be the God who prevails over the evil that afflicts his creation. And Plantinga, because he restricts his response to the 'problem of evil' to the free will defence, has not said anything about the God of the mystery of salvation. Logically coherent though it might be, the free will defence has to be reckoned to be *theologically incomplete* as a response to the 'problem of evil'.

Fourthly, to say, as Plantinga does, that God is morally justified in actualizing a world inhabited by free agents, provided it is logically possible for the evils caused by these agents to be countered by their good deeds, is, arguably, to provide an acceptable vindication of God's moral *blamelessness*. But is it adequate as a defence of his moral *perfection*? (Implicit here is the belief that there is more to moral perfection than simply leading a blameless existence.) Or indeed of divine *benevolence*? The Christian faith affirms God to be the One who brings salvation, and this God has surely to be a divinity who does more than simply tolerate human evil as the unavoidable consequence of having granted human agents free will. The God of salvation, on this (Christian) view, is the divine mystery who overcomes human wickedness in and through the historical presence of the Son. Plantinga's deity, in contrast, seems to have detached himself from the world and left its inhabitants to work out their own moral and spiritual destinies. This deistic Demiurge is hardly the God of salvation, and he may very likely be less. For, whether intentionally or otherwise, he is portrayed as a God who has to allow his status as a morally acceptable being to depend on the moral struggles of his creatures. And even the most wretched of human beings is not obliged to accept this constraint: we appear to have the advantage over Plantinga's God in as much as we are able to affect the issue of our moral standing by our *own* acts and omissions.[13]

To find a way of dealing with these objections, it will be necessary for Plantinga to provide an account of the responsibility that God bears for being the creator of this world. There has to be, in other words, a *justification* of God, provided by human beings, or, if this is not possible, then by God himself. This, in turn, might involve a quite radical change in the conception of God implicit in the free will defence. It may be that God can be justified, either by himself or by his creatures, only if he can properly be said to be the holy mystery who interrupts the course of history to bring salvation to his creation. And it may be that bearing responsibility for being the creator of this world, and thus enabling his ways with the world to be justified (either by himself or by his creatures) requires the divine mystery not just to constitute an interruption of human history, but also to participate in this history by (and here I crave the reader's indulgence for speaking anthropomorphically) bearing the burden of suffering that falls on creaturely beings.

But to do this – that is, to approach the 'problem of evil' at a level which presupposes the possibility of making sense of such a thing as divine *providence* – the free will defender has to consent to a change of identity and become a 'theodicist' (in Plantinga's understanding of the term). That is to say, she has to engage with the 'problem of evil' not just in terms of what it is logically possible for God and his creatures to be and to do, but also at the level of what the *truth* is about who God and we are, and what God and we can do and have done. Coming this far may require one more thing of the free will defender, namely, that she abandons a purely theoretical or 'aesthetic' approach to the 'problem of evil', and instead views it as an essentially practical problem (in the way distinguished in the previous chapter).[14] To propose that theodicy should be taken in this direction, however, is to anticipate certain moves that, on reflection, might turn out to be unnecessary. Even if it is conceded that a free will defence cannot stand on its own as a theologically adequate response to the 'problem of evil', it could nevertheless be argued that all that is needed to resolve the above-mentioned difficulties for the defence is for it to be augmented by an invocation of the mystery of divine providence. Nothing else is really needed. This would obviate the need to invoke the inescapably theological categories of 'divine interruption', 'divine participation' and 'divine salvation' (categories which are seemingly intrinsic to the viewpoint we are seeking to advocate). An account of God's providential agency would bypass the need for gratuitously complex theological 'hypotheses'. This is precisely what the so-called 'natural law' theodicy purports to achieve.

THE 'NATURAL LAW' THEODICY

Richard Swinburne has also used a version of the free will defence as an explanation of the existence of human evil. But he has ingeniously circumvented the need, felt by Plantinga and Stephen Davis, to ascribe the existence of *physical* evil to the agency of Satan and his legions by arguing that the existence of physical evil is a logically necessary condition of the existence (and of the avoidance) of moral or human evil. In Swinburne's scheme, the existence of physical or natural evil is viewed as a precondition of the viability of the free will defence.[15] He states his thesis in the following way:

> ... the existence of many natural evils ... is logically neces-
> sary ... if agents are to have *knowledge* of how to bring about
> evil or prevent its occurrence, knowledge which they must have if
> they are to have a genuine choice between bringing about evil
> and bringing about good.[16]

In short: human agents can make 'genuine choices' (the precondition of the adequacy of the free will defence) only if they have knowledge of how to perform, or to abstain from, evil actions; and the existence of 'many natural evils' is a necessary condition of the possession of this knowledge. Swinburne's argument for this thesis can be outlined thus:[17]

1 Agents acquire knowledge regarding the consequences of their actions by making an inductive inference from currently available evidence to what will occur in the future (*The Existence of God*, p. 203).

2 If agents are knowingly to bring about states of affairs, or to allow states of affairs to exist as a result of not preventing them from taking place, they must know that consequences follow from their actions. (p. 204).

3 Agents can know that certain of their actions will have harmful consequences only as a result of prior experience of such harmful consequences (p. 206).

4 Generally, agents can only know that their actions and omissions have bad consequences if *others* have experienced similar consequences before. In cases where illness and injury result in death this is obviously true; after all, an agent cannot really benefit, in the long term, from the knowledge gained through experiences that result in his *own* death (pp. 206–7).

5 For any evil which an agent knowingly inflicts on another, there must have been a first time in history at which this was done. There must have been a first act of arson, a first murder, a first blinding, a first emasculation, and so forth. The primal perpetrator of these evils cannot, by hypothesis, have known the consequences of his deeds through having observed another agent performing the same actions with the same consequences (p. 207).

6 The primal perpetrator must therefore have gained his knowledge of the consequences of performing a certain action from having seen or heard of this action accidentally having certain evil consequences (p. 207).

7 There must be natural evils, whether these occur accidentally or through natural causes, if an agent is to know how to cause evils himself or to prevent them from occurring. And there have to be many natural evils, since our knowledge of future events and processes is derived inductively from many past instances (p. 207).

Swinburne uses this argument to conclude that the existence of natural evil is a precondition of knowing how to perpetrate and to prevent human evil, and since this knowledge is the essential basis of responsible human action, it follows that God has a good reason for permitting evil, *both* physical and human, to exist:

> the fewer natural evils a God provides, the less opportunity he provides for man to exercise responsibility. For the less natural evil, the less knowledge he gives to man of how to produce or avoid suffering and disaster, the less opportunity for his exercise of the higher virtues, and the less experience of the harsh possibilities of existence; and the less he allows to men the opportunity to bring about large scale horrors, the less the freedom and responsibility which he gives to them (p. 219).

At this point, it could be objected that while there is

undoubtedly a case to be made for holding that a measure of suffering is needed so that men and women can develop morally and spiritually, the *actual* scale of suffering in the world is just too vast to make it reasonable for God to permit this suffering to exist. Swinburne is aware of the force of this objection, and he tries to counter it by saying:

> What in effect the objection is asking is that a God should make a toy-world, a world where things matter, but not very much; where we can choose and our choices can make a small difference, but the real choices remain God's. For he simply would not allow us the choice of doing real harm, or through our negligence allowing real harm to occur. He would be like the over-protective parent who will not let his child out of sight for a moment (pp. 219–20).

In order that human beings will not have to live in a 'toy-world', Swinburne implies, God is justified in allowing 'Hiroshima, Belsen, the Lisbon Earthquake, or the Black Death' (p. 219). Several purely philosophical objections can be raised against Swinburne's cleverly argued attempt to show that God has a moral warrant for allowing physical evil to exist. Far more relevent for our (mainly theological) purposes, however, is the real possibility that the conclusion of Swinburne's theodicy (that the natural realm must be characterized by regularity and orderliness if human beings are to know the consequences of their actions) is susceptible to objections that are not very different from those levelled against Plantinga's rendition of the free will defence.[18]

The first objection that can be raised against Swinburne's argument concerns its implications for the concept of divine *justice*. It may be acceptable in God's eyes that physical and human evils should exist so that men and women have the opportunity to *learn* to exercise their freedom in a responsible way. It may still be acceptable to God that these instrumentally valuable evils happen to include the terrible disasters at Hiroshima, Belsen, Lisbon (during the Great Earthquake), and in Europe at the time of the Black Death. It is possible for the theodicist to say this, however, only because she operates with an abstract conception of evil and suffering. For an inhabitant of Hiroshima in 1945, or a prisoner at Belsen during the Second

World War, the pain and desolation experienced in these places is not an abstract question. For such a victim, the reality of that which had to be endured in these places was too immediate, too pressing, for it to be otherwise. Which, for the victim (if not for the theodicist), must raise the question of God's justice: how can a just God allow so many innocent ones to suffer and to perish so that other human beings (some of whom have hardly suffered) can thereby learn to act responsibly? To question God's justice in this way is to endorse Ivan Karamazov's passionate claim that any good which might arise from a situation in which grievous and gratuitous suffering is inflicted on innocent persons is not a good that can outweigh or counter-balance the evil done to them. For this reason the 'natural law' theodicy will almost certainly be rejected by the 'protest' atheist. But to press this objection it will be necessary to elucidate and examine the claims made by the 'protest' atheist. This will be done shortly. For the time being it should be noted that Swinburne does in fact consider the hypothesis that God will use an after-life to compensate individuals for the ills they have suffered in this life. He professes to see 'very strong' reasons for holding this hypothesis, but maintains that adding it to the already complicated theistic hypothesis will diminish the prior probability of the latter.

The second objection to the 'natural law' theodicy poses the question of God's accountability for the existence and quantity of evil. Swinburne seems to believe that if God intervened with a fair degree of regularity to rescue human beings from their predicaments, we would be tempted to become hopelessly reliant on God, and would not therefore learn to help ourselves.[19] But what if at the end of time or the culmination of history, humans were still fundamentally unable to help themselves? And, moreover, what if we were still not terribly good at learning to be morally responsible agents, in the way depicted by Swinburne's theodicy? The ultimate responsibility for this state of affairs would then reside with the Architect of a natural order that had not turned out to be as pedagogically efficacious as its designer had perhaps intended. This (to say the least) would be a devastatingly unsatisfactory outcome for theism, and the only remotely convincing way to forestall it is for the theist to affirm that God is able to shape the evil that exists in the world to his own ultimate purposes.[20] Accepting this affirmation, however, would involve a concomitant assertion of all that Christians traditionally subsume under the rubric of the dogmas of incarnation, redemption, *parousia*, etc.

Swinburne's response to this suggestion is not difficult to anticipate. As was the case with the objection raised above, he would say that adding extra hypotheses to the already fairly complicated theistic hypothesis is undesirable because such a move reduces the prior probability of theism. Swinburne is doubtless correct when he says this. But using this ploy as a way of getting round certain objections is likely to have a cost. For while the theodicist manages to secure the prior probability of theism by not resorting to auxiliary hypotheses, at the same time she diminishes the *overall* or *final* probability of theism by leaving it vulnerable to crucial objections that would have been countered by the very supplementary hypotheses in question. In the end, economy is gained at the price of plausibility or truth. So it might be necessary, at some stage, for the 'natural law' theodicist drastically to modify her conception of divinity. Here, alas, the theodicist will find herself plunging even deeper into the mire. For resorting to the idea of an incarnate divinity, etc., implies, pragmatically, that the *existence* of divinity is not in doubt: it makes precious little sense to understand Jesus Christ as God's fathomless gift of himself (this being the central thrust of the mystery of incarnation) if God did not (already) exist as gift. Swinburne, however, understands theodicy to consist in the endeavour to reconcile the existence of evil with the being of a God who might, or might not, exist; depending on whether or not this reconciliation can be accomplished successfully. The consequences of affirming the mystery of incarnation would serve radically to undermine Swinburne's conception of what theodicy is all about: if our arguments are correct, and if we grant to Swinburne the concession of talking about divinity as if it were a 'thing', the theistic hypothesis would have to be confirmed *before* he is able to salvage his theodicy! Only a God whose existence is not in question, and who 'speaks' to us in history, will be of any use to the 'natural law' theodicist once her theodicy runs into this kind of difficulty.[21] But it would be a little premature for Swinburne's critics to jump to the conclusion that the theodicist has no alternative but to resort to the notion of incarnation if she is to solve or resolve the 'problem of evil'. For another way of dealing with the 'problem of evil' comes readily to mind, namely, denying that God has the power to overcome evil: if God did not have the power to overcome evil, then his existence would certainly *not* be incompatible with the existence of evil. This proposal is made by the exponents of 'process' theodicy.

We shall examine this theodicy in the next section, but I would like to conclude this discussion of Swinburne's theodicy by making a few rather aggressive remarks. It cannot be denied that my attempts to meet the above objections on Swinburne's behalf have been quite a bit less than half-hearted. However, I would venture to say that to presume for one moment that it is somehow possible to 'get it right' with regard to Swinburne's God is already to have got things terribly wrong. For to contemplate any 'agent' of whom the following can *truly* be said is to focus one's thoughts on a very strange kind of 'being':

> . . . a God who sees far more clearly than we do the consequences of quarrels may have duties very different from ours with respect to particular such quarrels. He may know that the suffering that A will cause B is not nearly as great as B's screams might suggest to us and will provide (unknown to us) an opportunity to C to help B recover and will thus give C a deep responsibility which he would otherwise not have.[22]

Even the screams of the innocent further the purposes of this (Swinburnean) God. D. Z. Phillips says that 'to ask of what use are the screams of the innocent, as Swinburne's defense would have us do, is to embark on a speculation we should not even contemplate', and that to speculate thus 'is a sign of a corrupt mind'.[23] In this reply to Phillips, Swinburne contends that

> when we are doing philosophy and are justified in doing so (as I hope that we are now) it is *never* a "sign of a corrupt mind" to be open-minded about things. In all areas of life what seems most obviously true sometimes turns out to be false, and it is not the sign of a corrupt mind but the sign of a seeker after truth to examine carefully views which initially seem obviously true. It seemed obvious to many men that the Earth was flat; we may, however, be grateful that despite this, they were prepared to listen to arguments to the contrary' (The stress is Swinburne's).[24]

It *is* precisely the sign of a corrupt mind to speak easily of two different realities, say, the world of the Flat Earth Society on the one hand and the world of Auschwitz on the other, as if they are interchangeable. To be 'open-minded' about certain realities, and 'more tellingly' to *insist* on retaining such a contemplative disposition, is to show oneself to be incapable of making certain exigent moral discriminations. In the worst of cases, this incapacity to acknowledge that a particular reality is mind-stopping betokens an irremissable moral blindness, in less serious occurrences it testifies to a real lack of moral imagination, to an unshakeable moral coarseness. But in *all* cases the failure to lend a voice to the cries of the innocent (and there can be few more glaring instances of this failure than the willingness to construct a divine teleology out of innocent suffering) is to have lost the capacity to tell the truth: 'The need to lend a voice to suffering is a condition of all truth. For suffering is objectivity that weighs upon the subject; its most subjective experience, its expression, is objectively conveyed.'[25]

In cases where human beings are *in extremis*, to be 'open-minded', and thus to deafen one's ears to their cries, is to repudiate their flesh-and-bloodness, their being human. And in this hedging of one's acknowledgement of the humanity of the other, one has lost one's own humanity.[26]

The mistake that Swinburne makes is to think that human beings can determine through reflection (whether detached or passionate) what a moral judgement is, can argue their way to certain 'rhymes or reasons' where morality is concerned.[27] He fails to realize that while it is possible to decide to *make* a moral issue out of a certain predicament, it is not possible to decide what it is that will *be* making this predicament a moral issue. There are moral reasons, and we can abide by them, spurn them, contemplate them, be convinced by them, and so forth. But we cannot 'invest' reasons with an essence called 'morality'. To think that morality is something that can be intellectually constructed in this way, that it can be slotted into a matrix of purposes (whether divine or otherwise), is to negate the concept of morality.[28] In the domain where human beings have to think and act, there are irreducible realities – realities 'extra-territorial to reason' (to borrow a phrase of George Steiner's) – which halt the tongue, afflict the mind with blankness. To be resolutely 'open-minded' when confronted with these morally surd realities is to have lost any possible accordance with the truth (Adorno). It is to have lost one's own humanity (Cavell). Consider Rivka Yosselevscka's narrative, produced at the trial of Adolf Eichmann, concerning an event that took place on the Sabbath at the beginning of Elul 1942 in Zagrodski, Pinsk district:

Attorney-General   Yes. And what happened towards sunrise?

Witness, Yosselevscka   And thus the children screamed. They wanted food, water. This was not the first time. But we took nothing with us. We had no food and no water, and we did not know the reason. The children were hungry and thirsty. We were held this way for 24 hours while they were searching the houses all the time – searching for valuables . . . .

I had my daughter in my arms and ran after the truck. There were mothers who had two or three children and held them in their arms running after the truck. We ran all the way. There were those who fell – we were not allowed to help them rise. They were shot – right there – wherever they fell . . . . When we all reached the destination, the people from the truck were already down and they were undressed – all lined up. All my family was there – undressed, lined up. The people from the truck, those who arrived before us . . . .

When I came up to the place – we saw people naked lined up. But we were still hoping this was only torture. Maybe there is hope – hope of living . . . . One could not leave the line, but I wished to see – what are they doing on the hillock? Is there anyone down below? I turned my head and saw that some three or four rows were already killed – on the ground. There were some twelve people amongst the dead. I also want to mention what my child said while we were lined up in the Ghetto, she said, 'Mother, why do you make me wear the Shabbat dress; we are going to be shot?'; and when we stood near the dug-outs, near the grave, she said, 'Mother, why are we waiting, let us run!' Some of the young people tried to run, but they were caught immediately, and they were shot right there. It was difficult to hold on to the children. We took all children, not ours, and we carried – we were anxious to get it all over – the suffering of the children was difficult; we all trudged along to come nearer to the place and to come nearer to the end of the torture of the children. The children were taking leave of their parents and parents of their elder people . . . .

We were driven; we were already undressed; the clothes were removed and taken away; our father did not want to undress; he remained in his underwear. We were driven up to the grave, this shallow . . . .

Attorney-General   And these garments were torn off his body, weren't they?

A   When it came to our turn, our father was beaten. We prayed, we begged with my father to undress, but he would not undress, he wanted to keep his underclothes. He did not want to stand naked.

Q   And then they tore them off?

A   Then they tore the clothing of (*sic*) the old man and he was shot. I saw it with my own eyes. And then they took my mother, and she said, let us go before her; but they caught mother and shot her too; and then there was my grandmother, my father's mother standing there; she was eighty years old and she had two children in her arms. And then there was my father's sister. She also had children in her arms and she was shot on the spot with the babies in her arms . . . .

And yet with my last strength I came up on top of the grave, and when I did, I did not know the place, so many bodies were lying all over, dead people; I wanted to see the end of this stretch of dead bodies but I could not. It was impossible. They were lying all over, all dying; suffering, not all of them dead, but in their last sufferings; naked, shot but not dead. Children crying 'Mother', 'Father'; but I could not stand on my feet . . . .

I was searching among the dead for my little girl, but I cried for her – Merkele was her name – Merkele! There were children crying 'Mother!' 'Father!' – but they were all smeared with blood and one could not recognize the children. I cried for my daughter . . . .

I was praying for death to come. I was praying for the grave to be opened and swallow me alive. Blood was spurting from the grave in many places, like a well of water, and whenever I pass a spring now, I remember the blood which spurted from the ground, from that grave. I dug with my fingernails, but the grave would not open. I did not have enough strength. I cried out to my mother, to my father, 'Why did they not kill me? What was my sin? I have no one to go to'. I saw them all being killed. Why was I spared? Why was I not killed?[29]

PROCESS THEODICY

Process theism is a philosophical theology based on the metaphysical system adumbrated by A. N. Whitehead (1861–1947). Whitehead, though he had an abiding interest in religion, was not himself a philosophical theologian, and it was left to Charles Hartshorne (1897–) to develop Whitehead's metaphysical and cosmological insights into a full theory of God's nature and activity.

The core of this conceptualization of divinity is supplied by the principle that God, while he is absolute and unsurpassable, is also personal, social and temporal. God is bi-polar, that is, he is a synthesis of concrete and abstract aspects: the latter comprising his 'necessary' attributes and the former his 'contingent' or 'accidental' attributes. The *abstract* pole of deity contains his absolute attributes – infinity, eternity, impassibility, immutability, self-existence, etc. – and it is this pole which makes God the ground of all reality. By contrast, the *concrete* pole of deity is divinity as eminently personal, temporal, social and relative – attributes such as love, wisdom and mercy belong to this pole. In this pole God is affected to a supreme degree by all reality. One way of characterizing the difference between the two poles would be to say, as Hartshorne in fact does, that the so-called God of philosophy is the God of the abstract pole, while the so-called God of religion is the God of the concrete pole (properly speaking, of course, the two 'Gods' represent *dual* aspects of the *one* deity).[30]

The distinctive feature of Hartshorne's concept of God is his thesis that God depends upon his creatures to affect or shape the course of his experience, that God, in his concrete aspect, is created by his creatures. God creates and includes the universe in himself, although the reality of God is not ultimately reducible to the reality of the universe: to say this would be to imply that the universe is infinite and thus self-identical with God, and Hartshorne is emphatic that God alone is infinite. Hartshorne is a *panentheist* and not a pantheist (if he did affirm that the reality of God could be reduced to the reality of the universe he would indeed be the latter). God, then, is not only an absolute and infinite being, he is also one who is supremely relative. This is apparent in the following conceptualization of the God who has both an objective and a subjective side:

None but God . . . can be infinitely passive, the endurer of all change, the adventurer through all novelty, the companion through all vicissitudes. He is the auditor of all speech who should be heard because he has heard, and who should change

our hearts because in every iota of our history we have changed
his. Unchangeably right and adequate is his manner of changing
in and with all things, and unchangeably immortal are all
changes, once they have occurred, in the never darkened expanse
of his memory, the treasure house of all fact and attained value.[31]

How is the existence of this God, who depends on his creatures,
to be reconciled with the existence and the scale of evil and
suffering in the world?

Hartshorne would first of all deny that the *existence* of God
can be disconfirmed in principle by the presence of evil in the
world. A renowned defender of the ontological argument for the
existence of God, Hartshorne believes that the assertion 'God
exists' is an *a priori* or necessary truth, and so cannot be negated
by the empirical or contingent truth 'evil exists'. Either God's
existence is logically impossible or it is logically necessary, in
which case empirical evidence, such as that furnished by the
existence of evil, has no bearing whatever on the question of the
existence or non-existence of deity. Hartshorne therefore
concludes that '[the 'problem of evil'] is a mistake, a
pseudoproblem'.[32] But why do so many apparently intelligent
persons not realize that the very attempt to do theodicy is
premised on an utterly egregious failure to perceive the true
logic of theism? Why do theodicists succumb to self-inflicted
logical blindness? Hartshorne's answer is that theodicists, and
very many theists, have an inadequate doctrine of God; and it is
precisely because they err in this respect that they are tempted
to think that God must somehow be absolved of any responsibility for the evils that exist in his creation. The need for theodicy
will vanish once 'classical theism's' 'self-contradictory' concept
of God is replaced by the bi-polar deity of process theology, or so
Hartshorne and his fellow process theologians maintain.

Hartshorne, it is clear from the foregoing, is an advocate of
the dissolution, as opposed to the solution or resolution, of the
'problem of evil'. There is something inherently unsatisfactory
about this procedure; it is almost philosophical sleight of hand.
It is perhaps significant that other process theodicists have not
elevated this strategy of dissolution into a general policy, and
prefer instead to confront the theodicy-issue head-on. In so
doing, they make 'classical theism's' conception of divine
omnipotence the main target of their critical and polemical
attentions.

'Classical theism', the process theodicists say, depicts God as an agent who has an absolute monopoly on power, a coercive power which consequently can only be exercised at the expense of all other beings. The upshot is a problematic divine determinism: since other beings do not possess any inherent power of their own, it follows that God alone is ultimately responsible for the ills that reside in the created realm. Dismantling the theodicy-problem will therefore require the theist to espouse a conception of divine omnipotence which does not entail that God is in total control of the course of history, and which allows a substantial degree of freedom to exist for all *organisms*. The reality of creaturely freedom necessitates an essential limitation upon the exercise of the divine will. If creaturely beings possess real freedom, they will be able to use their own powers to thwart God's designs for the created order. Evil arises because creatures misuse their inherent freedom to reject God's aims for them. In the words of John Cobb and David Griffin:

> . . . God seeks to pursuade each occasion towards that possibility for its own existence which would be best for it; but God cannot control the finite occasion's self-actualization. Accordingly, the divine creative activity involves risk. The obvious point is that, since God is not in complete control of the events of the world, the occurrence of genuine evil is not incompatible with God's benficence towards all his creatures.[33]

The 'problem of evil' is to be dismantled by denying the concept of omnipotence it presupposes: the God of process theism cannot control finite beings but can only set them goals which he then has to persuade them to actualize. The attenuation of divine omnipotence that is merely latent in, say, Plantinga's version of the free will defence, thus receives explicit endorsement from process theology.

In addition to its doctrine of the God who is necessarily merely a persuader, process theodicy possesses a number of other features that may enhance its appeal for some metaphysically-minded theologians. The first of these is its insistence that theodicy, in addition to dissolving the logical problem of *theism* vis-à-vis the fact of evil, should make *evil in itself* more intelligible. Only in this way, it is argued, will it be possible for the theist to show that the hypothesis that the world was created *by God* is more likely to be true than alternative hypotheses.[34] Making evil in itself intelligible will almost certainly require a complex explanatory theory of the universe; one able to account, in teleological terms, for the existence and activity of every entity. Process metaphysics purports to be just such a metaphysical system of the widest generality, and it therefore satisfies at least one of a number of conditions that have to be fulfilled by any theory which aspires to demonstrate the intelligibility of evil as such. A second attractive feature of process theodicy, one notably absent from the free will defence and the 'natural law' theodicy, is its positive attempt to give a comprehensive account of God's relation to his creation. According to his account, God not only institutes natural laws; he is also personally involved in the destinies of his creatures as the dynamic source of all value (value for the process theologian being that which resides in the conjunction of harmony and intensity), and as the one who savours and retains all creaturely experiences in his memory (and who transforms these experiences in the process).[35]

Another commendable feature of process theodicy in the eyes of some theologians is associated with Whitehead's *potentially* profound theological insight that God, far from being the one who detaches himself from the pain and desolation of those who are afflicted, is on the contrary '. . . the great companion – the fellow-sufferer, who understands'.[36] This principle, which lies at the heart of the theology of the cross, and which *must* be read in the light of a *theologia crucis* if it is to have real theological significance, effectively forestalls the objection (raised against the 'natural law' theodicy in the previous section) that God's justice is in jeopardy because of the manifestly incommensurable degrees of suffering undergone by different individuals. For if God is the co-sufferer of each and every victim, then quite clearly the justice of his ways with men and women cannot be in dispute: what is meted out to them is no less than what God himself has to endure. It is of course conceivable that the omnipotence or omniscience of this victim–God might be open to doubt, but the God who is a victim alongside every other victim will be the target of the very injustices that he is alleged to have not prevented from occurring in his creation.

The above-mentioned virtues notwithstanding, the process theodicy is still problematic in several respects. In the first place, it is questionable whether it really is a theodicy. Process theodicists, since they deny that God has unlimited power, cannot legitimately claim to have reconciled the proposition 'There is a God who is *omnipotent*, omniscient and benevolent' with the proposition 'Evil exists'. By denying, or at any rate attenuating, God's omnipotence, they effectively prevent the theodicy-problem from arising.[37] Process theism's denial that God is all-powerful has another, more crucial, implication for theology. The idea of an attenuated divine omnipotence might contribute to the resolution of the *theoretical* or *logical* aspect of the theodicy-problem, but a God too powerless to overcome evil will not conceivably be able to occupy the 'logical space' which circumscribes the afflicted individual, who will in all probability be more interested in the essentially practical matter of waiting and hoping for the conquest of evil and the cessation of pain. The merely suffering God might perhaps provide a half-consolation for the person who finds herself drinking the cup of suffering to its dregs, but this God is fundamentally unable to transform and to heal the world, or, to put it in more theological terms, to ensure that his Kingdom will become a reality.[38]

Indeed, the person in travail could well argue that there is no *practical* point in seeking to hold God responsible for the existence of evil, when this finite God would have been too powerless to have made any real difference to the world in the first place! To the person in urgent need of succour, it would conceivably be just as efficacious to look to unicorns and centaurs for salvation. It is simply not enough, given the 'logical space' occupied by the victims of evil, for God to be a mere fellow-sufferer. Whether or not one ought to *say* anything about God to the person who is on the verge of being broken by suffering is of course a very real and potentially pressing question, one that can only be answered in the light of the circumstances of the sufferer. But the theodicist has to take seriously the possibility that this is a time when *saying* anything at all might be the least appropriate thing to do. If, however, there is something that can *appropriately* be said by the theodicist to the sufferer, then the ultimately powerless divinity who happens to be no more than a co-sufferer is not really going to enhance the persuasiveness of the *Christian* theodicist's case. What the process theodicy lacks is an eschatology, a resurrection-perspective, in which the almighty God on the cross of the powerless Nazarene is affirmed in faith to have inaugurated a radically new world by this very deed on the cross. The Judaeo-Christian God is a God who acts decisively in history to bring about his rule on earth. This God, contrary to what the process theodicist affirms, is no merely persuasive co-sufferer.[39]

For these reasons the process theodicy is not the most formidable candidate when it comes to formulating a characteristically Christian response to the 'problem of evil'. A more suitable candidate would have to be one which was at least prepared to attach a greater significance to a specifically resurrection-perspective than does the process theodicy.

THE 'SOUL-MAKING' THEODICY

The 'soul-making' theodicy is associated above all with John Hick.[40] Central to any understanding of this theodicy is Hick's distinction between two basic kinds of 'answer' to the 'problem of evil'. One 'answer' – the Augustinian – excludes the idea that a God who endows his creatures with freedom and a modicum of power will intervene on the scale needed to prevent evil from occurring. Another 'answer' – the Irenaean – sees evil as an integral feature of an environment in which souls are shaped by a God who desires all creatures to grow into an ultimately perfect relationship with him. Hick's theodicy, as we have already indicated, stands within the Irenaean tradition. Its most noteworthy characteristic is its comprehensiveness. Many of the thorny theological and philosophical issues elided or overlooked by other theodicists are confronted by Hick, whose theodicy brings together, systematically, a number of themes treated separately by alternative theodicies.

Like Plantinga, Hick employs a version of the free will defence. But he differs from Plantinga in emphasizing the need to go beyond the mere affirmation that the fact of human freedom is sufficient to show that God's existence is logically compatible with the existence of evil. Hick believes that a defence of this kind must be incorporated into a theistic teleology, the cardinal tenet of which would be the affirmation that God creates us as free beings for a *purpose*, i.e., to enable us to fulfil our nature in relation to God by exercising our freedom

... in a universe which functions in accordance with its own laws ... [the] human being is free to acknowledge and worship God; and is free ... to doubt the reality of God.

Within such a situation there is the possibility of the human being coming freely to know and love one's Maker ... [The] end-state which God is seeking to bring about is one in which finite persons have come in their own freedom to know and love him ...[41]

This freedom is a '*cognitive* freedom' in relation to God:

The kind of distance between God and man that would make room for a degree of human autonomy is epistemic distance. In other words, the reality and presence of God must not be borne in upon men in the coercive way in which their natural environment forces itself upon their attention. The world must be to man, to some extent at least, *etsi deus non daretur*, 'as if there were no God'. God must be a hidden deity, veiled by His creation. He must be knowable, but only by a mode of knowledge that involves a free personal reponse on man's part ... Thus the world, as the environment of man's life, will be religiously ambiguous, both veiling God and revealing him.[42]

In this religiously neutral environment, human beings can undertake 'a hazardous adventure in individual freedom' (p. 292), so that God's purposes come to be fulfilled. Like Swinburne, Hick provides an instrumental account of the existence of evil. Evil and suffering, he believes, are constitutive of the 'soul-making process'. The often costly effort expended by individuals in their attempts to deal creatively with evil and suffering produces in them certain moral and spiritual qualities consonant with their being fashioned into 'children of God' (p. 293). Unlike Swinburne, however, Hick sees the need to posit a final state in which this pedagogy of human salvation will be completed. The process of 'soul-making' reaches its climax when all human beings enjoy a perfect relationship with their Maker, having finally been formed in his likeness.

Nevertheless, it is clear that in this present life the 'soul-making' process is still awaiting completion: the wicked prosper, the innocent and the righteous endure pain and misery. The evidence this side of death seems to favour the conclusion that God's purposes for his creatures have so far been unfulfilled, even thwarted. To counter this difficulty, Hick advocates a lengthening of historical perspective:

... if there is any eventual resolution of the interplay between good and evil, any decisive bringing of good out of evil, it must lie beyond this world and beyond the enigma of death. Therefore we cannot hope to state a Christian theodicy without taking seriously the doctrine of a life beyond the grave ... The Christian claim is that the ultimate life of man – after what further scenes of 'soul-making' we do not know – lies in that Kingdom of God which is depicted in the teaching of Jesus as a state of exaltant and blissful happiness, symbolized as a joyous banquet in which all and sundry, having accepted God's gracious invitation, rejoice together. And Christian theodicy must point to that final blessedness, and claim that this infinite future good will render worth while all the pain and travail and wickedness that has occurred on the way to it. Theodicy cannot be content to look to the past, seeking an explanation of evil in its origins, but must look towards the future, expecting a triumphant resolution in the eventual perfect fulfilment of God's good purpose.[43]

A theodicy such as Hick's, which seeks to resolve the 'problem of evil' by asking us (with no small degree of *prima facie* plausibility) to view occurrences of evil and suffering in the larger context of a total history which is leading to our eternal joy, will depend on the following assumptions: it presupposes the possibility (1) of a post-mortem existence; (2) of a consummation of the course of history; (3) that God can, and will, guarantee the ultimately salvific outcome of history.

It would be beyond the scope of this book to discuss (1). In any case, (1) is less important for theodicy than (2) and (3). (2) is entailed by (3), and since (3), rather than (2), expresses the core of the Christian understanding of salvation, I shall confine our discussion to (3).

For Hick's eschatological theodicy to work, God will have to guarantee that total joy will be ours at the consummation of history. Hence, if history terminated in catastrophe, then God would have failed to ensure the outcome specified by this theodicy. However, and herein lies the rub, if joy will be the *inevitable* outcome of history, what point can there be in undergoing the 'hazardous journey in individual freedom?' If the human soul fails to reach the final destination chosen by God, then her 'moral and spiritual training' has ultimately been in vain. On the other hand, if access to the termination-point of the journey is guaranteed for all, then questions must arise over the manifest differences in the severity of the training-schedules allocated to us by God: some individuals are dragged to a moral, spiritual and physical breaking-point, while others seem, by comparison, to be rather lightly taxed. No doubt it will take a detailed argument to press this point against the 'soul-making' theodicy; even so, it raises an issue that is likely to subvert this theodicy. This issue, which concerns the point or the purpose that can be ascribed to suffering, is not shirked by Hick. Hick wants to say that suffering constitutes the *means* by which human beings grow into a relationship with their creator.

Suffering, in one degree or another, is thus the *sine qua non* of attaining the perfect bliss that will be ours at the consummation of history. This condition, we have suggested, is *morally* dubious because not everyone is tested – morally, spiritually and physically – to the same degree. Hick proposes to get round this problem by maintaining that 'soul-making' continues after death. But a little reflection will indicate that this proposal is quite unsatisfactory. For exactly the same question that was asked about the *point* of suffering on earth can be asked about the point of suffering in the post-mortem Celestial City (it must be presumed that some souls will suffer in the Celestial City as they continue to undergo the 'soul-making' process): the eschatological theodicist does not resolve the issue simply by saying that suffering takes place at another time (after my death) and in another place (the Celestial City). If pointless suffering exists on earth, then it *can* exist in the Celestial City. (If gratuitous and haphazard instances of suffering are not to be found in the Celestial City, then, all else being equal, the 'soul-making' process located therein will be very much less arduous than the one that takes place on earth. This in turn will pose difficulties for the notion of divine justice.)

Moreover, it could be argued against the 'soul-making' theodicist that the degree and the variety of suffering that exists anywhere (the Celestial City included) is too great to justify whatever ultimate joy there is at the end of history. Thus Dorothee Soelle says, 'The God who causes suffering is not to be justified even by lifting the suffering later. No heaven can rectify Auschwitz'.[44] The sort of suffering that cannot be so justified goes under the name 'dysteleological suffering', or as Simone Weil calls it, 'affliction'.[45] Hick, to be fair, is well aware of the problem posed by pointless suffering. He says of such suffering:

Such suffering remains unjust and inexplicable, haphazard and cruelly excessive. The mystery of dysteleological suffering is a real mystery . . . It challenges Christian faith with its utterly baffling, alien destructive meaninglessness. And yet at the same time, detached theological reflection can note that this very irrationality and this lack of ethical meaning contribute to the character of the world as a place in which true human goodness can occur and in which loving sympathy and compassionate self-sacrifice can take place.[46]

Hick concludes his discussion of dysteleological suffering by citing H. H. Farmer's contention that 'paradoxically, the failure of theism to solve mysteries becomes part of its case!' (p. 372).[47] This appeal to mystery, coupled as it is with Hick's positing of an eschatological resolution of the plight of those who are afflicted, will carry very little conviction for the 'moral' atheist. Precisely why this is so we shall try to discover in the next section, when we will discuss the case of Dostoyevsky's character Ivan Karamazov. Ivan is someone who believes, or who had hitherto believed, in the love and power of God, and who is tormented by the terrible reality of the evil that surrounds him. If the eschatological theodicy, which combines salient features of the free will defence, the 'natural law' theodicy and the process theodicy, cannot carry conviction for him, then those theodicies must be deemed to be unsuccessful.

THE CRITIQUE OF TRADITIONAL THEODICY: THE CASE OF IVAN KARAMAZOV

Of God and the world he had created Ivan Karamazov says: 'I accept God plainly and simply . . . I accept his divine wisdom and his purpose . . . I believe in the underlying order and meaning of life. I believe in the eternal harmony into which we are all supposed to merge one day.'[48] However, almost immediately he tells his brother Alyosha: 'I refuse to accept this world of God's . . . Please understand, it is not God that I do not accept, but the world he has created. I do not accept God's world and I refuse to accept it'[49] Ivan then proceeds to explain why he cannot bring himself to accept this world of God's. He mentions a number of cases of extreme and gratuitous cruelty, in particular the report of an army general who fed an eight year-old boy to his hounds because the child had slightly injured his favourite dog with a stone. Ivan says:

> Listen: if all have to suffer so as to buy eternal harmony by their suffering, what have the children to do with it – tell me, please? It is entirely incomprehensible why they should have to buy harmony by their sufferings. Why should they, too, be used as dung for someone's future harmony?[50]

Ivan then conludes:

> I don't want harmony . . . too high a price has been placed on harmony. We cannot afford to pay so much for admission. And therefore I hasten to return my ticket of admission . . . It's not God that I do not accept, Alyosha. I merely most respectfully return him the ticket.[51]

This moral rebellion is not a species of 'atheism' in the conventional understanding of that term. As Stewart Sutherland points out in his philosophical study of *The Brothers Karamazov*, it is somewhat misleading to locate the atheism of Ivan in the context of (traditional) religious epistemology. As the above passages indicate, Ivan's atheism has nothing whatever to do with believing (or disbelieving) certain propositions relating to the existence of God.[52] Rather, the problem for Ivan is above all a moral problem: he rejects God not because he finds it impossible to believe that there is a God – on the contrary, he clearly believes that there is such a being – but because he finds it morally repugnant that God should (seem to) expect such a terrible price to be paid for the final bliss and harmony that he will bestow on humankind at the end of time. It is clear that, where Ivan is concerned, the problem is to do with the *morality* of *believing* in a God who exacts such an unbearable price for our salvation. Can the resources of the 'soul-making' theodicy (and *eo ipso* the other theodicies discussed in this chapter) be used to pursuade him that it is not immoral to believe in this divinity, implicitly identified by Ivan as the God of the Christian faith?[53] It will be recalled that for John Hick it is the case that

> If man's pain and sin are revealed in the final reckoning, and at the end of human time, as having . . . played a part in the

fulfilment of [God's purpose for his creatures], then in the ultimate perspective they have contributed to good.[54]

Where the 'soul-making' theodicy is concerned, all forms of suffering are ultimately constructive because they somehow advance God's purposes in creating the world. We live in a providential world where souls grow, despite their travails, into a true and lasting relationship with their Creator.

Is this eschatological theodicy likely to change the outlook of the 'protest' atheist? Will the Ivan Karamazovs of this world be persuaded to view the sufferings of humankind from the larger eschatological perspective of a total history which is moving towards a denouement that promises eternal happiness for the whole of humankind? The answer, one suggests, is: no. For Ivan already believes that the world is a providential place, he accepts, albeit most unwillingly, that history will probably take a course according with Christian eschatology (though he finds it quite wrong that one should acquiesce in the outcome promised by this scheme of things). What he cannot accept, therefore, is the price, in terms of innocent human suffering, that is exacted so that men and women may come to enjoy eternal harmony. God has a providential relationship with his creation, yes, but this divine providence is just too costly. Ivan, it seems, has steeled himself (in the end his spiritual turmoil drives him insane) to the point where he decides that he must decline to be the masochistic accomplice of this God – we ought not to allow ourselves to be loved by such a God. (Ivan, though, is in no way suggesting that we are worthy of the love of God. He tells Alyosha: 'And what is so strange . . . is not that God actually exists, but that such an idea – the idea of the necessity of God – should have entered the head of such a savage and vicious animal as man'.[55]) The 'soul-making' theodicist's central affirmation, that human suffering is the means by which supreme happiness is ultimately attained, is unacceptable to the 'protest' atheist: like Ivan, she questions the moral propriety of a process which submits innocent children to unbearable pain so that human beings can get to heaven. For Ivan, there is no possible moral justification for the belief that the sufferings of the innocent can be expiated or redeemed, either in this life or in a post-mortem existence. The idea of an eschatological resolution of humankind's earthly travails is one he rejects with great vehemence:

I understand, of course, what a cataclysm of the universe it will be when everything in heaven and on earth blends in one hymn of praise and everything that lives and has lived cries aloud: 'Thou art just, O Lord, for thy ways are revealed!' Then, indeed, the mother will embrace the torturer who had her child torn to pieces by his dogs, and all three will cry aloud: 'Thou art just, O Lord!' . . . But there's the rub: for it is that I cannot accept . . . I make haste to arm myself against it, and that is why I renounce higher harmony altogether. It is not worth one little tear of that tortured little girl who beat herself on the breast and prayed to her 'dear, kind Lord' in the stinking privy with her unexpiated tears! They must be expiated, for otherwise there can be no harmony. But, how, how are you to expiate them? Is it possible? I don't want harmony. I don't want it, out of the love I bear to mankind.[56]

Ivan, then, rejects the root-principle of the 'soul-making' theodicy, the principle that there can be a post-mortem transformation of the afflictions of humankind. As he sees it, the promised bliss of heaven cannot be a compensation or reward for the earthly travails of innocent human beings. With respect to Ivan, and any critic of the eschatological theodicy who happens to share his beliefs, it is certainly not self-evident that the 'soul-making' theodicist is wedded to the idea of a compensatory heaven. In fact, John Hick explicitly distances himself from this idea when he declares: 'The "good eschaton" will not be a reward or a compensation proportioned to each individual's trials, but an infinite good that would render worth while *any* finite suffering endured in the course of attaining to it'.[57] Since Hick's notion of a 'good eschaton' in which a transfiguration of innocent suffering will take place is certainly not logically incoherent, it is not likely that the 'protest' atheist will want to challenge him on this score. So although the passage from *The Brothers Karamazov* quoted above shows Ivan to be questioning the 'possibility' of an expiation of innocent suffering in the final reckoning, the 'possibility' mentioned therein is almost certainly not a specifically '*logical* possibility'; to assume this would be to assume, somewhat implausibly, that Ivan is bent on making a weak case from the outset. What 'possibility' can Ivan therefore be said to have in mind when he says of the tortured girl's tears that 'they must be expiated, for otherwise there can be no harmony. But how, how are you to expiate them? Is it possible?'

To gain a deeper insight into the kind of possibility that Ivan might be referring to in this passage, it is perhaps necessary to dwell on the urgent appeal which he makes when Alyosha accuses him of rebelling against God:

> . . . answer me: imagine that it is you yourself who are erecting the edifice of human destiny with the aim of making men happy in the end, of giving them peace and contentment at last, but that to do that is absolutely necessary, and indeed quite inevitable, to torture to death only one tiny creature, the little girl who beat her breast with her little fist, and to found the edifice on her unavenged tears – would you consent to be the architect on those conditions? Tell me and do not lie![58]

Only one answer can be given, and it is an answer that even God is (morally) constrained to give: ' "No, I wouldn't", Alyosha said softly.'

In other words, an all-powerful and all-knowing God cannot hope to create a world in which iniquity after iniquity is heaped on the heads of the innocent *and* be perfectly loving at the same time. Even a sinful Karamazov would not consent to create the world on these terms! Ivan is not calling theodicy into question. He is, after all, prepared to accept God, or at least to concede that human reason is not competent to discredit the idea of such a being. But what his moral sense forbids him to accept is God's *creation*; he cannot accept that this world, which is created by God, is at the same time the place where God *manifests* his love. Or to put it in another way: if *this* is how God displays his love (i.e. by creating such a world), then, says Ivan, what chance do mere mortals like us have of truly loving each other?[59]

If it is assumed that human beings have to exercise their capacity to love if their souls are to be formed in the image of God, then it must follow that the world (which, in Ivan's eyes, is such that it seemingly cannot be the locus of even a fathomless and unvanquishable divine love) is hardly the place where human beings can grow to love each other and their Maker. The eschatological theodicy, indeed all theodicy, has therefore to be rejected. But, this theodicist might interject, is Ivan really justified in suggesting, albeit indirectly, that God ought to have created a world that is a pain-free paradise, the kind of place in which there are no significant perils to be encountered, no real pain to be endured? Surely, John Hick and Richard Swinburne are right: it would be difficult, if not impossible, for human beings to develop into loving and compassionate creatures in so anodyne an environment? This objection can be given a Christological gloss: did Christ, the foundation of the world, according to the writer of the Fourth Gospel, not himself take the ultimate risk when he became the concrete embodiment of God's love for us? Alyosha, the novice monk, makes just this Christological point when he responds to Ivan's passionate denial that it is possible for anyone to forgive the person who causes an innocent child to suffer:

> . . . there is such a being, and he can forgive everything, everyone and everything and *for everything*, because he gave his innocent blood for all and for everything. You've forgotten him, but it is on him that the edifice is founded, and it is to him that they will cry aloud: 'Thou art just, O Lord, for thy ways are revealed!'[60]

Ivan, though, has anticipated this retort, and counters it by narrating the parable of the Grand Inquisitor. The gist of Ivan's parable is that though freedom might be God's greatest gift to humankind, this gift has left the human race 'in greater confusion and suffering', so much so that human beings would be happier if they surrendered their freedom in return for contentment (or so avers the Grand Inquisitor). For the 'protest' atheist, therefore, the two primary constitutive features of the 'soul-making' theodicy – the free will defence (and the providential teleology within which this defence is embedded) and the thesis of the eschatological resolution of human suffering – are to be rejected. Ivan repudiates these two key doctrines, but precisely by *accepting*, in a spirit of grim and mocking irony, the false and morally unacceptable deity of this teleology.[61] The very intelligibility and coherence of this theistic system is welcomed by Ivan – as a blasphemy that makes its God into an idol. It is easy to see that Ivan's struggle with the 'problem of evil' is bound to be inconclusive.[62]

The theoretical theodicies have been undermined by Ivan's corrosive scepticism. Not even the suggestion, made by John Hick and Brian Hebblethwaite, that we need to conduct theodicy from the standpoint of a longer historical perspective – in Hick's case one positing 'soul-making' in a post-mortem existence, in Hebblethwaite's case the perspective being that of the completed 'historical process'[63] – can confute Ivan's reservations (by indicating to him that his 'rebellion' might be premature because he has not employed a longer perspective). The person who thinks that Ivan's crisis can be resolved by constructing a more coherent, a more intuitively plausible, a more 'religiously adequate', a more personally moving *apologia* on behalf of the God who '*exists*' and who is '*good*', has utterly misperceived the nature of Ivan's epistemological crisis. For Ivan is not pleading to be convinced that there is a God, and that this God is benevolent, etc. Rather, Ivan is obsessively convinced that the affirmation of such a God serves only to make the 'problem of evil' more – much more – intractable. In his eyes, history has forced the theist to forgo, irrevocably, the 'grammar' of such expressions as 'divine benevolence' or 'divine providence'. We continue to use these expressions, but they lack application, and we are taken in by them. If we can only know God from his 'effects', then to say that X is 'divine' and 'benevolent' (and to mean it) is to relate X grammatically to a form of life in which we encounter, in some way and in some sense, the realities of healing and wholeness, of love and mercy. To use these expressions in contexts which betoken the *absence* of these realities is to run the danger of not knowing what we are saying, to be unable to activate our concepts. Ivan, at this level, is asking the question: 'how far may someone *in extremis* be justified in asserting that God is good, loving etc.?' (Or correspondingly: 'How far may we, when confronted by this person's sufferings, be justified in asserting that God is good, loving, etc?') And Ivan's answer is radical, namely, that neither this person nor us on her behalf, can give an answer to these questions. In these contexts, Ivan is suggesting, we no longer have the power to recognize a particular segment of reality as constituting a sphere in which (divine) healing, (divine) wholeness, and so on, are to be encountered. In these contexts, we can no longer be certain whether anything could conceivably count for this innocent sufferer as a manifestation of God's love, mercy, and so forth. There seems to be *absolutely* nothing that could, in a manner of speaking, compel us to assert that what has taken place is a manifestation of divine love, graciousness, etc. What Ivan is engaging in is best seen as a form of meta-linguistic reflection: he is attending here to the *a priori* possibility of applying those concepts which purport to express the reality of such love and graciousness. (He is thus engaged, generally, in the activity which Kant designated as 'transcendental logic', Hegel as logic, and Wittgenstein as 'grammar'.)

Now the issue of the 'grammar' of being 'justified in asserting' (that God is benevolent, gracious, etc.) is one that cannot be resolved empirically by citing counter-examples which show people to be the recipients of undeserved and unexpected good fortune (which can then be attributed to the 'work' of God) or by making the 'right' apologetic moves. It is highly significant that Alyosha does not attempt to resort to such empirical or apologetic stratagems. He does not try to give his brother the 'right' *description* of God and his ways. This, however, is the very thing that the metaphysical theodicist would like Alyosha to have done: most philosophical theodicists who discuss Ivan's situation assume implicitly that Alyosha's problem is that he simply does not have the right 'arguments' or descriptions to overturn the 'Euclidean mind' of his brother. These theodicists invariably conclude their examinations of *The Brothers Karamazov* by assembling a battery of the arguments that Alyosha *ought* to have deployed against his brother. In so doing, they fail to perceive that if Alyosha had sought to counter his brother's arguments by resorting to apologetics or by trying to share with his brother certain novel empirical discoveries that he had been able to make about God, he would certainly have failed to get to the essentially 'grammatical' *point* of what Ivan was endeavouring to say.

The really serious and important issue posed by Ivan is twofold. First, we have to determine, 'grammatically', whether or not things are such that it is inconceivable for the person *in extremis* to be in a position to speak of God as benevolent and gracious; or alternatively, whether we are in a position where we can somehow go on to imagine, and (far more crucially) to strive for, a form of life in which it will be possible to activate the concepts 'divine love', 'divine providence', and so forth. The Christian faith, of course, affirms that the latter is a real possibility because God, in the person of his Son, bears the weight of human history 'in the flesh'; that God has, as it were, inscribed his love in the text (and texture) of this history. But to *articulate* this possibility, from where we are situated *now*, the Christian has, like Job, to risk undertaking a sustained and perilous exploration of the categories of the unexplained, the arbitrary, the silent and the gratuitous. She also has to acknowledge that there are circumstances when this Christian 'grammar' will in all probability be forgone by the soul who finds herself *in extremis*.

Where Ivan is concerned, then, merely to say (as if one were actually describing something in so saying) that there is a good and gracious God only heightens and compounds the conundrum confronting the theodicist. Such saying only *reintroduces* the initial problem. Neither belief in an omnipotent, omniscient and morally benevolent divinity, nor its negation, can 'solve' the 'problem of evil'. This 'problem', if it is to be overcome, must be situated in a theological context void of any apologetic intent. That is, it will be a context which enables us to reconnect the concept of good and gracious 'godness' with the *reality* in which the sufferer is situated. The making of this reconnection is not a purely theoretical task, and its 'syntax' and 'vocabulary' are not confined to the discourse of *curiositas*, for this 'making' is precisely what it is, i.e., a '*doing*' or practical activity, and not just a thinking of lofty thoughts and a cultivation of noble sentiments (though of course having such thoughts and sentiments is not in itself incompatible with the *practice* demanded).[64] The task of making this reconnection calls for patterns of conduct on the part of the Christian which do not contradict and obscure the divine self-manifestation that is the ground and absolute presupposition of this reconnection. This proposal is in line with the suggestion of Boyce Gibson, who in this respect is one of Dostoyevsky's most helpful interpreters:

> Theoretically, Ivan's criticisms are unanswered: Alyosha, in particular, simply agrees with him: and Dostoevsky himself held them to be 'irrefutable'. The answer is to go forward from theory to practice: and Dostoevsky distinguished in the end between the yearning love which does nothing and submits, and the active love which has power to save.[65]

I am suggesting that perhaps the only discourse which can do justice to the radicality of Ivan's challenge is one that can in principle be heard – but maybe not *spoken* to those who are victims – by a community that stakes its very existence on the memory of suffering, on an inarticulate speech of the heart, a speech which opened itself to the mystery of God, a divine mystery which makes present the mystery of healing. For to speak is to imply that healing is *experienced* as healing, whereas to hear in silence is to acknowledge that someone's hurt can be so great that it betokens the very absence of the experience of healing and thus of divinity itself. This hearing can only be undertaken in a spirit of inviolable solidarity with those who are afflicted.[66]

NOTES

1 This classification is taken from Michael L. Peterson, 'Recent Work on the Problem of Evil', *American Philosophical Quarterly*, 20 (1983), pp. 321–39. Peterson merely uses this classification as a taxonomy, and does not set out to show that certain quite significant inter-relationships exist between the different kinds of theodicy. I hope to indicate some of these inter-relationships in this chapter.

2 For Plantinga's presentation of the free will defence, see 'The Free Will Defence', in W. L. Rowe and W. J. Wainwright, eds, *Philosophy of Religion: Selected Readings* (New York: Harcourt Brace Jovanovich, 1973), pp. 217–30; *God and Other Minds*, ch. 5; *The Nature of Necessity*, ch. 9; and *God, Freedom and Evil*. For alternative formulations, see Stephen Davis, 'A Defense of the Free Will Defence', *Religious Studies*, 18 (1982), pp. 335–44, and 'Free Will and Evil', in *Encountering Evil*, pp. 69–83; Stanley G. Kane, 'The Free Will Defence Defended', *The New Scholasticism*, 50 (1976), pp. 435–46; and Keith E. Yandell, 'Logic and the Problem of Evil: a Response to Hoitenga', in Yandell, ed., *God, Man, and Religion: readings in the philosophy of religion* (New York: McGraw-Hill, 1973), pp. 351–64.

3 See Plantinga, *The Nature of Necessity*, p. 165. Plantinga takes (1) to entail that God exists.

4 On this point, see Plantinga, *God, Freedom and Evil*, pp. 27–8.

5 Plantinga, *The Nature of Necessity*, pp. 165–6.

6 Plantinga, *God, Freedom and Evil*, p. 34. Plantinga's italics.

7 For Flew, see 'Compatibilism, Free Will and God', *Philosophy*, 48 (1973), pp. 231–44. For Mackie, see 'Evil and Omnipotence', in Rowe and Wainwright, eds, *Philosophy of Religion*, pp. 206–16. See also Mackie, *The Miracle of Theism* (Oxford: Clarendon, 1982), pp. 162–76.

8 Stephen Davis is another free will defender who attributes the

existence of physical evil to the agency of devils. See his 'Free Will and Evil' in Davis, ed., *Encountering Evil*.

9 Plantinga, *God, Freedom and Evil*, p. 63.

10 The article by Peterson, 'Recent work on the Problem of Evil', mentioned in note 1 above, reviews recent work on the free will defence.

11 Walter Kasper, *The God of Jesus Christ*, p. 158.

12 See Nelson Pike, 'Plantinga on Free Will and Evil', *Religious Studies*, 15 (1979), pp. 472–3. See also H. P. Owen, *Christian Theism: A Study in its Basic Principles* (Edinburgh: T. & T. Clark, 1984), pp. 86ff. The principle, upheld by Pike and Owen, that God will eventually transform evil into good in an eschatological consummation is of course the nub of John Hick's 'soul-making' theodicy. The theologian who shares Ivan Karamazov's belief that certain forms of evil are irredeemable would naturally be sceptical of this principle.

13 Robert Ackermann has objected (correctly in my opinion) that Plantinga's passive, non-intervening God cannot be reconciled with the Biblical account of divine agency. See his 'An Alternative Free Will Defence', *Religious Studies*, 18 (1982), pp. 365–72. I would want to go further than Ackermann and ask whether Plantinga's God is even remotely conceivable as the divine mystery involved in the bringing of *salvation* to humankind.

14 That several free will defenders have themselves acknowledged the necessity to take this defence in the direction of a fully-fledged theodicy is indicated by the works of Pike and Ackermann cited in notes 12 and 13 above. See also Davis, 'Free Will and Evil', cited in note 8 above. None of these writers, however, has seen the need to take theodicy into the sphere of a praxis-enabling enterprise.

15 For Swinburne's treatment of the problem of evil, see *The Existence of God*, ch. 11. See also 'Natural Evil', *American Philosophical Quarterly*, 15 (1978), pp. 295–301; and 'The Problem of Evil', Brown, ed., *Reason and Religion*, pp. 81–102, as well as the 'Postscript' on pp. 129–33.

16 *The Existence of God*, pp. 202–3.

17 References given in the text are to *The Existence of God*, pp. 202–20.

18 The reader who is interested in some of the specifically philosophical objections that have been raised against Swinburne's position is recommended to consult the following: D. Z. Phillips, 'The Problem of Evil: II', Brown, ed., *Reason and Religion*, pp. 103–22, and the 'Postscript' on pp. 134–9; Eleonore Stump, 'Knowledge, Freedom and the Problem of Evil', *International Journal of the Philosophy of Religion*, 14 (1983), pp. 49–58; David O'Connor, 'Swinburne on Natural Evil', *Religious Studies*, 19

(1983), pp. 65–73; Paul K. Moser, 'Natural Evil and the Free Will Defense', *International Journal of the Philosophy of Religion*, 15 (1984), pp. 49–56; and Brice R. Wachterhauser, 'The Problem of Evil and Moral Skepticism', *International Journal of the Philosophy of Religion*, 17 (1985), pp. 167–74. I am much indebted to these works.

19 *The Existence of God*, pp. 210–11.

20 It will be recalled that his point was also made in connection with the free will defence. See pp. 75–76 above. It has also to be remembered that such a divine transformation of evil into ultimate good is likely to be morally unacceptable to the 'protest' atheist. For a consideration of 'protest' atheism, see pp. 96–105 below.

21 John Hick is therefore correct when he says, in opposition to Plantinga and Swinburne, that 'the theodicy project stands . . . within an already operating belief in God'. See 'An Irenaean Theodicy' in Davis, ed., *Encountering Evil*, p. 39. Hick and I concur that theodicy is inaugurated by an act of *accusation*. That is to say, it is initiated by the theodicist's opponent, who, like Job, accuses God of creating a world in which the burden of suffering and evil is seen to be too onerous. In responding to her adversary, the theodicist engages in an attempt to convince, to persuade. She *does* something by *saying* something. Theodicy in this sense is a species of rhetoric, and is thus irreducibly performative. In this perspective God exists, *as* the One who is accused.

22 'The Problem of Evil: I', in Brown, ed., *Reason and Religion*, p. 92.

23 Brown, ed., *Reason and Religion*, p. 115.

24 Brown, ed., *Reason and Religion*, p. 130.

25 T. W. Adorno, *Negative Dialectics*, trans. E. B. Ashton, (London: Routledge & Kegan Paul, 1973), pp. 17–18.

26 For a quite brilliant treatment of the 'grammar' of this refusal to acknowledge the humanity of the other, to which I am indebted, see Stanley Cavell, *The Claim of Reason: Wittgenstein, Skepticism, Morality, and Tragedy* (Oxford: Clarendon, 1979), pp. 329–496. See also Cavell's essays 'Knowing and Acknowledging' and 'The Avoidance of Love: A Reading of *King Lear*', in his collection *Must we Mean what we Say?* (Cambridge: Cambridge University Press, 1976), chs. IX and X respectively.

27 Brown, ed., *Reason and Religion*, p. 131.

28 On this see Cavell, *The Claim of Reason*, pp. 289–90.

29 Quoted in Irving Greenberg, 'Cloud of Smoke, Pillar of Fire: Judaism, Christianity, and Modernity after the Holocaust', in Eva Fleischner, ed., *Auschwitz: Beginning of a New Era?* (New York: KTAV, 1977), pp. 15–17. Greenburg in turn quotes from the Eichmann trial records, as cited in Raul Hilberg, ed., *Documents of Destruction* (Chicago: Quandrangle, 1973), pp. 61–2.

30 For Hartshorne's characterization of God, see *The Divine Relativity: A Social Conception of God* (New Haven: Yale, 1948); *Man's Vision of God* (Hampden, Conn.: Archon, 1964); and 'The God of Religion and the God of Philosophy', in G. N. A. Vesey, ed., *Talk of God* (London: Macmillan, 1969), pp. 152–67. See also the essays in Section Two of D. Brown, R. E. James and G. Reeves, eds, *Process Philosophy and Christian Thought* (New York: Bobbs-Merrill, 1971).

31 Hartshorne, *Man's Vision of God*, p. 248.

32 Hartshorne, 'A New Look at the Problem of Evil', in F. C. Dommeyer, ed., *Current Philosophical Issues: essays in honor of C. J. Ducasse* (Springfield, Ill.: Thomas, 1966), p. 202. The claim that the 'problem of evil' is a 'pseudo-problem' is repeated in Hartshorne's *Creative Synthesis and Philosophical Method* (London: SCM, 1970), p. 258.

33 *Process Theology: an Introductory Exposition* (Belfast: Christian Journals, 1977), p 53. See also pp. 69–76. For a similar argument, see Lewis S. Ford, 'Divine Persuasion and the Triumph of Good', in Brown, James and Reeves, eds, *Process Philosophy*, p. 291.

34 For this argument, see Griffin, 'Creation out of Chaos', in Davis ed., *Encountering Evil*, p. 119.

35 On these points, see Ford, 'Divine Persuasion', in Brown, James and Reeves, eds., *Process Philosophy*, pp. 293ff.

36 A. N. Whitehead, *Process and Reality* (Cambridge: Cambridge University Press, 1923), p. 532.

37 As noted by John Hick in his response to Griffin's presentation in Davis, ed., *Encountering Evil*, p. 122.

38 Lewis Ford concedes that the God of process theism is unable in principle to change the world. See his 'Divine Persuasion', in Brown, James and Reeves, eds, *Process Philosophy*, pp. 302ff.

39 Lewis Ford attempts to deal with a similar criticism by suggesting that process theology does have an eschatology, but that it is not an eschatology focused on the *historical* realization of God's kingdom. Rather, it is an eschatology in which 'we are to seek a "a kingdom not of this world"' ('Divine Persuasion', p. 302). Ford in turn quotes from Whitehead, *Process and Reality*, p. 520. This recourse to biblical exegesis is rather stretched; I tend to agree with David Tracy that process theologians are hard pushed to show that their deity is the self-same God as the Judaeo-Christian God. See his *Blessed Rage for Order: The New Pluralism in Theology* (New York: Seabury, 1975), pp. 190–1.

40 The main texts are Hick, *Evil and the God of Love*, and 'An Irenaean Theodicy', In Davis, ed., *Encountering Evil*, pp. 39–52.

41 Hick, 'An Irenaean Theodicy', in Davis, ed., *Encountering Evil*, pp. 43. See also *Evil and the God of Love*, p. 318. All references cited in

parentheses within the text will be to *Evil and the God of Love*. Hick also espouses the free will defence in his *Philosophy of Religion* (Englewood Cliffs: Prentice-Hall, 1963), pp. 41ff.

42 Hick, *Evil and the God of Love*, pp. 317–18.

43 Hick, *Evil and the God of Love*, pp. 375–6.

44 Soelle, *Suffering* (London: Darton, Longman & Todd, 1975), p. 149.

45 By this Weil meant a form of suffering that is not *mere* pain and suffering. See her *Waiting on God* (London: Routledge & Kegan Paul, 1951).

46 Hick, *Evil and the God of Love*, pp. 371–2.

47 For Farmer's claim, see his *Towards Belief in God* (London: SCM, 1942), p. 234. Interestingly enough, the claim, made by Hick and Swinburne, that God would not advance his purposes by locating his creatures in a 'morally frictionless environment' (Hick), is also to be found in Thomas Malthus's *An Essay on the Principle of Population* (1798), ch. XIX. A 'morality of knowledge' would require us to confront all narratives which invoke the notion of a 'morally frictionless environment' with the shattering narrative that concluded our discussion of Swinburne's theodicy.

48 Dostoyevsky, *The Brothers Karamazov*, trans. D. Magarshack, (Harmondsworth: Penguin, 1958), pp. 274–5. All page references will be to this translation. The significance for theodicy of Dostoyevsky's portrayal of Ivan Karamazov cannot be gainsaid. In the words of A. Boyce Gibson: 'Henceforward, no justification of evil, by its outcome or its context, has been possible; Ivan Karamazov has seen to that'. See his *The Religion of Dostoevsky* (London: SCM, 1973), p. 176. My aim in this chapter is to let Ivan's narrative collide with those produced by our representative theodicists.

49 *The Brothers Karamazov*, p. 275.

50 *The Brothers Karamazov*, p. 286.

51 *The Brothers Karamazov*, p. 287.

52 Stewart Sutherland, *Atheism and the Rejection of God: Contemporary Philosophy and 'The Brothers Karamazov'* (Oxford: Blackwell, 1977). See especially pp. 25–39.

53 I do not propose to consider Dostoyevsky's own answer to the problem of evil as it is posed by Ivan. He himself believed Ivan's criticisms to be 'irrefutable'. See Boyce Gibson, *The Religion of Dostoevsky*.

54 Hick, *Evil and the God of Love*, pp. 374–5.

55 *The Brothers Karamazov*, p. 274.

56 *The Brothers Karamazov*, pp. 286–7.

57 Hick, *Evil and the God of Love*, p. 377

58 *The Brothers Karamazov*, pp. 287–8.

59 This is Sutherland's prespective on the argument of Chapter IV,
    Book V of *The Brothers Karamazov*. See Sutherland, *Atheism and
    the Rejection of God*, p. 74.

60 *The Brothers Karamazov*, p. 288.

61 Sutherland's explication of the concept of God espoused by Ivan to
    innervate his critique of theism is most illuminating. See his
    Atheism and the Rejection of God, pp. 25ff.

62 Janko Lavrin, *Dostoevsky: A Study* (London: Methuen, 1948),
    p. 139.

63 For Hick's suggestion, see (in addition to the references already
    given) his 'Remarks' in Brown, ed., *Reason and Religion*, pp. 127–8.
    For Hebblethwaite's, see his *Evil, Suffering and Religion*, p. 106.

64 Here I am applying Adorno's thesis that 'our metaphysical faculty
    is paralyzed because actual events have shattered the basis on
    which speculative metaphysical thought can be reconciled with
    experience'. See his *Negative Dialectics*, p. 362.

65 Boyce Gibson, *The Religion of Dostoevsky*, pp. 176–7. In my
    understanding of the nature of Ivan's problematic I have been
    profoundly indebted to the following essays of Stanley Cavell's:
    'Kierkegaard's *On Authority and Revelation*' and 'A Matter of
    Meaning It', in *Must we mean what we say?*, chaps. VI and VIII
    respectively. The fundamental ideas involved in my reconstruction
    of Ivan's espistemological crisis are of course derived from the work
    of Wittgenstein. See especially *The Philosophical Investigations*,
    trans. G. E. M. Anscombe, (Oxford: Blackwell, 1968), sections 19,
    23, and 241. See also pp. 174 and 226. The reader who is interested
    in the kind of syntax and the vocabulary that will be integral to this
    discourse of 'reconnection' is recommended to consult the chapter
    titled 'Correctness and Truth' in Nicholas Lash, *A Matter of Hope: A
    theologian's reflections on the thought of Karl Marx* (London:
    Darton, Longman & Todd, 1981), pp. 73–87.

66 Here I am mindful of a passage of Metz's which can be taken as the
    theological underpinning of the position adopted in this book:

> 'The history of . . . suffering has no goal, but it has a future. It is,
> moreover, not teleology, but the trace of suffering that provides us
> with an accessible continuity of this history. The essential dynamics
> of history consist of the memory of suffering as a negative
> consciousness of the future freedom and as a stimulus to overcome
> suffering withing the framework of that freedom. The history of
> freedom is therefore . . . only possible as a history of suffering'.

See his *Faith in History and Society*, trans. David Smith (London:
Burns & Oates, 1980), p. 108. It has to be borne in mind that Metz
sees himself as formulating a 'practical fundamental theology', and
that he would therefore be critical of my incorporation of themes

that belong essentially to the realm of a *dogmatic* theology. I cannot argue for this point here, but my response to Metz would be to say that theologians must resort to dogmatics if they are to articulate 'the memory of the passion, death and resurrection of Jesus Christ' (*memoria passionis, mortis et resurrectionis Jesu Christi*), a 'dangerous' memory which Metz takes to be intrinsic to a theology for those who are victims. Theologians cannot of course 'speak' this dogmatic language to those victims whose very experience is such that it confounds such speech.

CHAPTER 4

Theodicies with a 'Practical' Emphasis

In this chapter attention will be focused on three exponents of the 'practice'-oriented approach to the 'problem of evil', that is, the approach which concerns itself essentially with the question of the God of salvation who acts decisively to overcome evil. The three practitioners considered in this chapter are Dorothee Soelle, Jürgen Moltmann and P. T. Forsyth.

DOROTHEE SOELLE

Dorothee Soelle (1929–) writes about the theodicy-problem in her book *Suffering*.[1] *Suffering* begins with a sharp, even polemical, critique of what Soelle calls 'Christian masochism' and its concomitant 'theological sadism'. 'Christian masochism', she believes, is engendered by a theology which seeks 'the vindication of divine power through human powerlessness', and in which 'affliction is regarded as human weakness that serves to demonstrate divine strength'.[2] This assertion of God's majesty, a majesty that is inevitably affirmed at the expense of God's creatures, is complemented by a 'tendency . . . on the human side, to push for a willingness to suffer, which is called for as a universal Christian attitude'.[3] The injunction that the Christian should be willing to submit herself to suffering (because it is bestowed by God) has as its obverse a 'theological' sadism' which encourages the sufferer to become apathetic in the face of her suffering, by representing the human sufferer as a powerless and masochistic accomplice to this 'sadistic' God. If Christians ('masochistically') worship this all-powerful ('sadistic') God, who is necessarily the orginator of evil and suffering, it will be impossible for them to conceive of this God as one who suffers with the victims of history. In Soelle's eyes, therefore, it is necessary for Christians to purge themselves of this 'masochism' before they can legitimately aspire to work for less dehumanized and dehumanizing social formations.

The mode of argument adopted by Soelle is not ratiocinative. Unlike the exponents of the 'theoretical' approach to theodicy (and in particular Swinburne and Plantinga), Soelle does not set out to formulate a linear argument consisting of sets of premises from which certain irrecusable conclusions may be deduced. Instead, she prefers to meditate, often impressionistically and from several perspectives simultaneously, on a wide range of historical and fictional situations. Her meditations are shaped by a theological agenda which is headed by the following questions:

1 *What* are the different kinds and stages of suffering?
2 Who are the actual and typical *victims*?
3 Who are their actual and typical *oppressors*?
4 What social and historical *structures* enable the oppressors to afflict their victims?
5 How is suffering to be *overcome* by human beings?
6 What does *God* do when human beings suffer?

Soelle declines to provide abstract or merely theoretical 'answers' to these questions. Instead, she proposes to deal with them by adverting to specific and concrete fictional or non-fictional episodes. One such episode is the crucial conversation between Ivan and Alyosha Karamazov which culminates in the former's resolution to return his 'ticket' to heaven. Soelle, who characterizes Ivan as 'an atheist for love's sake',[4] centres her discussion on the attitude of Alyosha. The explanation conventionally advanced for Alyosha's invocation of the innocent suffering Christ (in his response to Ivan's 'rebellion') – namely, that this invocation reflects Alyosha's submission, in all humility, to the ineffable ways of the divinity – is rejected by Soelle. Alyosha, after all, agrees fully with Ivan in repudiating a future 'harmony' premised on the existence of innocent suffering. Soelle suggests that the difference between the two brothers is instead to be sought in their respective conceptions of what *follows* from the acknowledgement of the existence of gratuitous suffering. Ivan rejects the God who causes or permits such suffering. He blames God in the same breath as he justifies his rebellion. Alyosha, by contrast,

> directs his attention not to the power above but to the sufferers. He puts himself beside them. He bears their pain with them. He listens in agony as Ivan introduces examples of suffering he had assembled as witnesses against the compassion of God . . . He is silent, he shares the suffering, he embraces the others. Alyosha's strength is the silent sharing of suffering.[5]

Unlike his brother, who demands both the complete *intellectual* resolution of the theodicy-problem and the immediate cessation of all suffering, Alyosha follows the *practical* path of discipleship, in this way signifying his readiness to live without the metaphysical consolation of having an 'answer' to the 'problem of evil'. Where Ivan turns toward heaven in accusation, Alyosha pursues an earthly *imitatio Christi* that involves solidarity with those who suffer.

Soelle's treatment of the dialogue between Ivan and Alyosha reflects her radical historicization of the theodicy-question. According to this historicizing approach, the identities of victims, oppressors and spectators are defined by the historical and social contexts in which these individuals are situated, as too are the myriad forms of suffering (and actual and possible responses to occurrences of suffering) that exist on our planet. In Soelle's words:

> The issue we face today . . . is not about the necessity and possibility of eliminating misery but about the persons through whom this process is carried. *Who* is working for the abolition of social conditions which of necessity produce suffering?[6]

And further: 'That all suffering is social suffering . . . means that all suffering is to be worked on. No suffering can be clothed and transfigured any longer with the appearance of fate.'[7]

Human endeavour can therefore either maintain or diminish or enhance existing forms and magnitudes of even the most patently haphazard manifestations of suffering. Where the more extreme occurrences of suffering are concerned, the theodicist's almost irresistible urge to formulate explanations may have to be subdued by an imperative silence.[8] But even where the explanations of the theodicist have to give way to silence, the bystander, no matter how apparently detached he or she may be, is still confronted with a stark and inescapable choice: 'In the face of suffering you are either with the victim or the executioner – there is no option'.[9] Ivan professes to be on the side of the victims, but it is Alyosha who enacts this solidarity. It is Alyosha, therefore, who has learnt, in Bonhoeffer's words, 'to see the great events of world history from below, from the perspective of the outcast, the suspect, the maltreated, the powerless, the oppressed, the reviled'.[10]

The human being who lives in solidarity with the wretched of the earth is by that very fact living out a solidarity with the suffering Christ who represents God in the world. The individual who pursues this invariably painful *imitatio Christi* comes in the process to be God's representative on earth (albeit without supplanting or surpressing the precursory and paradigmatic Jesus of Nazareth). In making this point Soelle quotes with approval Bonhoeffer's well-known dictum that 'man is challenged to participate in the sufferings of God at the hands of a godless world'.[11]

The suffering Christ keeps a place in the world for the God in whose travails we are summoned to participate; but our participation in God's pain is possible only because the crucified Christ

> . . . identifies himself with the life of those who are condemned for life. He suffers everything which results from the destruction of hope. The Lamb of God who 'bears' the sin of the world is the man of God who 'bears' the world's inhumanity: that is, the consequences of the world's sin – destruction. Christ's entire life is determined by this unending identification with those who are the agents of their own punishment.[12]

Human beings can serve the pain of God with their own pain only through the mediation of Christ, who is both God's representative before us and our representative before God.[13] The proposition that the pain of Christ and that of all human beings *is* God's pain is virtually an axiom in Soelle's treatment of the theodicy-problem. Indeed, she wants to say that the resolution of this problem is to be sought in God's deed on the cross of his Son and in his indwelling in all the dark and shameful places where death, agony and degradation are inflicted on those who are weak and vulnerable. The 'problem of evil' is thus to be resolved by adverting to a theology of the cross. This is made plain by Soelle's interpretation of a story narrated by Elie Wiesel, a survivor of Auschwitz, in his book *Night*:

> One day when we came back from work, we saw three gallows rearing up in the assembly place, three black crows. Roll call. SS all round us, machine guns trained: the traditional ceremony. Three victims in chains – one of them, the little servant, the sad-eyed angel . . . All eyes were on the child. He was lividly pale, almost calm, biting his lips. The gallows threw its shadow over him. . . The three victims mounted together on to the chairs. The three necks were placed at the same moment within the nooses.
>
> 'Long live liberty!' cried the two adults.
>
> But the child was silent.
>
> 'Where is God? Where is He? someone behind me asked.
>
> 'At a sign from the head of the camp, the three chairs tipped over.
>
> Total silence throughout the camp. On the horizon the sun was setting.
>
> 'Bare your heads!' yelled the head of the camp. His voice was raucous. We were weeping.
>
> 'Cover your heads!'
>
> Then the march past began. The two adults were no longer alive. Their tongues hung swollen, blue-tinged. But the third rope was still moving; being so light, the child was still alive . . .
>
> For more than half an hour he stayed there, struggling between life and death, dying in slow agony under our eyes. And we had to look him full in the face. He was still alive when I passed in front of him. His tongue was still red, his eyes were not yet glazed.
>
> Behind me, I heard the same man asking:
>
> 'Where is God now?'
>
> And I heard a voice within me answer him:
>
> 'Where is he? Here He is – He is hanging here on this gallows . . .'[14]

The world inhabited by these tormented souls is a world that is, in George Steiner's words, 'extra-territorial to reason'. It is a great merit of *Suffering* that its author never ceases to forget Steiner's salutary truth, that she begins her discussion of this story by acknowledging the impossibility of finding a moral vocabulary capable of plumbing the depths of this unspeakably barbaric act: 'One has not yet travelled the way that leads from the question to the answer simply by reflecting on it theologically. The reflection stands in danger of missing the way itself since it is bound to other situations and thus cannot comprehend the question'.[15] The question asked by this anguished Jew, and the answer provided by the boy Wiesel, is indeed one that cannot be comprehended theologically. But the real test for any theodicy – perhaps the *only* test – is: how is it going to answer this man? Or perhaps even more fundamentally: *can* it answer this man?

John Hick, in his account of the 'Augustinian' pattern of theodicy, says that this kind of theodicy excludes the idea that God is so absolutely free and powerful that he will be able to prevent each and every human atrocity from happening: and this includes the monstrous crimes perpetrated in Auschwitz. This 'Augustinian' strategy is precisely the one espoused by Alvin Plantinga.[16] The other pattern of theodicy, the 'Irenaean' theodicy, which holds that occurrences of evil and suffering exist so that creatures have the opportunity to develop 'soul-making' qualities in the face of their afflictions, is preferred by Hick to its 'Augustinian' counterpart. The 'Irenaean' strategy, however, is entirely unsatisfactory when it comes to formulating a *victim*-oriented response to the plight of those who find themselves having to undergo the more gruelling forms of the 'soul-making' process. For it would surely be a blasphemy to announce to Wiesel's Jew that the innocent little child's death on the gallows was part of a divinely-ordained 'soul-making' process. This child's death – as were the millions of other deaths in Auschwitz, Dachau, Belsen, Treblinka and the other 'kingdoms of death' – was the culmination of a process which sought death absolutely, that is, as an end in itself. The horrific realities to be encountered in these 'kingdoms of death' make the thought of God an irrational, even impossible, thought. The notion of a 'soul-making' deity who 'operates' in these places becomes a literally unthinkable proposition. Besides, it could be argued that the first holocaust, far from assisting the 'soul-making' process, actually makes a second holocaust more, rather than less, likely. For has not the first holocaust shown that there are no final limits, be they of morality, common decency or simple forbearance, that human beings are not (now) capable of crossing? As Elie Wiesel asks pithily through his character Elisha: 'Where does suffering lead [man]? To purification or to bestiality?'.[17]

A world in which death is sought, systematically, as an end in itself, and in which it is conceivable that the devil now reigns in triumph, is a world that is *etsi deus non daretur*, 'as if there were no God'. In such a world – the world of the anguished Jew who cried out to the God who is in eclipse – the 'Augustinian' approach to the 'problem of evil' will certainly be less morally (and intellectually) inappropriate than its 'Irenaean' counterpart. But adopting the 'Augustinian' approach as a way of responding to the plight of the Jew who experienced the world *etsi deus non daretur*, while it may be less inherently problematic than the 'Irenaean' alternative, is nonetheless still somewhat unsatisfactory. For, surely, the inhabitants of Auschwitz would know that God, if he exists, is either (1) too indifferent to do anything about the sufferings of the child on the gallows; or (2) too helpless to do anything about it even if he wanted to. Alternative (2) will be the only remotely acceptable alternative for anyone who believes in the fundamental goodness of God. But espousing this alternative inevitably raises the following question: why is God helpless in the face of the little boy's suffering? The answer is given in Wiesel's story; God is helpless because 'he is hanging here on this gallows'. This, according to Soelle, is the only morally (and theologically) acceptable answer that we can give to the despairing Jew. Soelle, having opted for what is in outline an 'Augustinian' answer, accounts for the helplessness of God by invoking the divine presence or *shekinah* (within the specifically Jewish religious context of Wiesel's narrative) and the theology of the cross (within a specifically Christian – and more explicitly, a Lutheran – theological context). She characterizes this executed God thus:

> God is no executioner – and no almighty spectator (which would amount to the same thing). God is not the mighty tyrant. Between the sufferer and the one who causes the suffering, between the victim and the executioner, God, whatever people make of this world, is on the side of the sufferer. God is on the side of the victim, he is hanged.[18]

Theodicy resolves itself into *theophany*: the God who is not an executioner must become a co-sufferer, one who indwells (incarnates) himself in the suffering realities of his creation. With Soelle's claim that God is a co-sufferer goes the concomitant assertion that no suffering is ever justified: 'no heaven can rectify Auschwitz'.[19]

Ivan Karamazov, our paradigmatic 'protest' or 'moral' atheist, would certainly applaud Soelle's insistence that the terrible sufferings endured by innocent human beings cannot be recompensed by a 'heaven'. But what would he have made of the idea of a suffering God, a God who is tortured with those who are tortured, who is hanged with those who are sent to the gallows? If, perchance, Karamazov were acquainted with Wiesel's narrative, would he *still* think himself justified in 'returning his ticket' to God, especially the God who endures to the world's end all that the world has to endure? These are crucially important questions, but I shall postpone discussion of them until the similar positions of Jürgen Moltmann and P. T. Forsyth have been investigated in the next two sections of this chapter. Meanwhile, it is necessary to consider some issues that arise directly from Soelle's sponsorship of a theology of the cross.

Soelle, we have seen, demands that theology speak on behalf of those who are weak and powerless, that it should not function as a source of ideological strength and succour for those who are oppressors and executioners. She thereby implies that there is a clear-cut and easily-drawn distinction to be made between victim and executioner. She depicts Auschwitz very much as a place in which there were absolute agents: the Nazi guards who had the power to determine, at a whim, who should die and who should live the living death that was to be the destiny of those who did not perish immediately. These absolute agents were complemented by absolute subjects: the helpless inmates who were at the total disposal of their captors.[20] However, the testimonies of the survivors of the death camps show this account to be in need of qualification. These testimonies indicate: (1) that those who inhabited the concentration camps were seldom the unidimensional characters portrayed by many exponents of the victim-executioner dichotomy; and (2) that while this dichotomy was certainly implicit in the *organized* forms of terror employed by the Nazis, the inmates of the camps were at the same time beset by a more frightening (because random and *un*organized) kind of terror – that visited by the strong upon the weak – which manifested itself exclusively among the prisoners. Thus, Anna Pawelczynska, a sociologist who was herself a survivor of Auschwitz, has said:

> Besides the organized terror, another, more elemental terror came into being: of the stronger over the weaker. This was the inevitable consequence of the whole camp situation. That someone participated in the violence or became a victim of the violence . . . should . . . be evaluated in light of . . . the disease of starvation and the mental consequences of prolonged exposure to the action of a criminal apparatus of terror manifested in every possible way.
>
> Regardless of moral judgements, the fact is that the mechanisms of terror created a situation where some prisoners – by their very existence – restricted the chances of others to survive.[21]

When human beings are *in extremis* the distinction between victim and executioner ceases to be absolute, so that it becomes virtually inevitable that the victims will be driven, psychologically, to do the work of the executioners. Germane though this observation may be, it does not in any way alter the fact that the blurring of the victim–executioner distinction takes place only *because* of the situation in which the inmates of Auschwitz were forced to live: when it came to creating and maintaining this hellish system there was, in a sense, only one category of executioner and only one category of victim. But even though he evidently had in mind the state of individuals who were *in extremis*, Elie Wiesel still felt able to state the following truth about the generality of human beings: 'Deep down, I thought, man is not only an executioner, not only a victim, not only a spectator: he is all three at once'.[22] Implicit in this statement is the belief that human motives, desires, aversions and emotional responses are, in their innermost depths, strange and bafflingly complex, thereby making it possible (but certainly not necessary) for the executioner, the spectator and the victim to be the self-same individual. Nowhere is this obvious, but nonetheless salutary, truth more tellingly illustrated than in the only book written by Wiesel which deals directly with the holocaust. In *Night*, Wiesel recounts the railway journey made by a group of prisoners from the camp at Buna when they were being transferred to an unknown location in the middle of Germany. The train had stopped at a station in Germany, and a crowd of curious spectators dropped pieces of bread into the wagons. The passage narrating the outcome illustrates with an unbearable poignancy the truth of Wiesel's claim that he who is the victim can simultaneously be the executioner:

> A piece fell into our wagon. I decided that I would not move. Anyway, I knew that I would never have the strength to fight a dozen savage men! Not far away I noticed an old man dragging himself along on all fours. He was trying to disengage himself from the struggle. He held one hand to his heart. I thought at first he had received a blow in the chest. Then I understood; he had a bit of bread under his shirt. With remarkable speed he drew it out and put it to his mouth. His eyes gleamed; a smile, like a grimace, lit up his dead face. And was immediately extinguished. A shadow had just loomed up near him. The shadow threw itself upon him. Felled to the ground, stunned with blows, the old man cried:
>
> 'Meir. Meir, my boy! Don't you recognize me? I'm your father . . . you're hurting me . . . you're killing your father! I've got some bread . . . for you too . . . for you too . . .'
>
> He collapsed. His fist was still clenched around a small piece. He tried to carry it to his mouth. But the other one threw himself upon him and snatched it. The old man whispered something, let out a rattle, and died amid the general indifference. His son searched him, took the bread, and began to devour it. He was not able to get very far. Two men had seen and hurled themselves upon him. Others joined in. When they withdrew, next to me were two corpses, side by side, the father and the son.[23]

It is true of course that the son who killed his father, and the men who subsequently killed the parricidal son, were murderers by virtue of having first been victims: their descent into savagery must be seen in the context of their prior immurement in a system of unrelenting barbarism. In a sense, they meted out to others what had already been done to them. But if each one of us is simultaneously victim, executioner and spectator, then solidarity with victims will not on its own be sufficient to overcome oppression and injustice. The theologian who agrees with Soelle will certainly want to insist that the need for solidarity with the afflicted is given undeniable voice by the words, deeds and death of Jesus Christ. For the Christian faith, there can indeed be no discipleship without this solidarity. But the power which is sufficient to overcome human evil must be one which is capable of plumbing human malevolence to its uttermost depths, and, in so doing, of healing that brokenness which makes each one of us, at the same time, executioner, spectator and victim. Even so, the affirmation that the plight of the victims must be accorded an absolute priority is not to be gainsaid. The ideological appropriation of the notion of a universal and deep-seated human corruption to justify our inaction in the face of the suffering and degradation visited upon others must be strenuously resisted.

Nevertheless, the refusal to disengage ourselves from the plight of victims must be accompanied by the recognition that while our practical *efforts* to aid the conquest of evil confer on us the responsibility of supporting the victims and resisting their executioners, our *hopes* for overcoming evil and suffering must accommodate the perception that human wickedness has a depth which cannot be reached by even the most noble and heroic deeds of human solidarity. It therefore becomes an *anthropological* (and not just a theological) necessity to add a doctrine of prevenient grace to Soelle's affirmation of the principle of solidarity with those who suffer. (According to this doctrine, which owes its provenance to St Augustine, human beings are able to overcome sin only if they first receive from God the impulse to undergo a decisive transformation of self: without this prevenient grace creatruely beings cannot even begin their conquest of evil.[24] The doctrine of prevenient grace is certainly not incompatible with a theology of divine (and human) co-suffering. Soelle, however, has made no attempt to incorporate such a doctrine of prevenient grace into her theology. Indeed, it is debatable whether her theology can accommodate the very principle of such a doctrine. In repudiating what she regards as the apathetic and impartial God of 'traditional theism', Soelle virtually identifies God with the emancipatory aspirations of marginalized social groups: 'God is not above human parties and classes. He is involved. He is partisan. He is always on the side of the oppressed, and he exists only at the point where the oppressed take action.'[25] Soelle, it seems, views God as a grounding *principle* of human emancipatory endeavour; as a deity whose 'reality' is exhausted by the totality of human transformative practices. Soelle's theological intentions are very much in accord with the characterization of the work of Feuerbach provided by Marx in his fourth thesis on Feuerbach, namely, that Feuerbach was seeking a way of 'resolving the religious world into its secular basis'.[26] And it must be questioned whether a theological approach so *reductively* consonant with the Feuerbachian critique of religion can really accommodate the concept of prevenient grace. (In saying this I am mindful that there is scope for theology to come to terms with the Feuerbachian and Marxian critiques of religion in a way that avoids the danger of reductionism.))

Soelle takes great care, when she casts the episode of the boy's execution within a Christian framework, to acknowledge that there is a fundamental incongruence between the death of a first-century religious figure and the genocide which results from the relentless implementation of a twentieth-century technology of mass extermination. The two kinds of death are incomparable, so that if the theologian persists in making such a comparison, it becomes inevitable that '. . . in a sublime manner, the issue is robbed of clarity, indeed the modern horror is justified.'[27] A warrant for a Christian interpretation of this episode 'can only be established when it undergirds and clarifies what the story from Auschwitz contains'.[28] Her intentions to the contrary notwithstanding, Soelle's proposal that the Christian proclamation should 'undergird' and 'clarify' the narrative of events at Auschwitz will necessarily involve granting the Christian proclamation a priority in interpreting or understanding this narrative. In this interpretative task, it will, after all, be the central tenets of the Christian faith that serve as the *basis* for the imputation of any meaning or truth to the narrative, while the narrative will be the (mere) *object* of such an imputation. The Christian faith will be the *interpretans*, the Auschwitz narrative the *interpretandum*. The very thing that Soelle wishes to avoid – misrepresenting what happened at Auschwitz – will become unavoidable.

To circumvent the possibility of distorting the significance of what happened at Auschwitz, it will be necessary to reverse Soelle's supposition that it is the episode at Auschwitz which is the *interpretandum* and the Christian faith the *interpretans*. When this is done, the execution described by Wiesel (and, indeed, the descriptions of all the other ghastly events that occurred within the perimeter of Auschwitz) will be seen to be the 'active reinterpretation' of the Christian message. The Christian message will now be the *interpretandum*, the history of Auschwitz the *interpretans*. It is not, and indeed it cannot be,

Christianity's primary concern to 'make sense' of what happened at Auschwitz. If anything is Christianity's primary concern with regard to what took place at Auschwitz (apart from taking responsibility, in shame and penitence, for the centuries of Christian anti-semitism which made it possible for Auschwitz to become a reality), it is, rather, to allow itself to be reinterpreted, to be 'ruptured', by the pattern of events at Auschwitz.[29] Here I find myself in total agreement with Johann-Baptist Metz when he chides Soelle and Jürgen Moltmann for using Wiesel's account of the execution of the little boy to make a 'Christian-theological identification of God'. Metz is firm in his repudiation of such an identification:

> *Who* really has the right to give the answer to the God-question – 'Where is God? Here he is – he hangs on the gallows'? Who, if anyone at all, has the right to give it? As far as I am concerned, only the Jew threatened by death with all the children in Auschwitz has the right to say it – only he alone. There is no other 'identification' of God – neither as sublime as for instance in J. Moltmann nor as reserved and modest as in the case of D. Soelle . . . If at all, this can be done only by the Jew imprisoned together with his God in the abyss – it can be done only by him who himself finds himself in that hell 'where God and humankind full of terror look into each other's eyes' (Elie Wiesel). Only he, I think, can alone speak of a God 'on the gallows', not we Christians outside of Auschwitz who sent the Jew into such a situation of despair or at least left him in it.[30]

These grave reservations apart, Soelle's theology of the cross contains some of the ingredients integral to any sustained *theological* engagement with the phenomenon of 'protest' atheism. These ingredients – the idea of God as a co-sufferer; the denial that God is impassible; and the insistence that the crucial theodicy-question is not the question of the intelligibility of God, but that of his salvific activity to overcome evil – are given full expression in the writings of Jürgen Moltmann.

JÜRGEN MOLTMANN

In his great book, *The Crucified God*, Jürgen Moltmann (1926–) describes Elie Wiesel's narration of the little boy's execution as a 'shattering expression of the *theologia crucis*'.[31] Elsewhere, he says of Auschwitz in general and Wiesel's reply to the anguished Jew in particular:

> A theology after Auschwitz would be impossible, were not the *sch'ma* Isreal and the Lord's prayer prayed in Auschwitz itself, were not God himself in Auschwitz, suffering with the martyred and the murdered. Every other answer would be blasphemy. An absolute God would make us indifferent. The God of action and success would make us forget the dead, which we still cannot forget.[32]

So, like Soelle, Moltmann maintains that God is no passive onlooker who isolates himself from human pain and dereliction. He differs from Soelle, however, in claiming that it is not sufficient merely to cast the pain and death of Christ in the context of a Christian theodicy or a doctrine of salvation *simpliciter*. Before the event of the cross can be located in such a context – i.e. a context whose theological horizon is the justification of divine providence – it is necessary to relate the death of Christ to God himself, to the inner being of the Godhead.[33]

In delineating the relation between the passion of Christ and the reality of God, Moltmann invokes two cardinal principles. The first of these principles – that God is capable of undergoing change – is an implication of the incarnational truth that the Son of God is the representative and revealer of God. As a result of the incarnation, it is possible to affirm that Christ's passion is God's passion. Moltmann makes this point by adverting to Paul's saying, in 2 Cor. 5:19, that 'God (himself) was in Christ'. If God himself was in Christ, then God himself suffered in the event of the cross, and God himself died in Jesus.[34] But if God can suffer and die on the cross of Jesus, he must be changeable. Moltmann therefore jettisons the 'axiom of *apatheia*', which affirms the intrinsic unchangeableness of a God who, as pure actuality, is devoid of all potentiality (and hence is immune to change):

> In the metaphysical concept of God from ancient cosmology and the modern pyschological concept of God, the being of the Godhead . . . as the zone of the impossibility of death, stands in juxtaposition to human being as the zone of the necessity of

death. If this concept of God is applied to Christ's death on the cross, the cross *must* be 'evacuated' of deity, for by definition God cannot suffer and die. He is pure causality. But Christian theology must think of God's being in suffering and dying and finally in the death of Jesus, if it is not to surrender itself and lose its identity. Suffering, dying and similar negations simply cannot be predicated of that which is conceived of as pure causality and the unconditioned mover. The God who was the subject of suffering could not be truly God . . . With the Christian message of the cross of Christ, something new and strange has entered the metaphysical world. For this faith must understand the deity of God and thus bring about a fundamental change in the orders of being of metaphysical thought . . . It must think of the suffering of Christ as the power of God and death of Christ as God's potentiality.[35]

On Moltmann's view, then, the concept of God as an immutable and impassible being 'evacuates' the cross (and, *ipso facto*, the incarnation) of divinity. God must be able to suffer and change if the pain and death of the Son on Calvary is to be the pain and death of God himself.

The second underlying principle of Moltmann's elucidation of the relation between the cross of Christ and the being of God is already evident in the foregoing: if the passion of God is entailed by the passion of his Son, then the cross of Christ is a fully trinitarian event. 'The form of the crucified Christ is the Trinity'.[36] Moltmann's starting-point in this elucidation of the trinitarian form of the event of the cross is Luther's blunt assertion that '. . . faith tells us, not only that God is in [Christ] but therefore that Christ is God Himself'. Moltmann proposes to take Luther's affirmation of the divine Christ seriously, and goes on to say: 'what happened on the cross was a happening between God and God; there God disputes with God; there God cries out to God; there God dies in God.[37] In treating the cross as a fully trinitarian event, Moltmann is careful to secure himself against the heresies of patripassianism and theopaschitism. With regard to the former (which affirms that it is the Father who is the subject of Christ's human experiences), he says that we cannot say that the Father also suffered and died. For while Jesus suffers the process of dying, he cannot suffer death itself: suffering presupposes life, so the event of death cannot be suffered. The Father, however, can and does suffer the death of his Son.[38] With regard to theopaschitism (which affirms the death of one of the Trinity on the cross), Moltmann avoids using the locution 'the death of God', and stresses that although the Father and the Son both encounter death, it is only the Son who dies, and in confronting death on the cross the Father lives to endure the grief of losing his Son. God cannot die if he is to bring about the annihilation of death.[39]

Having asked himself the theologically primary question 'What does Jesus's death on the cross mean for God himself?', and having proposed a resolutely trinitarian answer to this question, Moltmann proceeds to locate Jesus's passion and death within the context of the doctrine of salvation (soteriology). Here, again, he diverges from Soelle. He accepts the characterization of God as a fellow-sufferer of those who suffer, but immediately qualifies his acceptance by indicating that, on its own, the principle of divine co-suffering is not sufficient.[40] For God not only participates in human suffering, he also makes this suffering his own:

> Only if all disaster, forsakenness by God, absolute death, the infinite curse of damnation and sinking into nothingness is in God himself, is community with this God eternal salvation, infinite joy, indestructible election and divine life.[41]

Or again:

> The misery that we cause and the unhappiness that we experience are [God's] misery and unhappiness. Our history of suffering is taken up into his history of suffering.'[42]

Moltmann, it could be said, resolves the 'problem of evil' by placing evil within the divine nature itself. In applying this principle he goes so far as to say that 'like the cross of Christ, even Auschwitz is in God himself'.[43] The cross and the events of Auschwitz and the other dark places on earth are incorporated into the inner being of the Godhead. Through this God becomes the God of the godless and the abandoned. Implicit in this theology of the cross – Moltmann's 'answer' to the 'problem of evil' – is a doctrine of justification articulated via the image of penal substitution. By dying in Jesus 'for us', God 'took upon himself the unforgivable sin and guilt for which there is no atonement, together with the rejection and anger that cannot be turned away, so that in Christ we might become his righteousness in the world'.[44] This divine deed of atonement, through which we are made righteous, is an 'objective' event. It is not enough, says Moltmann, to say that one comes to share the pain of the poor and the violated by allowing oneself to be crucified with Christ, that somehow the cross *derives* its significance from the crucifying solidarity that the believer displays towards the victims of oppression and injustice. On the contrary, this crucifying solidarity is possible, and has meaning, only because God has died for us in Jesus.[45] It is only through the 'objective' event enacted by God on the cross of his Son, the event in which our wounds are healed by the wounds of God, that we are able to live in solidarity with those who are suffering.[46] Through his self-humiliation on the cross God creates the conditions for the fellowship of sinners with himself, and through this fellowship, the real conditions for a solidarity with victims. Moltmann says that this communion with the crucified God 'involves man in a realistic divinization (*theosis*)', in which 'men live *in God and from God*, they "live, move and have their being in him" (Acts 17:28)'.[47] As a result of this 'realistic divinization', brought about by the passion and death of God, 'man is filled with the spirit of God. He becomes the friend of God, feels sympathy with God and for God . . . He is angry with God's wrath. He suffers with God's suffering. He loves with God's love. He hopes with God's hope'.[48] God's death for us on the cross is thus the source of our strength in the struggle against the powers that oppress and dehumanize our fellow beings. The cross is the basis of any liberating practice.

Moltmann's unrelenting emphasis on the salvific significance of the cross of Christ should not be taken to imply that he believes that Christians have no real cause to weep over the calamities that beset their world (given the decisive triumph over evil represented by the events of Gethsemane and Golgotha). To draw this conclusion would be to overlook his equally powerful claim that the cross is only the beginning of the trinitarian history of God. As one would expect of the author of the influential *Theology of Hope* (1967), Moltmann's theology of the cross is grounded in a thorough-going eschatology. He cites 1 Cor. 15, and says that only with the resurrection of the dead, the murdered and the gassed, only with the healing of those in despair who bear lifelong wounds, only with the abolition of all rule and authority, only with the annihilation of death will the Son hand over the kingdom to the Father. Then God will turn his sorrow into eternal joy. This will be the sign of the completion of the trinitarian history of God and the end of world history, the overcoming of the history of man's sorrow and the fulfilment of his history of hope.[49]

Only at the end of history will evil be finally overcome. For the present we have God's *promise*, embodied and given expression in the life, death and resurrection of Jesus Christ, that evil and suffering will not have the final word in the world's history. In faith, and with a suffering charity, the hope founded on this promise is enough to live by.[50]

Moltmann's assertion that God will turn his (and by implication our) sorrow into eternal joy at the consummation of history may be taken by some to indicate a striking *prima facie* affinity between Moltmann's theology of the cross and the eschatological theodicy of John Hick. To hasten to this conclusion, however, would be premature: Moltmann maintains that although human suffering is transfigured through its final integration into the being of God, it does not follow from this that evil is in any way justified. Moltmann refuses to grant sin and evil the positive status accorded to them by Hick in his characterization of the world as a 'vale of soul-making':

> *Post festum*, out of joy over grace, even sin can no doubt be thought of as *felix culpa*; but that does not give sin any positive quality. Consequently we cannot go beyond the fact of evil, for which no reason can be given, since every reason would be tantamount to an excuse. A dialectical trinitarian doctrine of the crucified Jesus does not lead with logical cogency to the declaration that evil is necessary for the sake of good. It really only leads to the removal of evil's potency: it is no longer necessary. Its compulsion is broken. Man has been freed.[51]

Although Moltmann refuses to accord evil a positive status by incorporating it into a divinely-ordained teleology (in the manner of the 'soul-making' theodicist), he nevertheless lays himself open to a serious objection when he claims that human

evil and suffering are finally overcome and transfigured
through being integrated into the inner being of the divinity at
the *eschaton*. It will be recalled that Hick's insistence that the
'soul-making' process continues in an after-life is vulnerable to
the charge that it merely reintroduces the question of unjust
suffering at another, post-mortem, level. Moltmann's 'dialectical trinitarian doctrine of the crucified Jesus', by integrating
suffering into the inner being of the Godhead, effectively
ontologizes suffering, and in so doing generates two significant
difficulties. First, it could be asked whether the problem of
innocent and undeserved suffering is in any way resolved by
this inner-trinitarian manoeuvre. Does the affirmation that
God himself suffers (unjustly and innocently) in his inner being
make this suffering any less unacceptable? Second, it could be
asked whether the traditional Christian understanding of evil
does really permit Moltmann to locate evil and suffering within
the innermost core of the divine being. If evil, and the suffering
that it causes, stem fundamentally from our non-identity with
self, others and God, then can such a *non-identity* be posited in
the very 'godness' of the One who is the author of our salvation;
the God who, in the course of annihilating evil and suffering,
will realize our true *identity* with self, others and himself?[52]

   The first of these two objections is not too difficult to answer if
the primacy of the practical dimension of the theodicy-problem
is acknowledged. Neither atheism nor theism, considered as
merely theoretical 'answers' to merely theoretical 'questions',
will help to eliminate or diminish the pain and desolation of the
person who is overcome by unbearable suffering. As Moltmann
says, quoting Ernst Bloch: 'Even if the answers have dis-
appeared, the questions and the agony have not been taken care
of'.[53] Neither theism nor atheism is able to resolve the question
of unjust or meaningless suffering. From the standpoint of those
who suffer, only the abatement and the abolition of the agony
will constitute an adequate 'answer' to this question. Moltmann
wants to say that the God who suffers in his innermost being is
the only hope for those who are alienated and injured because he
has taken up their alienation and hurt into his own being:

> The godforsaken and rejected man can accept himself where he
> comes to know the crucified God who is with him and has already
> accepted him. If God has taken upon himself death on the cross,

he has also taken upon himself all of life and real life, as it stands under death, law and guilt. In so doing he makes it possible to accept life whole and entire and death whole and entire. Man is taken, without limitations and conditions, into the life and suffering, the death and resurrection of God, and in faith participates corporeally in the fullness of God. There is nothing that can exclude him from the situation of God . . .[54]

The only 'answer' that will ultimately suffice for those who are in pain and dereliction, Moltmann suggests, is God's redemptive deed on the cross. For faith, it is this very deed which allows the word of liberation and succour to be spoken and heard.

The second objection strikes at the heart of Moltmann's position and is less easy to turn aside. By importing the cross and every trace of creaturely suffering into the very deity of God, Moltmann effectively abolishes any real distinction between the Trinity as it is encountered in the economy of salvation (the 'economic' Trinity or 'God for us') and that triunity which is constitutive of God's innermost being (the 'immanent' Trinity or 'God in himself'). Indeed, he wants to go so far as to maintain that the economic Trinity is the ground of the immanent Trinity: only in this way is it possible to say that 'the pain of the cross determines the inner life of the triune God from eternity to eternity'.[55] The trinitarian life of God therefore changes as the history of the world changes.[56] Moltmann's commendable intention in doing this is to secure the accessibility of the being of God to human history. But adhering to this intention exacts a price, namely, that of ontologizing evil and suffering (as Francis Fiorenza has pointed out). For if, as Moltmann avers, pain, anguish and death become entrenched in the divine being, it must then be the case that they have a positive quality, that they must retain their *potency* in the divine being if they are to be what they are. The outcome is bound to be highly problematic, not only for the concept of God, but also for the claim, central to the Christian faith, that in Christ God acted decisively in history to deprive evil of its power over human beings. The only sure way of forestalling this unacceptable outcome would be to restrict the event of the cross to the economic Trinity (albeit without positing an absolute disjunction between the economic and the immanent Trinity), and thus to ensure that the relation between God and the world is not understood as an unqualified incorporation of the world into the being of God.[57] Confining the event of the cross to the economic Trinity would still allow the proponent of the *theologia crucis* to retain the concept of a suffering God, and would not therefore jeopardize the doctrine of the atonement which is very much the root-principle of Moltmann's theodicy.

Finally, it must be said that Moltmann is vulnerable (to an even greater degree than Soelle) to J-B Metz's charge that those who seek to 'read' a theology of the cross into the event of Auschwitz are seeking to make an illegitimate 'Christian-theological' identification of the God of Auschwitz.[58]

P. T. FORSYTH

The principle that God's atonement on the cross of Christ is his self-justification in the face of the fact of human evil and suffering is merely stated, and therefore not fully thematized, in Moltmann's theology of the cross. This is understandable: Moltmann is not concerned to deal with the theodicy-problem in its own right. For a full-blown thematization of this principle – which is integral to the 'practical' approach to the theodicy-problem – we have to go back to the work of the great, but much-neglected, Scots theologian Peter Taylor Forsyth (1848–1921).

The socio-historical context of the composition and the reception of Forsyth's *The Justification of God: Lectures for War-Time in a Christian Theodicy* is provided by the First World War.[59] Forsyth perceived that the hellish disaster which had befallen mid-Europe had undermined once and for all the pretensions of the hopelessly optimistic philosophic theodicies of preceding centuries. These philosophic theodicies, which 'are only the poetry and majesty of thought', are 'apt to break in our hand when applied to the last anomalies of the soul'.[60] The philosophic theodicy is a theosophy rather than a theology, and it is therefore impervious to historical contingency. The philosophical theodicist is preoccupied 'with a wisdom instead of a work, with an impressive theory rather than a saving fact.'[61] The trenches of the European battlefields were the outcome of historical conditions which had confounded this wisdom and invalidated this theory. Spurning the philosophic theodicy, Forsyth proposes to 're-interrogate the Word of the historic Gospel for its word to the historic time, to leave the theosophies which rule the mystic hour for a theodicy with a historical base, a moral genius, and a mystic power . . .'.[62] This historical theodicy, rooted in the historic Gospel, will recognize the futility and the absurdity of our quest for a justification of God which is acceptable to the human conscience and to our powers of reason. Humankind cannot justify God. To the contrary, 'only God's justification of man gives the secret of man's justification of God. The justification at the root of all other is God's self-justification'.[63] And God justifies himself on the cross of Jesus Christ the Redeemer. The justification of God (theodicy) must therefore become God's justification of himself at Golgotha (the theology of the cross). This move from theodicy to *theologia crucis* is very much the explicit focal-point of *The Justification of God*:

> The whole world is re-constituted in the Cross as its last moral principle, its key, and its destiny. The Cross is at once creation's fatal jar and final recovery. And there is no theodicy in the world except in a theology of the Cross. The only final theodicy is that self-justification of God which was fundamental to His justification of man. No reason of man can justify God in a world like this. He must justify Himself, and He did so in the Cross of His Son.[64]

The emphasis in the philosophic theodicy is unavoidably anthropocentric, since it asks how God shall be just with human beings. Forsyth's theology, by contrast, is resolutely theocentric: it asks how shall human beings be just with God. And since God's justification of his creatures, and his self-justification, are embodied in the person of his Son, it follows that the theocentric theology is at the same time thoroughly Christocentric. Christ is the salvation of the world, and so a Christocentric theodicy must be a theodicy of salvation and vice versa:

> The only theodicy is that which redeems, and from the nettle of perdition plucks the flower of salvation. But it should be very clear that redemption is not a theodicy except by the way of an atonement which does justice to God's holiness . . . Salvation is a theodicy only by the way of a justification which places man in the position not of God's beneficiary only but of God's son in Christ.[65]

John Hick places Forsyth's theodicy under the rubric of the 'Irenaean' theodicy. He is right to the extent that Forsyth understands the history of the world to be the work and the goal of a providential God.[66] But Forsyth eschews any suggestion that the world is a 'vale of soul-making'; and it cannot be gainsaid that this theodicy is notably different from Hick's paradigmatically 'Irenaean' theodicy in several important respects. Forsyth's unremitting Christocentrism; his insistence that the Incarnation is the 'rational base' of the atonement (so that without incarnation there can be no salvation); his adoption of a doctrine of prevenient grace; and his espousal of an 'objective' conception of the atonement, are sufficient to set him in stark opposition to Hick. So too is Forsyth's determination to understand the event of the cross as God's final judgement on the world, and thus as the world's most profound crisis: 'Our faith . . . rose from the sharpest crisis, the deadliest death, and the deepest grave the world ever knew – in Christ's Cross'.[67]

The tragedy of the world can only be resolved by a unique and decisive divine Act, and not merely by having its citizens submit to a process of soul-formation: '. . . for man's historic and evil life . . . redemption [is] by something else than a diffused process – by a concentrated Act, with an eternal and universal bearing'.[68] For Forsyth, then, the divinely ordained teleology that Hick takes to be intrinsic to the 'Irenaean' pattern of theodicy is (no more than) the economy of salvation revealed and *enacted* in the life, death and resurrection of Jesus Christ.

In characterizing this divine act in the life, death and resurrection of his Son, Forsyth, like Soelle and Moltmann, states explicitly that it is God himself who suffers: 'He took on Himself there [the Cross] more than He ever inflicts; and His infliction from us there He turns into His redemption. The cross meant more change in God than in man.'[69] On the cross, God not only suffers, he also dies: '. . . the victory over evil, cosmical or ethical, cost . . . God His Life.'[70]

Again, like Moltmann and Soelle, Forsyth maintains that the divine rescue which is our redemption is social and not private and individual: 'that salvation of ours comes to us in the salvation of a world, and not of our soul single and alone'.[71]

In common with Soelle and Moltmann, Forsyth sees no point in seeking to provide a 'theoretical' answer to the theodicy-question. In *The Justification of God* Forsyth asks himself the questions: 'Why in His creation must the way upward lie through suffering?' and 'How can He allow the moral perdition even of those who were on the way to goodness, the fall even of the saint?', and says bluntly that 'these questions are quite unanswerable'.[72] At least, they are unanswerable if what is being sought is a merely 'theoretical' answer. The person looking for an 'answer' to these questions will be doomed to disappointment unless she can come to appreciate that 'the solution is in [God's] action . . .'[73] And God's action, which is the only possible theodicy, 'is an adequate atonement . . . holiness is not anything that can just be shown; it must be done. Here revelation is action'.[74] But what if the sceptic, an Ivan Karamazov say, persists in asking if God's creation is just too costly for those who have been left to shoulder the burden of suffering manifested within it? What if the suffering of the world is just not worth the candle? To this person, Forsyth says, God speaks thus:

> Do you stumble at the cost? It has cost Me more than you – Me who see and feel it all more than you who feel it . . . Yea, it has cost Me more than if the price paid were all Mankind. For it cost Me My only and beloved Son . . . Nor is its suffering the moral enormity that His Cross is. I am no spectator of the course of things, and no speculator on the result. I spared not My own Son. We carried the load that crushes you. It bowed Him into the ground. On the third day He rose with a new creation in His hand . . . and all things working together for good . . . And what He did I did. How I did it? How I do it? This you know not now, and could not, but you shall know hereafter. These are things the Father must keep in His own hand. Be still and know that I am God . . .[75]

'Be still and know that I am God'. This, in effect, is the reply that God gave to Job. But this passage also makes it clear that Forsyth, like Hick and Moltmann, believes that human suffering will be transfigured by God at the consummation of history, a consummation that has already been inaugurated by the event of the cross. The critic who endorses Soelle's dictum that 'no heaven can rectify Auschwitz' will of course be reluctant to accept the principle of an eschatological transformation of human suffering. From the standpoint of the innocent and hapless sufferer this principle is a blasphemy, one not in any way obviated by an appeal to the idea of a God who suffers in the sufferings of his creatures. Only a God who abolishes or diminishes the pain and misery of those who are in despair can help. It must be acknowledged, however, that it is not self-evident that the theology of the cross really needs to incorporate the principle of an eschatological resolution of human suffering. The theologian of the cross could conceivably affirm that our salvation has been wrought by God's cataclysmic deed on Calvary without having at the same time to claim that the unfathomable bliss to be shared by all in God's kingdom is a kind of recompense for our earthly travails. If this is so, then it will be possible to detach the concept of the eschatological transfiguration of human suffering from Forsyth's *theologia crucis* without vitiating the latter. Far more problematic, however, is Forsyth's assertion that the moral enormity of the cross outweighs that of any other deed of human malevolence. It is hard to see how one can *either* affirm or deny this proposition: both affirmation and denial presuppose the possibility of a moral appraisal of what happened at Auschwitz (thereby implying that our moral categories are somehow adequate to the task of expressing the reality of Auschwitz). Forsyth might have thought differently if he had been able to live long enough to know of all that took place in *l'univers concentrationnaire*. Then he might have shared Soelle's (and especially J–B Metz's) reluctance to compare or even to identify the sufferings of the Nazarene with all that had to be endured by the inmates of the kingdoms of night. It would be less unacceptable to say that the pain of these sufferers *is* the pain of God, that the theologian has to think of their history as God's history (in the way that Soelle and Moltmann propose).

COMMON THEMES

It has already been indicated that significant and undeniable differences exist between the respective theologies of the cross adumbrated by Soelle, Moltmann and Forsyth. Nevertheless, we are justified in placing their theologies under the same rubric – that of the so-called 'practical' approach to the theodicy-problem – because all these theologies display the following common features:

1 They affirm the principle that God is in some se
   who suffers with his creatures.
2 They maintain that the God who suffers in this world cannu.
   be an immutable and impassible deity.
3 They insist that the question of overwhelming import to the
   sufferer is not 'Is theism unintelligible because I am suffering?, but 'Is this God a God of salvation – is this a God who can
   help?'
4 They claim that it is a corollary of (1) and (3) that a *theological*
   approach to the 'problem of evil' from the standpoint of
   victims will necessarily lead to soteriology, or more precisely
   (given the framework of the Christian *mythos*), into the
   doctrine of the atonement.

Standing within the circle of the Christian *mythos*, one can
affirm that the God who shares the sufferings of his creatures to
the point of death is the God who is incarnate in the person of
Jesus of Nazareth. Or more simply: the 'practical' approach to
the 'problem of evil', presupposing as it does the atonement
wrought on the cross of the Son of God, rests finally on the
principle that the God who saves is the God who is incarnate in
his creation. The notion of an 'incarnate salvation' will need to
be examined. But first we need to consider the relation that any
theological rendition of this notion will have to the plight of
those who are spiritually broken and physically destroyed.

NOTES

1 Dorothee Soelle, *Suffering* (London: Darton, Longman & Todd,
   1975).
2 Soelle, *Suffering*, p. 17.
3 Ibid.
4 Soelle, *Suffering*, p. 175.
5 Ibid.
6 Soelle, *Suffering*, p. 2.
7 Soelle, *Suffering*, p. 106.
8 Soelle, *Suffering*, p. 69.
9 Soelle, *Suffering*, p. 32.
10 Quoted from Bonhoeffer, *Letters and Papers from Prison* (London:
   SCM, enlarged ed., 1971), p. 17. Bonhoeffer talks about 'identifying
   ourselves generously and unselfishly with . . . the sufferings of our
   fellow-men' on p. 299.

11 See Soelle's *Christ the Representative* (London: SCM, 1967), p. 148. For Bonhoeffer's saying, see his *Letters and Papers from Prison*, p. 361.

12 Soelle, *Christ the Representative*, p. 121.

13 Soelle, *Christ the Representative*, p. 130. The notion of 'serving the pain of God by our own pain' is derived by Soelle from the Japanese Lutheran theologian Kazoh Kitamori. See his *Theology of the Pain of God* (Richmond, Va.: John Knox, 1965), especially p. 50.

14 Soelle, *Suffering*, p. 145. For Wiesel's account of this episode, see *Night*, trans. Stella Rodway (London: Fontana/Collins, 1972), pp. 76–7.

15 Soelle, *Suffering*, p. 145.

16 This claim needs to be qualified. It is debatable whether Plantinga's God is really conceivable as a deity who brings salvation to humankind, and this conception is of course central to Augustine's approach to the 'problem of evil'.

17 See Elie Wiesel, *Dawn*, trans. Frances Frenaye, (New York: Avon, 1970), p. 24. This theme is explored in Emil L. Fackenheim, *God's Presence in History: Jewish Affirmations and Philosophical Reflections* (New York: Harper Torchbooks, 1972), pp. 75 and 81. Fackenheim dedicates his book to Wiesel, and says that both Christians and Jews must ask themselves the question: '. . . at Auschwitz, did the grave win after all, or, worse than the grave, did the devil himself win?' (p. 75).

18 Soelle, *Suffering*, p. 148.

19 Soelle, *Suffering*, p. 149.

20 A similar rendition of the victim-executioner dichotomy is to be found in Rebecca Chopp, 'The Interruption of the Forgotten', in *Concilium 175: The Holocaust as Interruption* (Edinburgh: T. & T. Clark, 1984), p. 19.

21 Anna Pawelczynska, *Values and Violence in Auschwitz*, trans. Catherine S. Leach, (Berkeley: University of California, 1979), pp. 66–7. As Adorno notes, in the extermination camps 'topsy-turviness perpetuates itself: domination is propagated by the dominated'. See his *Minima Moralia*, p. 183.

22 Wiesel, *The Town Beyond the Wall*, trans. Stephen Barker, (New York: Avon, 1970), p. 174.

23 Wiesel, *Night*, pp. 112–13.

24 See St. Augustine, *Enchiridion* 32 and *de nat et grat* 35.

25 Soelle quoted in James Bentley, *Between Marx and Christ* (London: Verso, 1982), p. 130.

26 For Marx's fourth thesis on Feuerbach, see 'Concerning Marx', in *Karl Marx: Early Writings*, trans. R. Livingstone and G. Benton, (Harmondsworth: Penguin, 1975), p. 422.

27 Soelle, *Suffering*, p. 146.

28 Soelle, *Suffering*, p. 147.
29 This line of thought has been prompted by my reading of Nicholas Lash, 'What might martyrdom mean?', in William Horbury and Brian MacNeil, eds, *Suffering and Martyrdom in the New Testament* (Cambridge: Cambridge University Press, 1981), pp. 183–98. See also W. F. Flemington, 'On the Interpretation of Colossians 1:24', in Horbury and MacNeil, eds, *Suffering and Martyrdom in the New Testament*, pp. 84–90.
30 J–B Metz, 'Facing the Jews: Christian Theology after Auschwitz', *The Holocaust as Interruption*, pp. 29–30. The central thesis of Metz's essay is that Christians can form and understand their identity only in the face of the Jews and their experiences in Auschwitz.
31 Moltmann, *The Crucified God*, trans. R. A. Wilson and John Bowden, (London: SCM, 1974), p. 273.
32 'The Crucified God and the Apathetic Man', in Moltmann's collection of essays *The Experiment Hope*, trans. M. Douglas Meeks, (London: SCM, 1975), p. 73. See also *the Crucified God*, pp. 222ff and 274. J–B Metz was asked the question whether after Auschwitz there could still be prayers on the part of Christians. His reply to his interlocutor (the Czech philosopher Milan Machovec) is similar to Moltmann's, namely, that 'we can pray after Auschwitz, because there were prayers in Auschwitz'. See his 'Facing the Jews', *The Holocaust as Interruption*, p. 29. Metz, however, declines to interpret Auschwitz in terms of a *theologia crucis*.
33 See 'The Theology of the Cross Today', in Moltmann's collection of essays *The Future of Creation*, trans. Margaret Kohl, (London SCM, 1977), p. 61.
34 Moltmann, *The Crucified God*, p. 192.
35 Moltmann, *The Crucified God*, pp. 214–15.
36 Moltmann, *The Crucified God*, pp. 246.
37 'The Theology of the Cross', *The Future of Creation*, p. 65. See also 'God and Resurrection', in Moltmann's collection of essays *Hope and Planning*, trans. Margaret Clarkson, (London: SCM, 1971), p. 43, and *The Crucified God*, p. 192. Also relevant is the following statement in Moltmann's treatise on the Trinity: 'The pain of the cross determines the inner being of the triune God from eternity to eternity'. See *The Trinity and the Kingdom of God*, trans. Margaret Kohl (London: SCM, 1981), p. 161.
38 Moltmann, *The Crucified God*, p. 243; *The Trinity and the Kingdom of God*, p. 81.
39 Moltmann, *The Trinity and the Kingdom of God*, p. 81; *The Future of Creation*, p. 73.
40 Moltmann, *The Experiment Hope*, p. 80.
41 Moltmann, *The Crucified God*, p. 246.

42 Moltmann, *The Experiment Hope*, p. 83.

43 Moltmann, *The Crucified God*, p. 278.

44 Moltmann, *The Crucified God*, p. 192.

45 Moltmann makes it clear that he disagrees with Bultmann and Soelle, who imply that the cross of Christ can be preached only if the believer is prepared to be crucified with Christ. Against this 'subjective' viewpoint, Moltmann espouses the 'objective' principle that 'not until Christ has taken on our cross as his own is it meaningful to take up our cross in order to follow him' (*The Crucified God*, p. 62). See also *the Trinity and the Kingdom of God*, pp. 39–41. For his criticism of Soelle, see, pp. 61–3 and p. 78 n. 50.

46 For this see Moltmann's *The Open Church: Invitation to a Messianic Life-Style*, trans. M. Douglas Meeks, (London: SCM, 1978), p. 25. See also 'Political Theology and Political Hermeneutic of the Gospel', in Moltmann's *On Human Dignity: Political Theology and Ethics*, trans. M. Douglas Meeks, (London: SCM, 1984), p. 103; and his 'The Theology of Mystical Experience', in *Experiences of God*, trans. Margaret Kohl, (London: SCM, 1980), p. 75.

47 Moltmann, *The Crucified God*, p. 277.

48 Moltmann, *The Crucified God*, p. 192.

49 Moltmann, *The Crucified God*, p. 278.

50 Moltmann, *The Trinity and the Kingdom of God*, pp. 42, 60.

51 Moltmann, *The Future of Creation*, p. 77.

52 The second of these objections has been posed by Francis Schüssler Fiorenza in his 'Joy and Pain as Paradigmatic for Language about God', *Concilium*, 5 (1974), pp. 67–80; and 'Critical Social Theory and Christology', *Proceedings of the Catholic Theological Society of America*, 30 (1975), pp. 86–7.

53 Moltmann, *Hope and Planning*, p. 33.

54 Moltmann, *The Crucified God*, p. 277.

55 Moltmann, *The Trinity and the Kingdom of God*, p. 161; See also *The Future of Creation*, p. 76.

56 There is a penetrating discussion of this issue in Roger Olson, 'Trinity and Eschatology: The Historical Being of God in Jürgen Moltmann and Wolfhart Pannenberg', *Scottish Journal of Theology*, 36 (1983), pp. 213–27.

57 This, in essence, is the position of Karl Barth and Karl Rahner. Barth warns that 'we should be repeating the error of Philo and Gnosticism, which was unhesitatingly repudiated by the Early Church, if we tried . . . to introduce the world in some sense as a necessary element, a divine mode, into the life of the Godhead'. See his *Church Dogmatics* II/1 (Edinburgh: T. & T. Clark, 1957), p. 317. Rahner argues that while it is God himself who suffers, and not just the man Jesus, the unchangeability of God in himself means that

God 'changes *in* another'. See his 'On the Theology of the Incarnation', in *Theological Investigations*, vol. 4 (London: Darton, Longman & Todd, 1974), pp. 113–14 n3.

58 For Metz's stricture, see note 30 above.

59 *The Justification of God: Lectures for War-Time on a Christian Theodicy* (London: Duckworth, 1916). In his 'Preface' Forsyth says: '. . . it is hard to believe that the word [theodicy] can be so strange at a time when when the passion for the thing has, by the magnitude for our present calamity, become for multitudes the keynote of their religion' (p. v). All page references given within the text will be to this work.

60 Forsyth, *The Justification of God*, pp. 137, 146.

61 Forsyth, *The Justification of God*, p. 150.

62 Forsyth, *The Justification of God*, p. 7.

63 Forsyth, *The Justification of God*, p. 35.

64 Forsyth, *The Justification of God*, pp. 124–5.

65 Forsyth, *The Justification of God*, p. 161.

66 For Hick's discussion of Forsyth, see *Evil and the God of Love*, pp. 246–50.

67 Forsyth, *The Justification of God*, p. 54.

68 Forsyth, *The Justification of God*, pp. 72–3.

69 Forsyth, *The Justification of God*, p. 32.

70 Forsyth, *The Justification of God*, p. 151.

71 Forsyth, *The Justification of God*, p. 62.

72 Forsyth, *The Justification of God*, p. 139.

73 Ibid.

74 Forsyth, *The Justification of God*, p. 172.

75 Forsyth, *The Justification of God*, pp. 169–70.

CHAPTER 5

'Taking Suffering Seriously'

The principle that the self-revelation of God on the cross of Christ is the self-justification of God is integral to the 'practical' approach to the theodicy-problem. In the face of this divine self-justification the attempt by the *human* thinker to justify God vis-à-vis the fact of evil (which of course is what theodicy essentially is) becomes superfluous. The Christian who takes the atonement seriously has no real need for theodicy. ('Theodicy' in this context refers specifically to the 'theoretical' aspect of the theodicy-question.) Theodicy, we are suggesting, has to wait on what God reveals to humankind about the pain and suffering that exist in his creation. In this way theodicy (thus conceived) becomes a 'speaking-out' of the event of revelation, a revelation with a texture to be articulated in terms of a *theologia crucis*. What God reveals is that divinity itself, through the cross of the Son, endures the sufferings that afflict us. Divinity is 'accessible', without being 'knowable', to humankind by this action of God on the cross.[1]

(It is highly contentious theological issue whether the 'involvement' of God with suffering creatures must involve suffering on the part of the Godhead. We have seen that the exponents of the 'practical' approach to theodicy – Soelle, Moltmann and Forsyth – waive the 'axiom of *apatheia*' in the course of affirming this intimate divine involvement with the pain of his creation. Herbert McCabe has challenged this view in a recent essay titled 'The Involvement of God'.[2] Invoking the classical teaching of Augustine and Aquinas, McCabe argues that it is not in the nature of God to be an 'object' in history, a being alongside other beings, and so God cannot depend on his creatures in any way. It follows from this that God cannot suffer, though he does have the 'most intimate possible involvement with the sufferings of his creatures'. It would be impossible to do justice to McCabe's fascinating essay in a short digression like this, but it is not entirely clear how God can have the capacity to be *concerned* about the travails of his creatures if he does not have some kind of 'attitude' towards them, and the possession of this 'attitude' would seem willy-nilly to imply that God is more than just notionally related to those who are the object of his concern. Whether the having of this concern requires us to say that God *is* a co-sufferer is of course another matter altogether. I am inclined to think that it does not.)[3]

The revelation that constitutes the core of 'theodicy' is (if it is genuine) only secondarily, and not primarily, an impartation of knowledge, a 'gnosis'; primarily it is, and can only be, God's action to bring salvation to humankind in and through the life, death and resurrection of Jesus Christ. The Christian 'answer' to the 'problem of evil' is the hesitant, stammering bringing of this reconciling action to speech. This, one hopes, is the only approach to the 'problem of evil' that can even aspire to reflect the true dimensions of the epistemological crises, and the spiritual predicaments, of the Ivan Karamazovs of this world. Of course for the person in a different situation and with a correspondingly different intellectual horizon (say, the professor motivated by apologetic considerations who, in the tranquillity of her study, seeks to present a theoretical justification of God in the face of the fact of evil), the primary question when reflecting on the 'problem of evil' may well be the issue of the intelligibility of theism.[4] In chapter 1 it was suggested that theodicy is a signifying practice, and the theodicist a producer of a system of signification. In the context of a *theologia crucis*, the putatively objective basis of such signification is supplied by the texts which contain the narratives of the passion of Jesus Christ and of the passion of all victims. This *theologia* emerges from the theologian's confrontation with, and interrogation by, the events of the passion of the Son of God and of the passion of all innocent victims. The manner of the theodicist's confrontation with these narratives, and with the *events* presented for representation in these narratives, depends in part on what theological problems, issues or questions she identifies as important. Or to put it in the parlance of the philosophy of social science: her 'theologizing' (which in this context will take the form of the creation of a narrative) is always 'interest-relative'. It is vital, therefore, that we attend to the 'grammar' of such 'interest-relative' narrative formations before we proceed to consider the specific 'grammar' of the atonement, that is, the material form of the 'practical' approach to theodicy.

THE INTEREST-RELATIVITY OF THEODICY

Alan Garfinkel (1945–) has drawn attention to the 'interest-relativity' of explanation and argues that a 'why-question' (for example, the question 'Why does God allow evil to exist?') always presupposes a 'space' of relevant alternatives. Garfinkel makes this point by referring to the famous (or perhaps one should say infamous) American bank robber Willie Sutton, who is supposed to have been asked the question 'Why do you rob banks?' by a clergyman anxious to reform him. Sutton's reply was: 'Well, that's where the money is.' Garfinkel argues that two conceivable 'spaces' surround the question asked by the clergyman: (1) the space which surrounds the clergyman's *own* asking of the question, whereby the question really means: 'why do you rob at all?'; and (2) the space which surrounds the question to which Sutton's answer would have been the appropriate answer; that is, a question like 'Why do you rob banks, as opposed to, say, jeweller's shops?'. That is to say, where the *clergyman's* question is concerned, the object of explanation (or narrative rendition) and its surrounding alternatives are

$$
\text{Sutton} \left\{ \begin{array}{l} \text{does not rob} \\ \\ \text{robs} \end{array} \right\} \text{banks,}
$$

whereas *Sutton's* object of explanation is

$$
\text{Sutton robs} \left\{ \begin{array}{l} \text{jeweller's shops.} \\ \text{petrol kiosks.} \\ \text{banks.} \end{array} \right.
$$

Applied to theodicy, Garfinkel's argument reminds us that the explanations provided by the theodicist are always 'interest-relative', and that we must therefore ask ourselves the question, 'What "space" is being presupposed by our asking of the questions that fall under the rubric of theodicy?'[5] Where the 'theoretical' theodicist is concerned, the object of explanation (or narrativization) and its surrounding alternatives are

Evil exists because
$$\left\{ \begin{array}{l} \text{the world is a 'vale of soul-making'.} \\ \text{we are free beings.} \\ \text{good is impossible without the} \\ \text{possibility of evil.} \end{array} \right\}$$

whereas for the victim of such evil (and hence for the 'praxis-oriented' theodicist) the object of explanation and its surrounding spaces are more likely to be

Evil exists because
$$\left\{ \begin{array}{l} I \text{ am imprisoned } here. \\ We \text{ are being tortured } now. \\ You \text{ are indifferent to } our \text{ hunger.} \\ God \text{ is an indifferent spectator.} \end{array} \right\}$$

The 'praxis-oriented' theodicist, unlike her theoretically-minded counterpart, will locate the 'problem of evil' in the 'space' occupied by victims, and will invariably discuss it with a quite different context of narrative construction in mind. The presuppositions that underlie the explanations advanced by the two approaches are radically different.[6] In the case of the 'theoretical' approach, the implicit or explicit question being answered is

Given that there is evil (*in general*), why does evil (*in general*) exist?

whereas for the victim-oriented theodicy, the implicit or explicit question being asked is

Why is *this* (specific evil) being done to *me/us*, by *you/them*, *here* and *now*?[7]

Given that this is the 'logical' or 'explanatory space' occupied by the victims of evil, the proponent of the principle that 'the only "acceptable" theodicy is an adequate atonement' must ask herself the question: can the 'syntax' and 'vocabulary' of an 'incarnate salvation' be inserted into this 'explanatory space'? Or is this space fundamentally such that no narrative of salvation and atonement can be grounded in it? This question must be addressed before the 'grammar' of an 'incarnate salvation' can be delineated in substantive terms. There are doubtless many who will say that *all* theological speech in the dark places of this world is inherently mystifying, even the words 'And the Word became flesh, and dwelt amongst us.' For those of this persuasion, even the stammeringly uttered and deeply felt truth that God himself keeps company with those who are oppressed, excluded and finally eliminated will almost certainly be an utterance which is ideologically tainted.[8]

Central to this application of the principle of the 'interest-relativity' of explanation is the notion that the only theological discourse *about* Auschwitz which can be permitted is a discourse which could have been enunciated *in* Auschwitz by its inmates. As Metz says, there can be prayer after Auschwitz because there was prayer in Auschwitz. But, and this is now the crucial question, was there 'theodicy' in Auschwitz? *Could* there have been 'theodicy' in Auschwitz? Does the 'language' of Auschwitz contain the 'grammatical' resources for undertaking 'theodicy'? In trying to resolve these questions we come up against an immediate problem, one posed by the very nature of the 'language' of Auschwitz itself. Elie Wiesel has said that

> the language of night was not human, it was primitive, almost animal – hoarse shouting, screams, muffled moaning, savage howling, the sound of beating . . . This is the concentration camp language. It negated all other language and took its place.[9]

There can be no possibility of rational speech in such conditions. This is virtually a truism (except, of course, for the metaphysical theodicist). The person who is not already convinced that this is the case needs to dwell on an absolutely unspeakable episode which took place in Auschwitz in the summer of 1944. This episode was recounted in the testimony of S. Szmaglewska, a Polish guard, to the Nuremberg War Crimes Tribunal:

> *Witness* ... women carrying children were [always] sent with them to the crematorium. [Children were of no labour value so they were killed. The mothers were sent along, too, because separation might lead to panic and hysteria, which might slow up the destruction process, and this could not be afforded. It was simpler to condemn the mothers too and keep things quiet and smooth.] The children were then torn from their parents outside the crematorium and sent to the gas chambers separately. [At that point, crowding more people into the gas chambers became the most urgent consideration. Separating meant that more children could be packed in separately, or they could be thrown in over the heads of adults once the chambers were packed.] When the extermination of the Jews in the gas chambers was at its height, orders were issued that children were to be thrown straight into the crematorium furnaces, or into a pit near the crematorium, without being gassed first.
>
> *Smirnov (Russian prosecutor)* How am I to understand this? Did they throw them into the fire alive, or did they kill them first?
>
> *Witness* They threw them in alive. Their screams could be heard at the camp. It is difficult to say how many children were killed in this way.
>
> *Smirnov* Why did they do this?
>
> *Witness* Its very difficult to say. We don't know whether they wanted to economize on gas, or if it was because there was not enough room in the gas chambers.[10]

Greenberg proposes that this episode should serve as an 'orienting event' or litmus-test for post-Auschwitz theological formulation: 'No statement, theological or otherwise, should be made that would not be credible in the presence of the burning children.'[11] No attempted justification of God on the part of human beings can aspire to meet this test; indeed, the very thought that it is possible for someone to say, with the sufferings of these children in mind, that God is justified, is a blasphemy. This episode can only prompt penance and conversion; it cannot motivate a theodicy, even one which takes the form of an atonement. In saying that this episode cannot ground the narrative of such an atonement it is not being implied that there cannot, in principle, be a collision or engagement between such a narrative of faith and the narratives generated by Auschwitz. Indeed, Wiesel himself allows for a similar possibility in *The Gates of the Forest*, when Gregor, whose faith had been destroyed by the holocaust, has a passionate exchange with the Hasidic rebbe:

> Gregor was angry. 'After what happened to us, how can you believe in God?'
> What an understanding smile on his lips the Rebbe answered, 'How can you *not* believe in God after what has happened?'.[12]

The narrative of faith collides with the narrative of its negation, but neither achieves an ascendancy over the other. At the level of belief, Auschwitz gives one reason *both* to believe and to disbelieve: the testimony of its witnesses speaks for both these seemingly irreconcilable moments, moments which must nevertheless be simultaneously affirmed. At the level of cognition, the affirmation of the one moment at the expense of its counterpart testimony of negation, and vice versa.[13] The safeguard the possibility of truth it is necessary to hold the one moment as the necessary dialectical negation or counterpoise of the other. The testimony of affirmation needs to be 'ruptured' by its counterpart testimony of negation, and vice versa.[13] The acknowledgement of the inescapable need for such a linguistic 'rupture', however, can only take place at the level of (mere) cognition. But is it enough for us, when confronted with the brute reality of Auschwitz, to be content with a purely cognitional grasp of the implications of the testimony of its victims? Or does this testimony point us beyond the dialectic of belief and unbelief? The Hasidic Rebbe in *The Gates of the Forest* indicates that this dialectic is doomed to be unresolved if it is confined to the realm of cognition. In his words, God 'has become the ally of evil, of death, of murder, but the problem is still not solved. I ask you a question and dare you to answer: "What is there left for us to do?"'.[14] If this dialectic is to be overcome, the Rebbe avers, it must be tranposed from the sphere of cognition to the field of *action*.[15] Or in terms of our discussion, there must be a transposition from the realm of a theological (or more specifically, soteriological) discourse to that of a discourse which facilitates a messianic praxis. This praxis-facilitating discourse will perhaps be the only one which is capable of being grounded in the 'explanatory space' occupied by victims. The irreducibly *theological* affirmation of an 'incarnate salvation' can only be made from within the circle of faith, and we have seen that it is hard to dispute the suggestion that it would be blasphemous to assume that there is going to be room for this 'circle' (and its accompanying theological affirmations) in the utterly unique 'explanatory space' inhabited by the citizens of *l'univers concentrationnaire*.

'THEODICY' AS SECOND-ORDER THEOLOGICAL DISCOURSE

Our discussion has gravitated towards the insight that theodicy is best conceived as a second-order theological discourse ranging over a first-order praxis-generating discourse. This discourse has to confess its inability to address the 'problem of evil' from a cosmic perspective which enables us to justify God. Reflection on the testimonies and testaments of those who were inhabitants of the kingdoms of night indicates that the person who wishes to speak theologically in response to these narratives must acknowledge that the God who disengages himself from the afflictions of victims cannot be justified, either by human beings or himself. The God who is a mere onlooker when confronted with gratuitous suffering is a demon and not a God. For those who suffer, however, the utterance of this truth, no matter how deeply it is felt by those who utter it, can only be half a consolation.

The most pressing question for any person interested in the possibility of a (first-order) praxis-facilitating discourse is bound to be: what is the conceivable structure and content of such a discourse? Susan Shapiro has pointed out that three pervasive experiences underpin the 'rupture' of language brought about by the holocaust. It seems to me that our first-order language (which will almost certainly *not* be a specifically theological discourse) must, at the very least, seek to articulate these experiences; only in this way will it be possible for our theological languages to be 'chastised' by narratives of pain and godforsakeness, thereby allowing themselves to be broken into by the reality which is 'spoken' by these narratives. According to Shapiro, the first of these linguistically normative experiences is the almost universal experience of having been abandoned by God. She quotes Wiesel's words in *Night*: 'Theirs was the kingdom of night. Forgotten by God, forsaken by Him, they lived alone, suffered alone, fought alone'.[16] The second experience is the concerted and relentless endeavour of the Nazis to dehumanize their victims prior to eliminating them.[17] The third experience was the world's almost total indifference to the fate of the Jews. Again, Shapiro cites Wiesel: 'Alone. That is the key word, the haunting theme . . . The world knew and kept silent . . . Mankind let them suffer and agonise and perish alone. And yet, and yet, they did not die alone, for something in all of us died with them.'[18] The first-order language that we need to allow for would be a language that promoted solidarity with those who were forced to undergo these experiences. It would be a language premised upon Wiesel's own injunction to allow the stories of the victims to be communicated:

> Let us tell tales. Let us tell tales – all the rest can wait, all the rest can wait. Let us tell tales – that is our primary obligation . . .
> Tales of children so wise and so old. Tales of old men mute with fear. Tales of victims welcoming death as an old acquaintance. Tales that bring men close to the abyss and beyond – and others that lift him up to heaven and beyond. Tales of despair, tales of longing. Tales of immense flames reaching out to the sky, tales of night consuming life and hope and eternity.
> Let us tell tales so as to remember how vulnerable man is when faced with overwhelming evil. Let us tell tales so as not to allow the executioner to have the last word. The last word belongs to the victim. It is up to the witness to capture it, shape it, transmit it and still keep it as a secret, and then communicate that secret to others.[19]

Our first-order language would therefore be one that registered, formed and communicated the stories of victims. In doing this it would bear in mind Wiesel's stricture that 'not all tales can be, should be, communicated in language'.[20] In many cases, the first-order discourse would, so to speak, be no more than a set of quotation marks round the narratives of these stories. In the context of the aftermath of the holocaust, it would be a language that aimed (in Metz's words) to further 'a kind of coalition of messianic trust between Jews and Christians in opposition to the apotheosis of banality and hatred present in our world'.[21] Only by engendering and sustaining the praxis of such a messianic trust will this first-order discourse be able to serve as an instrument of interrogation and critique for all (second-order) theological affirmations. In short, it would rivet the attention of the makers of these essentially theological affirmations on Irving Greenberg's devastating reminder: take burning children seriously.

NOTES

1 In seeking to ground the *theologia crucis* in God's salvific deed of revelation on the cross I am bearing in mind Wolfhart Pannenberg's formula that God is 'accessible ... by his own action'. Pannenberg makes this point in *Theology and the Philosophy of Science* (London: Darton, Longman & Todd, 1976), p. 310. Nicholas Lash rightly says that Pannenberg's formula is a necessary condition for the enterprise of critical theology. See his *Theology on Dover Beach* (London: Darton, Longman and Todd, 1979), pp. 16–23. To quote Lash: 'unless God is accessible by his own action, Christian faith expresses only man's hope, and theology is rendered incapable of speaking of God' (p. 17).

2 Herbert McCabe, 'The Involvement of God', *New Blackfriars*, 66 (1985), pp. 464–76.

3 In my articles 'The Impassibility of God and the Problem of Evil', *Scottish Journal of Theology*, 35 (1982), pp. 97–115, and 'Theodicy?', *Harvard Theological Review*, 76 (1983), pp. 225–47, I argued against the 'axiom of *apatheia*'. I am now less certain that the denial of this axiom is a pre-condition of affirming that God is 'involved' in the sufferings of his creatures. For a lucid conspectus of recent work on the theme of divine suffering, see Warren McWilliams, 'Divine Suffering in Contemporary Theology', *Scottish Journal of Theology*, 33 (1980), pp. 35–53. A more general survey is to be found in Richard Bauckham, '"Only the suffering God can help": divine passibility in modern theology', *Themelios*, 9 (1984), pp. 6–12.

4 Such a person may even believe that it is possible to have an explanation which makes evil and suffering intelligible. The perspective assumed in this book agrees with the author of *The Brothers Karamazov* that it is not possible – in principle – to provide such an explanation.

5 For Garfinkel's discussion, see *Forms of Explanation: Rethinking the Question in Social Theory* (New Haven: Yale University, 1981), ch. 1. See Hilary Putnam, *Meaning and the Moral Sciences* (London: Routledge & Kegan Paul, 1978), pp. 42–3, for another discussion of the 'interest-relativity' of explanation.

6 In characterizing the differences between the two 'explanatory spaces' I have borne in mind Lucien Goldmann's injunction that 'if we want to study a human phenomenon we must circumscribe the object in a certain way and try to determine the essential questions: Who is the subject? In whose life and practical activities (*praxis*) did the mental structures and categories and the forms of thought and affectivity arise which determined the origin and behaviour of the object studied?' See his 'Structure: Human Reality and Methodological Concept', in R. Macksey and E. Donato, eds., *The Languages of Criticism and the Sciences of Man* (Baltimore: Johns Hopkins, 1970), p. 94.

7 In arriving at this formulation I have been guided by J–B Metz's cautionary reminder: 'After Auschwitz, every theological "profundity" which is unrelated to people and their concrete situations must cease to exist. Such a theology would be the very essence of superficiality'. See his *The Emergent Church: the Future of Christianity in a Postbourgeois World*, trans. Peter Mann, (London: SCM, 1981), p. 22.

8 J–B Metz asks himself how Christians can come to terms with Auschwitz and says: 'We will in any case forgo the temptation to interpret the saving of the Jewish people from our standpoint, in terms of saving history. Under no circumstances is it *our* task to mystify this suffering! *We* encounter in this suffering first of all only the riddle of our own lack of feeling, the mystery of our own apathy, not, however, the traces of God'. See *The Emergent Church*, p. 19.

9 Elie Wiesel, 'Why I Write', in Alvin H. Rosenfeld and Irving Greenberg, eds., *Confronting the Holocaust: The Impact of Elie Wiesel* (Bloomington: Indiana University, 1978), p. 201. Elsewhere Wiesel says: '. . . Treblinka means death – absolute death – death of language and of the imagination. Its mystery is doomed to remain intact'. See his essay 'Art and Culture After the Holocaust', in Fleischner, ed., *Auschwitz*, p. 405.

10 Quoted from Irving Greenberg, 'Cloud of Smoke, Pillar of Fire: Judaism, Christianity, and Modernity after the Holocaust', in Fleischner, ed., *Auschwitz*, pp. 9–10.

11 Irving Greenberg, 'Cloud of Smoke, Pillar of Fire', p. 23.

12 *The Gates of the Forest* (New York: Avon, 1967), p. 192. Wiesel has said in an essay that 'this event [the holocaust] could not have been without God, nor could it have been with God'. See 'Freedom of

Conscience – A Jewish Commentary', *Journal of Ecumenical Studies*, 14 (1977), p. 643. See also Wiesel's contribution to the symposium 'Jewish Values in the Post-Holocaust Future', *Judaism*, 16 (1967), p. 281: '. . . the Holocaust has terrifying theological implications . . . It can be explained neither with God nor without Him'.

13 For accounts of this dialectical hermeneutics of testimony, see Robert McAfee Brown, *Elie Wiesel: Messenger to all Humanity* (Notre Dame: University Press, 1983), pp. 162ff; and Susan Shapiro, 'Hearing the Testimony of Radical Negation', in *The Holocaust as Interruption*, p. 9. To quote Irving Greenberg: 'The holocaust offers us only dialectical moves and understandings – often moves that stretch our capacity to the limit and torment us with their irresolvable tensions'. See his 'Cloud of Smoke, Pillar of Fire', p. 22.

14 Wiesel, *The Gates of the Forest*, p. 197.

15 On the Hasidic rebbe's exploration of the question of doing (as opposed to the question of cognition), see Ted L. Estess's informative essay, 'Elie Wiesel and the Drama of Interrogation', *The Journal of Religious Studies*, 56 (1976), p. 29.

16 Susan Shapiro, 'Hearing the Testimony', *The Holocaust as Interruption*, p. 3.

17 Shapiro, 'Hearing the Testimony', p. 3.

18 Shapiro, 'Hearing the Testimony', p. 3. Wiesel is quoted from his 'The Holocaust as Literary Inspiration' in Lucy Baldwin Smith, ed., *Dimensions of the Holocaust* (Evanston, Ill.: Northwestern University, 1977), p. 7. See also 'Art and Culture After the Holocaust' (p. 407), where Wiesel says: 'Had they [the inmates in the murder factories] been aware that the outside world knew – and knew everything – many would have wanted to die sooner . . . as several hundred children did after their liberation. They who had managed to resist and survive the wickedness of the executioner, were helpless and desperate when they discovered the truth: the world knew and was indifferent.'

19 Wiesel, 'Art and Culture After the Holocaust', Fleischner, ed., *Auschwitz*, p. 403.

20 Wiesel, 'Art and Culture After the Holocaust', Fleischner, ed., *Auschwitz*.

21 J–B Metz, *The Emergent Church*, p. 32. See also his 'Facing the Jews', in *The Holocaust as Interruption*, p. 33.

CHAPTER 6

'Salvation Incarnate'

A putative 'answer' to the 'problem of evil' that invokes the theology of the cross will inevitably create its own problems, since it is, necessarily, an answer circumscribed by an 'incarnational' faith. Such an 'answer' will be acceptable in principle only to the person who is not prepared to dismiss as patently absurd the suggestion that the 'grammar' of God incorporates a 'rule' to the effect that, as a consequence of the life, death and resurrection of Jesus of Nazareth, speech about human suffering is in some sense speech 'about' divinity's very own history.[1] The only real alternative to not incorporating this 'rule' into the 'grammar' of God is silence (in this case a silence that bespeaks the absolute absence, as opposed to the *hiddenness*, of divinity). Indeed, it was acknowledged in the previous chapter that it is very often the case that silence – a silence that is 'neutral' as regards the 'absolute absence' or the 'hiddenness' of divinity – is the *only* morally appropriate response to occurrences of extreme and gratuitous suffering. It would seem that these two alternatives, speech about divinity, and a profoundly moral reticence about God's 'ways' with sufferers (which, provided they are expressed in separate levels of language, are not *necessarily* mutually exclusive) are the only conceivable responses to the objections of the 'protest' atheist.

The principle of a *theologia crucis* is not one that can be vindicated by philosophical or systematic theology. That salvation should be proffered to humankind in and through a Nazarene who died on a cross at Golgotha nearly two thousand years ago is a truth that in the end can only be spoken by resorting to a theology of revelation open to the Word of God as 'given' in Holy Scripture.[2] If this is the case, then theodicy is a form of speech that must be moved away from philosophical theology (where in current practice it takes the form of an articulation or defence of a specious 'theism') into the realm of dogmatics (which understands theological truth as precisely that which gives voice to the history of the crucified Nazarene). The very real danger in trying to say so much about 'godness' is that we cease to be sufficiently dialectical, that we do not really give enough emphasis to the notions of paradox and mystery, notions which must lie at the heart of any theology of the cross that hopes to be taken seriously. A 'morality of knowledge' places us under an obligation to the victims of evil not to overlook the sheerly intractable features of the 'problem of evil'.[3] Theodicy, we saw in chapter 1, is inherently flawed: it requires us to be articulate, rational and reasonable in the face of the unspeakable. Theodicy, one suspects, is doomed always to be at variance with the profound truth that the 'problem of evil' will cease to be a problem only when evil and suffering no longer exist on this earth. Until that time there is much substance in the charge that the theodicist's presumption (that words can express the reality of the unspeakable) only trivializes the pain and suffering of this world. It is therefore necessary to stress, once again, that the reflections undertaken in this chapter belong to a second-order *theological* discourse, that is, a kind of discourse which if (mistakenly!) regarded as a first-order discourse, would be starkly incommensurable with the 'explanatory (or narrative) space' occupied by countless innocent victims.

THE 'GRAMMAR' OF SALVATION

In a suggestive essay on the atonement in the *Festschrift* for H. H. Farmer, Donald MacKinnon has argued that an adequate conception of the atonement must bring out very clearly 'the dark ambivalence of human action intended somehow to rectify an inherently false situation, and restore perception of its truth'.[4] In the context of our discussion, therefore, the application of MacKinnon's insight would seem to suggest that our deeds of solidarity with victims, while they might be highly desirable and commendable, are nevertheless afflicted by 'the dark ambivalence of human action'; so that we urgently need are the linguistic, conceptual and theological resources to elucidate this 'dark ambivalence' (and in so doing to advance the cause of human solidarity with the afflicted). To achieve this clarity, we need, according to MacKinnon, two things: (1) 'a phenomenology of moral evil'; and (2) the resources of 'ontological metaphysics'. A 'phenomenology of moral evil' is needed because the place of the atoning life and death of Jesus Christ is precisely this ambivalent world of ours, and its ambivalence, as MacKinnon see it, constitutes the very essence of tragedy. The resources of 'ontological metaphysics' are required because the atonement necessarily involves the idea of incarnation, and these resources must be employed to bring out the significance of incarnation for the atonement (or so MacKinnon maintains). MacKinnon's claim that the Christian understanding of atonement needs a 'phenomenology of moral evil' and the resources of 'ontological metaphysics' is one that we shall address later in this chapter. He is also right, from the standpoint of the Christian tradition, in saying that the atonement necessarily involves incarnation. For the Christian faith, traditionally understood, has confessed that the atoning life and death of Jesus brings salvation to humankind precisely because in and through this life divinity has identified with men and women: quite simply, without incarnation there can be no atonement. Or, as MacKinnon puts it, there *can* be salvation without the atonement (and hence without incarnation), but it would be a redemption which could be wrought by a *deus ex machina*, a deity who saves humankind but who does not identify with humankind in the process. This question can be stated 'grammatically', by asking what connection there is between the (incarnational) proposition 'The "logical space" in which 'godness' is located is the self-same "space" in which Jesus of Nazareth is located' and the (soteriological) proposition 'This identity of "spaces", and the reality it presupposes, is (through the cross of Christ) of decisive salvific significance for human beings'. Or to put it much more simply: why is incarnation necessary in order for there to be salvation?

The atonement, it could be said, brings together our depth of wickedness and the work of Jesus, especially his deed wrought on Golgotha. A truly acceptable salvation-scheme would, on this view, be a set of 'grammatical' principles which governed faith's expression of this reconciling work in and through the utmost depths of human malevolence. In MacKinnon's words, such a salvation-scheme would touch 'the deepest contradictions of human life, those contradictions which writers of tragedy have not hesitated to recognize, and to recognize without the distorting consolation of belief in a happy ending'.[5] Precisely such a salvation-scheme, MacKinnon believes, is to be found in the Passion narratives of the gospels.

One of the necessary requirements of a properly-constituted salvation-scheme (and here we include the salvation-schemes which belong to non-Christian faiths as well) is to 'tell the truth of what we are', and in so doing make explicit the malevolence which permeates the very depths of our lives.[6] (The necessity for such a decisive and implacable reckoning with the 'truth of what we are', so that we do not escape judgement when we succumb to forms of self-deception that are palpably evil, is nowhere more clearly indicated than in Heinrich Himmler's assertion to Felix Kersten, his masseur, that 'some higher Being . . . is behind Nature . . . If we refused to recognize that we should be no better than the Marxists . . . I insist that members of the SS must believe in God'.)[7] It is only when our capacity for evil has been rendered explicit that we have a realistic basis for undergoing that transformation or *metanoia*, that healing, which constitutes our salvation. A truly acceptable salvation-scheme, therefore, must contain the theme of divine judgement as well as the one of divine reconciliation. It is in this judgement that we are shown the truth about ourselves, the truth which makes our wickedness explicit.

Central to the Christian faith is the affirmation that God's work of judging and reconciling human beings to himself is one which requires divinity to *identify* with his creation through Jesus Christ. For many theologians with an interest in Christology this affirmation is not, in itself, likely to be controversial: for these theologians the real problems are likely to creep in only when attempts are made the spell-out the nature of this divine identification with creation through Christ. For the theological or philosophical *anthropologist*, however, this affirmation *in itself* is likely to be vastly problematic. Why is this 'identification' of God with humankind so necessary for salvation? Why does atonement presuppose incarnation? To satisfy this sceptical anthropologist, it seems to me, we need to resort to an anthropology of conversion. It would be outside the scope of this book fully to develop this account of conversion; here we can only hint at its bare bones and sinews. Integral to this anthropology of conversion would be the principle referred to in the paragraph above, namely, that only the person who sees herself for what she really is can experience true sorrow and forgiveness. As Rowan Williams puts it, 'If we believe we can experience our healing without deepening our hurt, we have understood nothing of the roots of our faith'.[8] In other words: before we can undergo this healing we have at the very least to experience the truth of our evil, and its accompanying hurt, at its worst. Faith invites us to seek, and to accept, such judgement. To quote Sebastian Moore: 'Christianity . . . invites us to experience our evil as never before, at last unmasked, . . . and in that experience to feel for the first time the love that overpowers evil.'[9]

The salvation of humankind, grounded in the infinite mercy of God, arises from this confrontation of suffering, sorrow and healing; to quote Moore again, '. . . evil made totally explicit is resolved in the forgiveness of God'.[10] God, as faith sees it, resolves humankind's evil in his forgiveness, by identifying with it. By accepting us at our worst, God's love brings about our salvation. For faith, this saving deed of acceptance was made on the cross. At this point the Christian anthropology of conversion has already acquired a Christological focus; for it is a basal assertion of the Christian faith that it is in and through Jesus Christ that God identifies with, and overcomes, the evil and suffering inherent in the human condition. On the cross God breaks into the reality of our lives, shows us the truth of what we are, and thereby heals us. God 'interrupts' us, and shows the truth of what we are, because on the cross the 'being' of God is the 'being' of the Nazarene. For faith there is thus an intrinsic connection between 'truth' and 'interruption'. This connection is expressed thus by Eberhard Jüngel:

> . . . of all creatures, man is that being to whom God wishes to draw near . . . so near, in fact, that he, God, is closer than anyone to man. Thus it is not man who can be closest to himself. It is precisely in his desire to be closest to himself in his self-correspondence that man is interrupted by God. God wants to draw nearer to man than man is ever able to be himself. It is just for this that man is created as man in such a way that he can be interrupted, and he is human precisely in that he allows himself

to be interrupted. God is man's original interruption. He intervenes. For this reason God is, at the same time, the truth of life. He is this as the one who intervenes.[11]

Jüngel, of course, wants to say that God breaks into our lives by *being* the truth in Jesus Christ, that God's intervenient identification with the evil and suffering of humankind is grounded in the historical particularity of Jesus Christ. In no other way can we confront the ultimate depths of our malevolence and indifference. According to Jüngel, God interrupts the continuity (a continuity-*in*-evil) of our lives by allowing our sin and death to interrupt *his* own life in and through the death of Jesus Christ. (Exponents of the 'practical' approach to the theodicy-problem would of course want to extend this principle by saying that God's life is 'interrupted' by all manifestations of innocent and gratuitous suffering.) 'Incarnation' therefore has its place in a 'grammar' which regulates our linguistic representations of God's decisive and unsurpassable 'interruption' of humankind's continuity-in-evil, an 'interruption' that can take place precisely because God *is* the truth in Jesus Christ. Incarnational propositions, we are suggesting, function as presuppositions for (soteriological) propositions by expressing the truth of this saving divine identification, an identification that is the presupposition for this saving 'interruption'.

We can make this point by resorting to philosophical logic, and in particular to P. F. Strawson's well-known paper criticizing Russell's Theory of Descriptions. In this paper, Strawson argues that the assignation of a truth-value to a proposition in certain cases *presupposes* the truth of one or more other propositions. A proposition Q is said to presuppose a proposition P if and only if Q is neither true nor false unless P is true. For example, the truth of the following proposition

(P) *Mrs Brown has a dog*

is a *necessary condition* for the following proposition to be either true or false

(Q) *Mrs Brown indulges her dog*

In short: the proposition 'Mrs Brown indulges her dog'

presupposes the proposition 'Mrs Brown has a dog'.[12] Using the notion of a presupposition, we could argue that incarnational propositions are precisely those propositions whose truth has to be presupposed in order that we may assign a truth-value to soteriological propositions. Thus, for example, it could be argued that the following incarnational proposition

(P) *The 'logical space' in which 'godness' is located is the self-same 'space' in which Jesus of Nazareth is located*

is a necessary condition for the following soteriological proposition to be either true or false

(Q) *This identity of 'logical spaces', and the reality it presupposes, is (through the cross of Christ) of decisive salvific significance for human beings.*

Or to put it in bluntly 'realist' language: it is a necessary condition of determining whether or not humankind is redeemed that God salvifically identifies with human beings by being incarnate in Jesus of Nazareth. Without incarnational propositions we could not even say that it is *false* that God brought salvation to humankind, because the question of salvation cannot arise unless the depth of evil that confronts us has been rendered explicit, and this, as our typical salvation-scheme indicates, can only be done by divine engagement with the very depths of this evil.

While the Christian faith has from its very beginnings stressed the intrinsic connection between incarnation and the salvation wrought by God on the cross of Jesus Christ, it is important that we should not at the same time divorce incarnation from God's *continuing* work in creation. The salvation of human beings is enacted by God in the realm of humanity. This important principle was espoused by Irenaeus, who grounds the soteriological theme (of Jesus Christ as the re-creator of a humanity whose relationship with God has been distorted by sin) in a doctrine of creation, or more specifically, re-creation. Irenaeus, we have seen, emphasizes the continuity of God's creative and redemptive activity, and God's saving deed in Jesus Christ is seen by him as a part of this continuing re-creation, in which communion is restored between God and human beings as a result of the life, death and resurrection of Jesus Christ. Irenaeus does this by adverting to the notion of 'recapitulation'.[13] The governing principle in the Irenaean doctrine of recapitulation is the comparison and contrast between Adam, who fell into disobedience and thereby distorted his and his descendants' relationship with God, and Jesus Christ, whose unfailing and total obedience 'reversed' the disobedience of Adam and thus restored us to a proper relationship with God; or as Irenaeus puts it, 'The Son of God became the Son of Man that man . . . might become the Son of God'.[14] Jesus Christ, according to this view, is thus the 'archetype' of a re-created humanity. We attain to our salvation by conforming our lives to the pattern established by his. Or in terms of our typical salvation-scheme: it is by following the pattern established by the life, death and resurrection of Jesus Christ that we are enabled to transform our evil and sin into that healing which lies at the heart of salvation.[15] The divinely enacted justification emphasized by the theology of the cross needs in turn to be complemented and augmented by the doctrine of creation's stress on the importance of sanctification. No person of faith who has glanced at the merest fragment of a memoir by an inmate of Auschwitz can readily overlook our desparate and overwhelming need for that divine power which works for an overcoming of human bestiality and indifference, that is, that divine power which makes possible the sanctification of human beings. Given the massive complicity, and indeed the active participation, of countless Christians in the technology of torture and death created by the Nazi state, it cannot be denied that we are in the most dire need of forgiveness and healing. On this matter Christians have no choice. That Christians acknowledge their need for forgiveness is of course no consolation for those who have perished. Nevertheless, after Auschwitz, the Christian crucified hope – a 'hope against hope' – for re-creation is constrained by two imperatives:

1 That Christians *must* allow the beliefs and practices which underpin this hope, and the language in which it is expressed, to be 'interrupted' by the history of the beliefs and practices of Jews (and more generally, by the beliefs and practices of all who suffer innocently).
2 That the prayer and confessions which are constitutive

elements of the process of sanctification cannot be pursued in isolation from the *practice* of a messianic solidarity with all Jews (and more generally, with all who are oppressed, dispossessed and dehumanized). This solidarity will of course be one which strives to combat all the forces which make places like Auschwitz possible.

Where theodicy is concerned, (1) entails that all theological affirmations – including that of a God who suffers with those who suffer because he indwells his creation (a *second-order* affirmation crucial to the perspective we have espoused) – must be 'interrupted' by the narratives of those who are victims. Again, where theodicy is concerned, (2) reminds us that theological assertions, even when they happen to motivate and sustain prayer and confession, are nonetheless significant only insofar as they guide and inspire action designed to overcome pain and misery. But even here the theodicist has to bear in mind a very necessary proviso. Evil, in its root and essence, is a mystery. How the mystery of the triune God engages with, and overcomes its historically-textured realities is a mystery too, one that the theologian must ponder over and then hesitatingly articulate in the grasp of the triune God's infinite, but always costly and self-giving, love. We have the assurance of the victory of this love, but we cannot use this assurance (nor the truth that evil is ultimately a mystery) either as a warrant for indifference or to provide easy consolation, a premature palliative, for those who are victims. If we do, we become like the friends of Job, whose all too rational, and ostensibly plausible, explanations of his plight only added to his torment. The theologian who reflects on the 'problem of evil' must begin from this sense of failure, this awareness of the poverty and brokeness of her linguistic and conceptual resources. She must above all, *sustain* this sense of failure, as she proceeds to reflect on the 'problem of evil': 'True thoughts are those alone which do not understand themselves' (T. W. Adorno).[16] Then, and only then, will the theologian's reflections begin to approximate to the form of understanding demanded by a truly Christian reponse to the 'problem of evil', that is, an understanding which forsakes the attempt to seek a ('theoretical') justification of God in order to engage in a historically-conditioned articulation of what is involved in justifying *sinners*.[17] Because of what 'godness' is, the speech in which God justifies himself by justifying sinners is necessarily one that is not transparent to itself. But there is something else: *any* speech which allowed itself to be 'interrupted' by the narratives of what happened in Auschwitz and the other kingdoms of night would perforce be one that was *not* transparent to itself.

NOTES

1 It is precisely for this reason that John Hick rejects the 'classic' atonement doctrine. According to him, this doctrine is inextricably bound up with the notion of the incarnation, and it therefore makes Christology the effective ground of soteriology. Hick of course rejects this incarnational Christology because of the so-called 'scandal of particularity' which surrounds the incarnation. Salvation, thus conceived, will *eo ipso* be confined to the adherents of an incarnational faith, and this is unacceptable in a world that is characterized by a plurality of faiths. See John Hick, 'Evil and Incarnation', in Michael Goulder, ed., *Incarnation and Myth: The Debate Continued* (London: SCM, 1979), pp. 77–84.

2 My remarks here are necessarily programmatic and vastly in need of clarification and elaboration. To unravel the implications of the locution 'the Word of God is given in Holy Scripture' alone would take a book (or even several books). The reader's indulgence is begged.

2 See T. W. Adorno, *Minima Moralia*, p. 197. 'Intelligence is a moral category.'

4 Donald MacKinnon, 'Subjective and Objective Conceptions of Atonement', in F. G. Healey, ed., *Prospect for Theology: Essays in Honour of H. H. Farmer* (London: Nisbet, 1966), pp. 169–82, p. 170. In this essay MacKinnon attempts a *rapprochement* between 'subjective' and 'objective' conceptions of atonement. Roughly speaking, he regards the former conception as involving fundamentally the moral consciousness of human beings, whereas the latter conception has to do with (the overcoming of) that tragic ambivalence which seems inherent in the very fabric of the universe, and which therefore transcends the sphere of human moral powers. Unless otherwise specified, all page references to MacKinnon given within the text will be to this essay.

5 MacKinnon, 'Subjective and Objective' in Healey, ed., *Prospect for Theology*, p. 172.

6 MacKinnon, 'Subjective and Objective' in Healey, ed., *Prospect for Theology*, p. 181.

7 Quoted in Irving Greenberg, 'Cloud of Smoke, Pillar of Fire', *Auschwitz*, p. 46, which in turn quotes from Roger Manvell, *SS and Gestapo* (New York: Ballantine, 1969), p. 109.

8 Rowan Williams, *The Wound of Knowledge* (London: Darton, Longman & Todd, 1979), p. 30. I have attempted a fuller sketch of this anthropology of conversion in my 'Atonement and Christology', *Neue Zeitschrift für Systematische Theologie und Religionsphilosophie*, 24 (1982), pp. 131–49.

9 Sebastian Moore, *The Crucified is no Stranger* (London: Darton Longman & Todd, 1977), p. 14. This marvellous little book is indispensable reading for anyone interested in the anthropology of coversion.

10 Moore, *The Crucified is no Stranger*, p. x.

11 Eberhard Jüngel, 'The Truth of Life: Observations on Truth as the Interruption of the Continuity of Life', in R. W. A. McKinney, ed., *Christ, Creation and Culture: Studies in Honour of T. F. Torrance* (Edinburgh: T. & T. Clark, 1976), p. 234.

12 P. F. Strawson, 'On Referring', in G. H. R. Parkinson, ed., *The Theory of Meaning* (Oxford: Oxford University Press, 1968), pp. 61–85. For a more extended treatment of the notion of a *presupposition,* see James D. McCawley, *Everything that Linguists have always Wanted to Know about Logic* (Oxford: Blackwell, 1981), pp. 235–72.

13 Irenaeus, *Against Heresies*, V, 1 and 10–23 (pp. 526–7 and 536–52).

14 Irenaeus, *Against Heresies*, V, 6, 1.

15 For a similar insistence on the continuity between atonement and creation, see Geoffrey Lampe, *God as Spirit: the Bampton Lectures 1976* (Oxford: Oxford University Press, 1978), pp. 14–24.

16 Adorno, *Minima Moralia*, p. 192.

17 On this, see Walter Kasper, *The God of Jesus Christ*, pp. 158–64.

Bibliography

Only works quoted or cited in the text have been included in this bibliography.

I THE FREE WILL DEFENCE (ALVIN PLANTINGA)

Plantinga, Alvin, *God and Other Minds: A Study of the Rational Justification of Belief in God* (Ithaca and London: Cornell University, 1967).

Plantinga, Alvin, *The Nature of Necessity* (Oxford: Clarendon, 1974).

Plantinga, Alvin, *God, Freedom and Evil* (London: Allen & Unwin, 1974).

Plantinga, Alvin, 'The Free Will Defence', in Rowe and Wainwright, eds, *Philosophy of Religion*, pp. 217–230.

Ackermann, Robert, 'An Alternative Free Will Defence', *Religious Studies*, 18 (1982), pp. 365–72.

Davis, Stephen, 'Free Will and Evil', in Davis, ed., *Encountering Evil*, pp. 69–83.

Davis, Stephen, 'A Defense of the Free Will Defense', *Religious Studies*, 18 (1982), pp. 335–44.

Flew, Antony, 'Compatibilism, Free Will and God', *Philosophy*, 48 (1973), pp. 231–44.

Kane, Stanley G., 'The Free Will Defence Defended', *The New Scholasticism*, 50 (1976), pp. 435–46.

Mackie, J. L. 'Evil and Omnipotence', in Rowe and Wainwright, eds, *Philosophy of Religion*, pp. 206–16.

Pike, Nelson, 'Plantinga on Free Will and Evil', *Religious Studies*, 15 (1979), pp. 449–74.

Yandell, Keith W., 'Logic and the Problem of Evil: a Response to Hoitenga', in Yandell, ed., *God, Man, and Religion: readings in the philosophy of religion* (New York: McGraw–Hill, 1973), pp. 351–64.

II THE NATURAL LAW THEODICY (RICHARD SWINBURNE)

Swinburne, Richard, *The Coherence of Theism* (Oxford: Clarendon, 1977).

Swinburne, Richard, *The Existence of God* (Oxford: Clarendon, 1979).

Swinburne, Richard, 'The Problem of Evil: I', in Brown, ed., *Reason and Religion*, pp. 81–101 and 129–33 (postscript).

Swinburne, Richard, 'Natural Evil', *American Philosophical Quarterly*, 15 (1978), pp. 295–301.

Moser, Paul K., 'Natural Evil and the Free Will Defense', *International Journal of the Philosophy of Religion*, 15 (1984), pp. 49–56.

O'Connor, David, 'Swinburne on Natural Evil', *Religious Studies*, 19 (1983), pp. 65–73.

Phillips, D. Z., 'The Problem of Evil: II' in Brown, ed., *Reason and Religion*, pp. 103–21 and 134–9 (postscript).

Stump, Eleonore, 'Knowledge, Freedom and the Problem of Evil', *International Journal of the Philosophy of Religion*, 14 (1983), pp. 49–58.

Wachterhauser, Brice R., 'The Problem of Evil and Moral Skepticism', *International Journal of the Philosophy of Religion*, 17 (1985), pp. 167–74.

III THE 'PROCESS' THEODICY

Brown, Delwin, James, Ralph E., and Reeves, Gene eds, *Process Philosophy and Christian Thought* (New York: Bobbs-Merrill, 1971).

Cobb, John B., and Griffin, David R., *Process Theology: an Introductory Exposition* (Belfast: Christian Journals, 1977).

Ford, Lewis S. 'Divine Persuasion and the Triumph of Good', in Brown, et al., eds, *Process Philosophy and Christian Thought*, pp. 287–304.

Griffin, David R., 'Creation Out of Chaos and the Problem of Evil', in Davis, ed., *Encountering Evil*, pp. 101–19.

Hartshorne, Charles, *The Divine Relativity: A Social Conception of God* (New Haven: Yale, 1948).

Hartshorne, Charles, *Man's Vision of God* (Hampden, Conn.: Archon, 1964).

Hartshorne, Charles, *Creative Synthesis and Philosophic Method* (London: SCM, 1970).

Hartshorne, Charles, 'A New Look at the Problem of Evil', in F. C. Dommeyer, ed., *Current Philosophical Issues: essays in honor of C. J. Ducasse* (Springfield, Ill.: Thomas, 1966), pp. 201–12.

Hartshorne, Charles, 'The God of Religion and the God of Philosophy', in G. N. A. Vesey, ed., *Talk of God* (London: Macmillan, 1969), pp. 152–67.

Whitehead, A. N., *Process and Reality* (Cambridge: Cambridge University Press, 1923).

IV   THE 'THE SOUL-MAKING' THEODICY (JOHN HICK)

Hick, John, *Philosophy of Religion* (Englewood Cliffs, NJ: Prentice-Hall, 1963).
Hick, John, *Evil and the God of Love* (London: Fontana/Collins, 1968).
Hick, John, 'An Irenaean Theodicy', in Davis, ed., *Encountering Evil*, pp. 39–52.
Hick, John 'The Problem of Evil: Remarks', in Brown, ed., *Reason and Religion*, pp. 122–9.

V   DOROTHEE SOELLE

Soelle, Dorothee, *Christ the Representative* (London: SCM, 1967).
Soelle, Dorothee, *Suffering* (London: Darton, Longman & Todd, 1975).

Bentley, James, *Between Marx and Christ* (London: Verso, 1982).
Metz, J–B, 'Facing the Jews: Christian Theology after Auschwitz', in E. Fiorenza and D. Tracy, eds, *The Holocaust as Interruption*, pp. 26–33.

VI   JÜRGEN MOLTMANN

Moltmann, Jürgen, *Hope and Planning*, trans. Margaret Clarkson (London: SCM, 1971).
Moltmann, Jürgen, *The Crucified God*, trans. R. A. Wilson and John Bowden (London: SCM, 1974).
Moltmann, Jürgen, *The Experiment Hope*, trans. M. Douglas Meeks (London: SCM, 1975).
Moltmann, Jürgen, *The Future of Creation*, trans. Margaret Kohl (London: SCM, 1977).
Moltmann, Jürgen, *The Open Church: Invitation to a Messianic Life-Style*, trans. M. Douglas Meeks (London: SCM, 1978).
Moltmann, Jürgen, *Experiences of God*, trans. Margaret Kohl (London: SCM, 1980).
Moltmann, Jürgen, *The Trinity and the Kingdom of God*, trans. Margaret Kohl (London: SCM, 1981).

Moltmann, Jürgen, *On Human Dignity: Political Theology and Ethics*, trans. M. Douglas Meeks (London: SCM, 1984).

Fiorenza, Francis Schüssler, 'Joy and Pain as Paradigmatic for Language about God', *Concilium*, 5 (1974), pp. 67–80.

Fiorenza, Francis Schüssler, 'Critical Social Theory and Christology'. *Proceedings of the Catholic Theological Society of America*, 30 (1975), pp. 63–110.

Olson, Roger, 'Trinity and Eschatology: The Historical Being of God in Jürgen Moltmann and Wolfhart Pannenberg', *Scottish Journal of Theology*, 36 (1983), pp. 213–27.

VII   P.T. FORSYTH

Forsyth, P. T., *The Justification of God: Lectures for War-Time on a Christian Theodicy* (London: Duckworth, 1916).

Hick, John, *Evil and the God of Love*, pp. 246–50.

VIII   OTHER WORKS DEALING WITH THEODICY

Becker, Ernest, *The Structure of Evil: An Essay on the Unification of the Science of Man* (New York: The Free Press, 1976).

Davis, Stephen T., ed., *Encountering Evil: live options in theodicy* (Edinburgh: T. & T. Clark, 1981).

Geach, P. T., *Providence and Evil* (Cambridge: Cambridge University Press, 1977).

Hebblethwaite, Brian, *Evil, Suffering and Religion* (London: Sheldon, 1979).

Kant, Immanuel, *On the Failure of all Attempted Philosophical Theodicies* (1791), translated as an appendix in Michel Despland, *Kant on History and Religion* (London and Montreal: McGill-Queen's University, 1973), pp. 283–97.

McCabe, Herbert, 'God: Evil', *New Blackfriars*, 62 (1981), pp. 4–17.

Peterson, Michael L., 'Recent Work on the Problem of Evil', *American Philosophical Quarterly*, 20 (1983), pp. 321–39.

Rowe, William L., 'The Problem of Evil and Some Varieties of Atheism', *American Philosophical Quarterly*, 16 (1979), pp. 335–41.

Surin, Kenneth, 'The Impassibility of God and the Problem of Evil', *Scottish Journal of Theology*, 35 (1982), pp. 97–115.

Surin, Kenneth, 'Theodicy?', *Harvard Theological Review*, 76 (1983), pp. 225–47.

IX OTHER WORKS CONSULTED

Adorno, T. W., *Negative Dialetics*, trans. E. B. Ashton, (London: Routledge & Kegan Paul, 1973).

Adorno, T. W., *Minima Moralia: Reflections from Damaged Life*, trans. E. F. N. Jephcott (London: Verso, 1974).

Adorno, T. W., The Essay as Form', trans. B. Hullot-Kentor and F. Will, *New German Critique*, no. 32 (1984), pp. 151–71.

Armstrong, A. H., 'St. Augustine and Christian Plantonism', in Markus, ed., *Augustine*, pp. 3–37.

Augustine, Bishop of Hippo, *Enchiridion*, i–iv, in the translation of the Library of Christian Classics, vol. VII, ed. and trans. Albert C. Outler (London: SCM, 1955).

Augustine, Bishop of Hippo, *Our Lord's Sermon on the Mount*, in the translation of the Nicene and post-Nicene Library, vol. VI (Grand Rapids: Eerdmans, 1979).

Augustine, Bishop of Hippo *Retractions*, in *Augustine: Earlier Writings*: in the translation of the Library of Christian Classics, ed. J. H. S. Burleigh, (Philadelphia: Westminster, 1953), pp. 17–18.

Augustine, Bishop of Hippo, *Confessions*, in the translation of the Library of Christian Classics, vol. VII, ed. and trans. Albert C. Outler, (London: SCM, 1955).

Augustine, Bishop of Hippo, *The Trinity*, in the translation of the Nicene and Post-Nicene Library, vol VIII, (Grand Rapids: Eerdmans, 1978).

Augustine, Bishop of Hippo, *The City of God*, in the translation of the Nicene and Post-Nicene Library vol. II, (Grand Rapids: Eerdmans, 1977).

Augustine, Bishop of Hippo, *Soliloquies* in *Augustine: Earlier Writings*, pp. 23–63.

Augustine, Bishop of Hippo, *On the Gospel of St John*, in the translation of the Nicene and Post-Nicene Library, vol VII.

Augustine, Bishop of Hippo, *De Natura et Gratia*, J. P. Migne, *Patrologia Latina*.

Baier, Annette, 'Secular Faith', in Stanley Hauerwas and Alasdair MacIntyre, eds, *Revisions: Changing Perspectives in Moral Philosophy* (Notre Dame: University Press, 1983), pp. 203–21.

Barth, Karl, *Church Dogmatics* II/1 (Edinburgh: T. & T. Clark, 1957).

Bellow, Saul, *Herzog* (Harmondsworth: Penguin, 1965).

Bernstein, Richard J., *Beyond Objectivism and Relativism: Science, Hermeneutics and Praxis* (Oxford: Blackwell, 1983).

Bonhoeffer, Dietrich, *Letters and Papers from Prison* (London: SCM, enlarged ed., 1971).

Brown, Peter, *Augustine of Hippo: A Biography* (London: Faber & Faber, 1967).

Brown, Peter 'Saint Augustine: Politcal Society', in Markus, ed., *Augustine*, pp. 311–29.

Brown, Robert McAfee, *Elie Wiesel: Messenger to all Humanity* (Notre Dame: University Press, 1983).

Brown, Stuart C., ed., *Reason and Religion* (London and Ithaca: Cornell University, 1977).

Burrell, David, *Exercises in Religious Understanding* (Notre Dame: University Press, 1974).

Burtt, E. A., *The Metaphysical Foundations of Modern Science* (London: Routledge & Kegan Paul, 2nd rev. ed., 1932).

Cavell, Stanley, *Must We Mean What We Say?* Cambridge: Cambridge University Press, 1976).

Cavell, Stanley, *The Claim of Reason: Wittgenstein, Skepticism, Morality, and Tragedy* (Oxford: Clarendon, 1979).

Childs, Brevard S., *Introduction to the Old Testament as Scripture* (Philadelphia: Fortress, 1979).

Chopp, Rebecca, 'The Interruption of the Forgotten', in E. Fiorenza and D. Tracy (eds), *The Holocaust as Interruption*, pp. 19–25.

Conrad, Joseph, *Tales of Unrest* (Harmondsworth: Penguin, 1977).

Daniélou, Jean, *Gospel Message and Hellenistic Culture*, trans. John Austin Baker (London: Darton, Longman & Todd, 1973).

Descartes, René, *Meditations*, in F. E. Sutcliffe (trans.), *Descartes: Discourse on Method and Other Writings* (Harmondsworth: Penguin, 1968).

Dostoyevsky, Fyodor, *The Brothers Karamazov*, trans. D. Magarshack, (Harmondsworth: Penguin, 1958).

Drake, Stillman (ed. and tr.), *Discoveries of Galileo* (New York: Doubleday, 1957).

Estess, Ted L. 'Elie Wiesel and the Drama of Interrogation', *The Journal of Religion*, 56 (1976), pp. 18–35.

Evans, G. R. *Augustine on Evil* (Cambridge: Cambridge University Press, 1982).

Fackenheim , Emil L., *God's Presence in History: Jewish Affirmations and Philosophical Reflections* (New York: Harper Torchbooks, 1972).

Farmer, H. H., *Towards Belief in God* (London: SCM, 1942).

Fiorenza, Elisabeth Schüssler, and Tracy, David, eds, *The Holocaust as Interruption (Concilium 175)* (Edinburgh: T. & T. Clark, 1984).

Fleischner, Eva, ed., *Auschwitz: Beginning of a New Era?* (New York: KTAV, 1977).

Flemington, W. F., 'On the Interpretation of Colossians 1: 24', in Horbury and MacNeil eds, *Suffering and Martyrdom in the New Testament*, pp. 84–90.

Foucault, Michel, *The Archaeology of Knowledge*, trans. A. M. Sheridan, (New York: Harper Colophon, 1972).

Foucault, Michel, *The Order of Things: An Archaeology of the Human Sciences* (New York: Vintage, 1973).

Foucault, Michel, *Power/Knowledge: Selected Interviews and Other Writings by Michel Foucault, 1972–1977*, ed. Colin Gordon (New York: Pantheon, 1980).

Garfinkel, Alan, *Forms of Explanation: Rethinking the Question in Social Theory* (New Haven: Yale University, 1981).

Gibson, Boyce, *The Religion of Dostoevsky* (London: SCM, 1973).

Goldmann, Lucien, 'Structure: Human Reality and Methodological Subject', in R. Macksey and E. Donato, eds, *The Languages of Criticism and the Sciences of Man* (Baltimore: Johns Hopkins, 1970), pp. 98–124.

Gordis, Robert, *The Book of God and Man: A Study of Job* (Chicago and London: University of Chicago, 1978).

Greenberg, Irving, 'Cloud of Smoke, Pillar of Fire: Judaism, Christianity and Modernity after the Holocaust', in Fleischner, ed., *Auschwitz*, pp. 7–55.

Hacking, Ian, *The Emergence of Probability* (Cambridge: University Press, 1975).

Hacking, Ian, 'Five Parables', in Rorty, Schneewind and Skinner, eds, *Philosophy in History*, pp. 103–24.

Hick, John, 'Evil and Incarnation', in Michael Goulder, ed., *Incarnation and Myth: The Debate Continued* (London: SCM, 1979), pp. 77–84.

Hick, John, 'Towards a Philosophy of Religious Pluralism', *Neue Zeitschrift für Systematische Theologie und Religionsphilosophie*, 22 (1980), pp. 131–49.

Hick, John, *Problems of Religious Pluralism* (London: Macmillan, 1985).

Hilberg, Raul, ed., *Documents of Destruction* (Chicago: Quadrangle, 1973).

Hippolytus, *The Refutation of All Heresies*, VI, 2–37, in the translation of the Ante-Nicene Library, vol. V, (Grand Rapids: Eerdmans, 1978).

Horbury, William, and MacNeil, Brian, eds., *Suffering and Martyrdom in the New Testament* (Cambridge: Cambridge University Press, 1981).

Hume, David, *A Treatise of Human Nature*, ed. L. A. Selby-Bigge (Oxford: Clarendon, 1888).

Hume, David, *Dialogues Concerning Natural Religion*, ed. H. D. Aiken, (New York: Harper, 1948).

Irenaeus, Bishop of Lyons, *Against Heresies*, in the translation of the Ante-Nicene Library, vol. I, (Grand Rapids: Eerdmans, 1979).

Jaeger, Werner, *Paideia: the Ideals of Greek Culture* (3 vols), (Oxford: University Press, 1944).

Jameson, Frederic, *The Political Unconscious: Narrative as a Socially Symbolic Act* (London: Methuen, 1981).

Jennings, T. W., *Beyond Theism* (Oxford: Oxford University Press, 1985).

Jüngel, Eberhard, *God as the Mystery of the World*, trans. D. L. Guder, (Edinburgh: T. & T. Clark, 1983).

Jüngel, Eberhard, 'The Truth of Life: Observations on Truth as the Interruption of the Continuity of Life', in R. W. A. McKinney, ed., *Christ, Creation and Culture: Studies in Honour of T. F. Torrance* (Edinburgh: T. & T. Clark, 1976), pp. 231–6.

Kant, Immanuel, *Critique of Pure Reason*, trans. N. Kemp Smith (London and New York: Macmillan, 1964).

Kasper, Walter, *The God of Jesus Christ*, trans. M. J. O'Connell (London: SCM, 1984).

Kelly, J. N. D., *Early Christian Doctrines* (London: Black, 5th ed., 1977).

Kitamori, Kazoh, *Theology of the Pain of God* (Richmond, Va.: John Knox, 1965).

Ladner, G. B., *The Idea of Reform: its Impact on Christian Thought and Action in the Age of the Fathers* (Cambridge, Mass.: Harvard University, 1959).

Lampe, Geoffrey, *God as Spirit: the Bampton Lectures 1976* (Oxford: Oxford University Press, 1978).

Lash, Nicholas, *Theology on Dover Beach* (London: Darton, Longman & Todd, 1979).

Lash, Nicholas, *A Matter of Hope: A theologian's reflections on the thought of Karl Marx* (London: Darton, Longman & Todd, 1981).

Lash, Nicholas, 'What might martyrdom mean?', in William Horbury and Brian MacNeil, eds, *Suffering and Martyrdom in the New Testament*, pp. 183–98.

Lash, Nicholas, 'Considering the Trinity', *Modern Theology*, 2 (1986), pp. 183–194.

Lavrin, Janko *Dostoevsky: A Study* (London: Methuen, 1948).

Lloyd, A. C., 'On Augustine's Concept of a Person', in Markus, ed., *Augustine*, pp. 91–205.

Locke, John, *in Epistola de Tolerantia* (*A Letter on Toleration*), ed. J. W. Gough and R. Klibansky (Oxford: Clarendon, 1968).

Louth, Andrew, *The Origins of the Christian Mystical Tradition: From Plato to Denys* (Oxford: Clarendon, 1981).

Louth, Andrew, *Discerning the Mystery: An essay on the nature of theology* (Oxford: Clarendon, 1983).

McCabe, Herbert, 'The Involvement of God', *New Blackfriars*, 66 (1985), pp. 464–76.

McCawley, James D., *Everything that Linguists have Always Wanted to Know about Logic* (Oxford: Blackwell, 1981).

MacIntyre, Alasdair, 'The Debate About God: Victorian Relevance and Contemporary Irrelevance', in MacIntyre and Paul Ricoeur, *The*

Religious Significance of Atheism (New York: Columbia University, 1969), pp. 3–55.

MacIntyre, Alasdair, 'Is Understanding Religion Compatible with Believing?', in Bryan R. Wilson, ed., *Rationality* Oxford: Blackwell, 1974), pp. 62–77.

MacIntyre, Alasdair, 'Epistemological Crises, Dramatic Narrative and the Philosophy of Science', *The Monist*, 60 (1977), pp. 453–72.

MacIntyre, Alasdair, 'The Relation of Philosophy to its Past', in Rorty, Schneewind and Skinner, eds., *Philosophy in History*, pp. 31–48.

Mackie, J. L., *The Miracle of Theism* (Oxford: Clarendon, 1982).

MacKinnon, Donald, *The Problem of Metaphysics* (Cambridge: Cambridge University Press, 1974).

MacKinnon, Donald, 'Subjective and Objective Conceptions of Atonement', in F. G. Healey, ed., *Prospect for Theology: Essays In Honour of H. H. Farmer* (London: Nisbet, 1966), pp. 169–82.

Madsen, Peter, 'Semiotics and Dialectics', *Poetics*, 6 (1972), pp. 29–42.

Malthus, Thomas, *An Essay on the Principle of Population*, ed. A. Flew (Harmondsworth: Penguin, 1970).

Manvell, Roger, *SS and Gestapo* (New York: Ballantine, 1969).

Markus, R. A. 'Marius Victorinus and Augustine', in A. H. Armstrong, ed., *The Cambridge History of Later Greek and Early Medieval Philosophy* (Cambridge: Cambridge University Press, 1967), Part V.

Markus, R. A., ed., *Augustine: A Collection of Critical Essays* (new York: Doubleday/Anchor, 1972).

Marx, Karl, *Early Writings*, trans. R. Livingstone and G. Benton (Harmondsworth: Penguin, 1975).

Metz, Johann-Baptist, *Faith in History and Society: Toward a Practical Fundamental Theology*, trans. David Smith (London: Burns & Oates, 1980).

Metz, Johann-Baptist, *The Emergent Church: The Future of Christianity in a Postbourgeois World*, trans. Peter Mann, (London: SCM, 1981).

Miles, Margaret, 'Vision: The Eye of the Body and the Eye of the Mind in Saint Augustine's *De trinitate* and *Confessions*', *The Journal of Religion*, 63 (1983), pp. 125–42.

Moore, Sebastian, *The Crucified is No Stranger* (London: Darton, Longman & Todd, 1977).

Nash, Ronald H., *The Light of the Mind: St Augustine's Theory of Knowledge* (Lexington: University Press of Kentucky, 1969).

Nicholls, Aidan, *The Art of God Incarnate: Theology and Image in Christian Tradition* (London: Darton, Longman & Todd, 1980).

Norris, Richard, 'The Transcendence and Freedom of God: Irenaeus, the Greek Tradition and Gnosticism', in Schoedel and Wilken, eds, *Early Christian Literature*, pp. 87–100.

O'Connell, Robert J., 'Action and Contemplation', in Markus, ed., *Augustine*, pp. 38–58.

Owen, Huw Parri, *Christian Theism* (Edinburgh: T. & T. Clark, 1984).

Pannenberg, Wolfhart, *Theology and the Philosophy of Science* (London: Darton, Longman & Todd, 1976).

Pawelczynska, Anna, *Values and Violence in Auschwitz*, trans. Catherine S. Leach (Berkeley: University of California, 1979).

Phillips, D. Z., 'The Friends of Cleanthes', *Modern Theology*, 1 (1985), pp. 91–104.

Plato, *Timaeus*, trans. H. D. P. Lee (Harmondsworth: Penguin, 1971).

Putnam, Hilary, *Meaning and the Moral Sciences* (London: Routledge & Kegan Paul, 1978).

Quasten, Johannes, *Patrology: vol. 1 (The Beginnings of Patristic Literature)* (Utrecht-Antwerp: Spectrum, 1975).

Rahner, Karl, 'On the Theology of the Incarnation', in *Theological Investigations*, vol 4 (London: Darton, Longman & Todd, 1974).

Ricoeur, Paul, *The Symbolism of Evil*, trans. E. Buchanan, (Boston: Beacon, 1969).

Ricoeur, Paul, *The Conflict of Interpretations*, ed. Don Ihde, (Evanston: Northwestern University, 1974).

Rorty, Richard, *Philosophy and the Mirror of Nature* (Oxford: Blackwell, 1980).

Rorty, Richard, 'The historiography of philosophy: four genres', in Rorty, Schneewind and Skinner, eds., *Philosophy in History*, pp. 49–76.

Rorty, R., Schneewind, J. B., and Skinner, Q., eds., *Philosophy in History* (Cambridge: Cambridge University Press, 1984).

Rowe, W. L. and Wainwright, W. J. eds., *Philosophy of Religion: Selected Readings* (New York: Harcourt Brace Jovanovich, 1973).

Said, Edward, W., *Orientalism: Western Conceptions of the Orient* (Harmondsworth: Penguin, 1985).

Said, Edward W., 'The Problem of Textuality: Two Exemplary Positions', *Critical Inquiry*, 4 (1978), pp. 673–714.

Said, Edward W., 'Opponents, Audiences, Constituences, and Community', *Critical Inquiry*, 9 (1982), pp. 1–26.

Sartre, Jean-Paul, *What is Literature?*, trans. B. Frechtman, (London: Methuen, 1950).

Schillebeeckx, Edward, *Jesus: an Experiment in Christology*, trans. Hubert Hoskins, (London: Collins, 1979).

Schoedel, William R. and Wilken, Robert L. eds, *Early Christian Literature and the Classical Intellectual Tradition* (Paris: Beauchesne, 1979).

Schouls, Peter A., *The Imposition of Method: A Study of Descartes and Locke* (Oxford: Clarendon, 1980).

Sellars, Wilfrid, 'Empiricism in the Philosophy of Mind', in his *Science,*

Perception and Reality (London: Routledge & Kegan Paul, 1963).

Shapiro, Susan, 'Hearing the Testimony of Radical Negation', in E. Fiorenza and D. Tracy, eds, *The Holocaust as Interruption*, pp. 3–10.

Spinoza, *Ethics*, trans. R. H. M. Elwes, in *The Rationalists* (New York: Doubleday, 1960).

Stout, Jeffrey, *The Flight from Authority* (Notre Dame: Notre Dame University Press, 1981).

Strawson, P. F. 'On Referring', in G. H. R. Parkinson, ed., *The Theory of Meaning* (Oxford: Oxford University Press, 1968), pp. 61–85.

Stroup, George W., *The Promise of Narrative Theology* (Atlanta: John Knox, 1981).

Surin, Kenneth, 'Atonement and Christology', *Neue Zeitschrift für Systematische Theologie und Religionsphilosophie*, 24 (1982), pp. 131–49.

Surin, Kenneth, 'Atonement and Moral Apocalypticism: William Styron's *Sophie's Choice*', *New Blackfriars*, 64 (1983), pp. 300–15.

Surin, Kenneth, 'Philosophical Reflection and the Trinity', *Modern Theology*, 2 (1986), pp. 235–56.

Sutherland, Stewart, *Atheism and the Rejection of God: Contemporary Philosophy and 'The Brothers Karamazov'* (Oxford: Blackwell, 1977).

Taylor, Charles, 'Philosophy and its History', in R. Rorty, J. B. Schneewind and Q. Skinner, eds, *Philosophy in History*, pp. 17–30.

Tracy, David, *Blessed Rage for Order: The New Pluralism in Theology* (New York: Seabury, 1975).

Turner, Denys, 'De-centring Theology', *Modern Theology*, 2 (1986), pp. 125–43.

von Balthasar, Hans Urs, *The von Balthasar Reader*, ed. M. Kehl and W. Löser (New York: Cross Roads, 1982).

von Balthasar, Hans Urs, *The Glory of the Lord: A Theological Aesthetics: vol. II*, trans. A. Louth, F. McDonagh and B. McNeil (Edinburgh: T. & T. Clark, 1984).

Weber, Max, 'The Social Psychology of the World Religions', in H. H. Gerth and C. Wright Mills, eds, *From Max Weber* (New York: Oxford University, 1958), pp. 267–301.

Weil, Simone, *Waiting on God* (London: Routledge & Kegan Paul, 1951).

White, Hayden, 'The Value of Narrativity in the Representation of Reality', *Critical Inquiry*, 7 (1980), pp. 5–27.

Wiesel, Elie, *The Gates of the Forest* (New York: Avon, 1967).

Wiesel, Elie, *Dawn*, trans. Frances Frenaye (New York: Avon, 1970).

Wiesel, Elie, *The Town Beyond the Wall*, trans. Stephen Barker (New York: Avon, 1970).

Wiesel, Elie, *Night*, trans. Stella Rodway (London: Fontana/Collins, 1972).

Wiesel, Elie, 'Jewish Values in the Post-Holocaust Future', *Judaism*, 16 (1967), pp. 266–99.

Wiesel, Elie, 'Art and Culture After the Holocaust', in E. Fleischner, ed., *Auschwitz*, pp. 403–16.

Wiesel, Elie, 'Freedom of Conscience – A Jewish Commentary', *Journal of Ecumenical Studies*, 14 (1977), pp. 638–49.

Wiesel, Elie, 'The Holocaust as Literary Inspiration', in Lucy Baldwin Smith, ed., *Dimensions of the Holocaust* (Evanston, I11.: Northwestern University, 1977), pp. 5–17.

Wiesel, Elie, 'Why I Write', in Alvin H. Rosenfeld and Irving Greenberg, eds, *Confronting the Holocaust: The Impact of Elie Wiesel* (Bloomington: Indiana University, 1978), pp. 200–6.

Williams, Rowan, *The Wound of Knowledge* (London: Darton, Longman & Todd, 1979).

Wittgenstein, Ludwig, *The Philosophical Investigations*, trans. G. E. M. Anscombe (Oxford: Blackwell, 1968).

Wolfson, Harry Austryn, *The Philosophy of the Church Fathers* (Cambridge, Mass.: Harvard University, 3rd rev. ed., 1970).

Young, Frances M. 'The God of the Greeks and the Nature of Religious Language', in Schoedel and Wilken, eds, *Early Christian Literature*, pp. 45–74.

Young, Frances M., *Sacrifice and the Death of Christ* (London: SPCK, 1975).

Index